Divine Interpretation

"An invaluable resource for any serious student of Torrance, bringing together a rich and rewarding collection of his essays. Highly recommended."

—**Alister McGrath**, University of Oxford

"It is not too much to say that without a proper hermeneutics shaped by the unique nature of its object, theology would be lost. This impressive collection of essays from Thomas F. Torrance helpfully gathers together many of his most important writings on the subject displaying an amazing grasp of history and theology. Familiar themes emerge: the important connection between the incarnation and atonement, the nature of scientific knowledge of God as knowledge grounded in God and personally conveyed through his Word and Spirit by grace through faith, and more. But the really important impression that this book will convey to its readers is the way Torrance's own thinking is not only shaped by Scripture but by the early church Fathers, and especially by Calvin and Barth. There are contextual discussions of just how Calvin related experience and knowledge of God that will illuminate Torrance's own important discussions of the Trinity and Christology. This is a book that Torrance scholars and theologians interested in Reformation history, as it relates to Augustine and Mediaeval theology generally, will want to read."

—**Paul Molnar**, St. John's University, Queens, New York

"T. F. Torrance's extensive studies on the history of hermeneutics deserve to remain important reading for students of theology and scriptural interpretation. This volume presents a very valuable collection of some of Torrance's most significant texts in the field, set out somewhat after the fashion of the ambitious general history of hermeneutics which he originally envisioned as corollary to his work on theological epistemology and Christian doctrine. For all who wish to gain an understanding of Torrance's provocative ways of reading historical theology and its legacies, this book is an essential asset."

—**Ivor J. Davidson**, University of Aberdeen

"One might think a work on hermeneutics would be mired in stodgy prose and consumed with literary and secular hermeneutical theory. This volume exhibits neither tendency. Hermeneutics for Torrance is Christology in another key, and that means his hermeneutics is distinctly Christian. As we have come to expect from Torrance, the tradition is examined (here especially significant late medieval thinkers, Reformers, and of course Karl Barth) not merely for its own sake but for the cause of following the mind of the catholic Church in order to make clear what it means for Christ to be the Truth and the one who fully reveals God. Gathered together in one accessible volume, the editors have done a service to the church with these carefully chosen essays which form a companion volume of sorts to Torrance's earlier study in hermeneutics, *Divine Meaning*, which explored the patristic consensus."

—**Myk Habets**, Carey Baptist College

"T. F. Torrance's writings on the history of biblical hermeneutics deserve to be much more widely known than they presently are, for they have a great deal to teach both academic theologians and members of the church. These collected essays put some important texts within easy reach and provide all who care about biblical interpretation with a great deal of food for thought."

—**Darren Sarisky**, Wycliffe Hall, University of Oxford

Divine Interpretation:
Studies in Medieval and Modern Hermeneutics

THOMAS F. TORRANCE COLLECTED STUDIES 2

Thomas F. Torrance

EDITED BY

Adam Nigh and Todd Speidell

☙PICKWICK *Publications* · Eugene, Oregon

DIVINE INTERPRETATION
Studies in Medieval and Modern Hermeneutics

Thomas F. Torrance Collected Studies 2

Copyright © 2017 T. F. Torrance. All rights reserved. Except for brief quotations in critical publications or reviews, no part of this book may be reproduced in any manner without prior written permission from the publisher. Write: Permissions, Wipf and Stock Publishers, 199 W. 8th Ave., Suite 3, Eugene, OR 97401.

Pickwick Publications
An Imprint of Wipf and Stock Publishers
199 W. 8th Ave., Suite 3
Eugene, OR 97401

www.wipfandstock.com

PAPERBACK ISBN: 978-1-60899-941-5
HARDCOVER ISBN: 978-1-4982-8849-1
EBOOK ISBN: 978-1-4982-4369-8

Cataloguing-in-Publication data:

Names: Torrance, Thomas F. (Thomas Forsyth), 1913–2007 | Nigh, Adam, editor | Speidell, Todd, editor

Title: Divine interpretation : studies in medieval and modern hermeneutics / Thomas F. Torrance, edited by Adam Nigh and Todd Speidell.

Description: Eugene, OR: Pickwick Publications, 2017 | Series: Thomas F. Torrance Collected Studies | Includes bibliographical references and index.

Identifiers: ISBN 978-1-60899-941-5 (paperback) | ISBN 978-1-4982-8849-1 (hardcover) | ISBN 978-1-4982-4369-8 (ebook)

Subjects: LCSH: Bible—Hermeneutics | Hermeneutics—Religious aspects—Christianity | Theology, Doctrinal

Classification: BS467 T67 2017 (print) | BS467 (ebook)

Manufactured in the U.S.A.   AUGUST 7, 2017

Contents

Preface and Acknowledgments   vii

Introduction: The History of Hermeneutics according to T. F. Torrance   1

Part 1: Foundations for the History of Hermeneutics   10

    1. Biblical Hermeneutics and General Hermeneutics   11

    2. The Complex Background of Biblical Interpretation   20

    3. Karl Barth and the Latin Heresy   44

Part 2: Medieval and Modern Hermeneutics   68

    4. The Place of Word and Truth in Theological Inquiry according to St Anselm   69

    5. Scientific Hermeneutics according to St Thomas Aquinas   97

    6. The Hermeneutics of John Reuchlin, 1455–1522   132

    7. The Hermeneutics of Erasmus   151

    8. Hermeneutics according to F. D. E. Schleiermacher   180

    9. Karl Barth, Theologian of the Word   191

General Index   225

Scripture Index   227

Preface and Acknowledgments

THE FIRST VOLUME OF the Thomas F. Torrance Collected Studies was *Gospel, Church, and Ministry*, edited by Jock Stein. The present volume, *Divine Interpretation: Studies in Medieval and Modern Hermeneutics*, is its sequel, thus constituting Thomas F. Torrance Collected Studies 2. The essays of this volume may also be read as a companion piece to T. F. Torrance's *Divine Meaning: Studies in Patristic Hermeneutics* and *The Hermeneutics of John Calvin*, both of which are currently available through Bloomsbury Publishers. Torrance's essays on Augustine and Luther, part of the Thomas F. Torrance Manuscript Collection at Princeton Theological Seminary, were not available for inclusion in this book.

We wish to thank Jim Tedrick, Managing Editor at Wipf and Stock Publishers, who supported the publication of this book and gave us liberty of editorial oversight. We decided to preserve the original customs and preferences of T. F. Torrance regarding spelling, punctuation, and capitalization. We have only made minor and occasional changes to ensure consistency and clarity and to correct errors introduced by the scanning process of these essays. We are grateful to Wipf and Stock Publishers for making available the Thomas F. Torrance Collected Studies.

Adam Nigh deserves primary credit for collecting, organizing, and introducing these previously published essays (see his Introduction to this volume). Several editors of *Participatio: The Journal of the Thomas F. Torrance Theological Fellowship* deserve a special word of thanks for their careful work in reading, correcting, and preparing these essays for publication: Assistant Editors Steve Chaffee, Kate Dugdale, Jonathan Kleis, Jason Radcliff, and Albert Shepherd V, and Production Editor Jock Stein. Iain Torrance provided invaluable information for Adam Nigh's introductory essay.

Todd Speidell

As an additional acknowledgement, I would like to thank Jock Stein and Todd Speidell for their patience and persistence in working with me to get this project completed. The only greater gratitude I owe is to my wife, Rachel Nigh, who has endured hours of my absence after work and on weekends stretched across years in order to have this book see publication.

Adam Nigh

INTRODUCTION

The History of Hermeneutics according to T. F. Torrance

This book gathers together several of T. F. Torrance's essays on the history of the Christian church's biblical hermeneutics to see the larger picture that emerges. It is a large and detailed picture that was to find expression in a massive study, publishable either as "one very large volume or three smaller books."[1] Although Torrance put a good deal of effort into this project in the 1960s, thereafter other interests claimed his attention.[2] He published some of its essays individually in various journals and books over the following decades, leaving several other draft essays, including illuminating discussions of the hermeneutics of Augustine, Luther, and Bultmann unpublished to this day.[3] To later readers, his decision not to

---

1 Torrance, *Theological Science* (London: Oxford University Press, 1969), viii.

2 Torrance offers brief accounts of the development of these writings on the history of hermeneutics in the preface to *Theological Science*, vii–viii, and *The Hermeneutics of John Calvin* (Edinburgh: Scottish Academic Press, 1988), vii–ix.

3 These unpublished essays can be found in Princeton Seminary's "Thomas F. Torrance Manuscript Collection." The essay on Augustine's hermeneutics is titled there simply "Augustine" and can be found in Box 33 labeled "Hermeneutics" (1 of 6), folder labeled "Notes 285a–306." While "Augustine" begins on page 286, it is preceded by an essay on the hermeneutics of John Chrysostom given odd pagination as pp. 285a–285g, the purpose of which is to provide a picture of Antiochene exegesis as the rival of Alexandrian exegesis, all of this serving as background to Augustine's synthesis. Pages 299–306 can be seen either as an extension of the Augustine essay dealing with his legacy in the early Middle Ages, or, as is indicated in the draft tables of contents also contained in the hermeneutics boxes at Princeton, a distinct essay titled "The Augustinian Tradition." The Luther essay is titled "The Reformation" and can be found in Box 35 labeled "Hermeneutics" (6 of 6) in a folder labeled "'The Reformation' (typescript).(1)." Despite the title, this sixty-three-page essay is, after about four and a half pages on the influence of biblical humanism on the Reformation, all about Luther's hermeneutics. The essay on Bultmann is titled "Interpretation according to Bultmann" and can be found in Box 31 labeled "Hermeneutics" (2 of 6).

1

proceed with the project may be a disappointment. This introductory essay will outline the big picture of hermeneutical history Torrance envisioned and commend this collection of Torrance's essays as offering a satisfying contribution.

In preparing to publish his Hewett Lectures on "The Nature of Theology and Scientific Method" delivered at several seminaries in the American northeast[4] in 1959 and which Torrance's readers know as the book *Theological Science*, he attempted to add a new chapter on hermeneutics but found there was too much material for just one chapter, too much probably even for one book. He envisioned three volumes: *The Hermeneutics of the Fathers*, *The Hermeneutics of the Medievals and Reformers*, and *The Hermeneutics of the Moderns, from Spinoza to Bultmann*.[5] Had it been published as a single volume, a table of contents for the study would have resembled the following[6]:

Introduction
    i. General and Biblical Hermeneutics
    ii. The Two-Fold Source

1. *The Ancient Problem*
A. Patristic Interpretation
    (1) Early Patristic Interpretation
        Melito, Irenaeus
    (2) Alexandrian Interpretation
        Clement
    (3) Antiochene Interpretation
        Chrysostom
    (4) Athanasius

---

4 Those seminaries were Union Theological Seminary, Andover Newton Theological School, the Episcopal Theological School and Princeton Theological Seminary. See Torrance, *Theological Science*, vii.

5 Torrance, *The Hermeneutics of John Calvin*, vii.

6 Three typed versions of possible outlines for this study exist in the first folder of box 32 in Princeton Seminary's "Thomas F. Torrance Manuscript Collection," labeled "Hermeneutics" (3 of 6). The most developed appears exactly as seen here from the introduction to section 3, *The Modern Problem*. None of those outlines fill in what that third section would contain, but it can be constructed from an unpublished essay titled "Interpretation" in Box 31 of Princeton's collection labeled "Hermeneutics" (2 of 6). This essay is headed by a "III" and addresses itself to the "modern problem" of hermeneutics. The outline given here under section 3, *The Modern Problem* has been constructed from the subheadings of "Interpretation."

Introduction

 (5) Hilary
 (6) Augustine

B. Medieval Interpretation (Augustinian Tradition)[7]
 (1) Anselm
 (2) Aquinas
 (3) Duns Scotus, William of Ockham

2. *Transition*
A. Transition to the Reformation
 (1) Reuchlin
 (2) Erasmus
B. The Reformation
 (1) Luther
 (2) Calvin
C. Protestant Scholasticism and Rationalism
 (1) The Problem of Method
 (2) Spinoza

3. *The Modern Problem*
A. Erroneous Ways of Interpretation
 (1) Truth and Error in Realism
 (2) Truth and Error in Idealism
 (3) Truth and Error in Subjectivism
  (a) The Influence of subjective-idealism: Schleiermacher
  (b) The Influence of Romanticism: Winkleman and Herder
  (c) The influence of historicism: Dilthey
 (4) Truth and Error in Existentialism: Heidegger
B. Interpretation According to Bultmann

The two essays of the introduction and almost all of the essays on patristic interpretation were published together in 1995 as the book *Divine Meaning: Studies in Patristic Hermeneutics*.[8] Torrance included the essays

---

 7 This is not just a section heading but, as noted above in fn. 3, itself an unpublished essay titled "The Augustinian Tradition." It traces Augustine's legacy in the hermeneutics of John Cassian, Vincent of Lerins, Pseudo Dionysius, Boethius, Hugh of St. Victor, and Peter Lombard.

 8 Torrance, *Divine Meaning* (Edinburgh; T. & T. Clark, 1995). The two patristic essays left out of that volume and remaining regrettably unpublished are those on the hermeneutics of Chrysostom and Augustine.

on Duns Scotus and William of Ockham together with a newer essay on the hermeneutics of John Major as contextualizing background to Calvin, along with a lengthier study of Calvin's work, in the 1988 book *The Hermeneutics of John Calvin*. The book you are holding serves as a companion to these two earlier collections (though both are currently out of print), presenting Torrance's published essays on medieval and modern hermeneutics. Together, these three books offer a nearly complete picture of Torrance's envisioned project.

Why collect these different studies into one volume? What is wrong with reading them as discrete studies of the hermeneutics of distinct thinkers as Torrance eventually published them? The problem with this approach is that on their own the titles of these essays are misleading. A reader, approaching an essay with the title "Scientific Hermeneutics, According to Thomas Aquinas," will likely view it as a study of Thomas Aquinas' approach to biblical interpretation and expect the essay to describe the methods by which he interprets particular passages, attending especially to his biblical commentaries. But that is *not* what Torrance is really doing. What he means by "hermeneutics" is not a general methodology of textual interpretation but the theological and philosophical commitments interpreters bring with them about the world's relation to God and the nature of God's activity in the world. For Torrance, these issues are governed by and understood through Christology, Trinity, creation, and soteriology; it is in the person and work of Jesus Christ that God has given us to know who he is, who we are, what the world is, and how all of these relate to one another. That is to say, when Torrance studies someone's hermeneutics, he primarily wants to know what they think it means for God to reveal himself and what it has to do with their Christology. But what is missed when these studies are separated is his intention of tracing the church's understanding on this question throughout its history. Telling that story as a whole was the original intention behind the composition of these essays, which was obscured by their separate publication.

Taken together, that story goes something like this: God taught Israel, and thereby the first Christians, to know him through his covenantal acts of redemption. Together, these acts form a history that reaches its intended fulfillment in the incarnation of Jesus Christ and his atoning work, the ultimate salvific act of God. Torrance uses the word "realist" for understanding these acts to be nothing less than God's own actions in

Introduction

our world.⁹ Beginning with the Hellenistic world's Platonic philosophy, the church has had to assert its realist understanding of God's presence and activity in the world against "dualist" ways of thinking that keep the spiritual and physical aspects of the world strictly separate, and thus deny the logic of Scripture's description of God's action in the world. Such dualist thinking seeks to find in such narratives symbolic or allegorical expression of spiritual truth in the physical realm.

Dualism was explicit in those schools of thought that the early church's (basically realist) ecumenical councils anathematized, but then continued in more covert forms in the West through the massive medieval influence of Augustine's sacramental cosmology, the notion that all of creation signifies divine reality. This Augustinian influence, which Torrance calls the "Latin heresy," directs our minds to follow the signs imbedded in all temporal creation to its eternal Creator. Torrance sees this migration of thought as dualist because it requires the mind to move across a chasm that remains latently acknowledged between creation and God, whereas the realism Torrance advocates directs us to see the presence and activity of God in creation through the incarnation in such a way that our minds are not to move from creation to Creator, but rather to behold the Creator *in* the man Jesus Christ. Scripture's reference, then, is not directly vertical, so that our minds ought to move from its statements to God in his transcendent eternity, but horizontal to the historical humanity of Jesus Christ in which God himself has already made the vertical move down to us in the incarnation.¹⁰

The Reformation was, in Torrance's narrative, a recovery of this kind of christocentric realism. Modernism, however, developed a new form of dualism, especially in Immanuel Kant, whose philosophy was more concerned to bar the mind from its object than spirit from matter, but it amounts to the same thing as the ancient dualism. With this modern perspective, the exegete takes Scripture's theological statements as

---

9 This is admittedly a severely simplified account of Torrance's realism. For a fuller account, attending to the greater nuances of Torrance's hermeneutics, see my "The Depth Dimension of Scripture: A Prolegomenon to Evangelical Calvinism" in *Evangelical Calvinism*, eds. Myk Habets and Bobby Grow (Eugene, OR: Wipf and Stock Publishers, 2012), 67–93 and my doctoral dissertation, *The Depth Dimension: Scripture and Hermeneutics in the Theology of T. F. Torrance* (2013) available in the library of the University of Aberdeen.

10 Torrance has called Christ's humanity the "real text" of Scripture. Cf. Torrance, *Theological Science*, 193, *The Mediation of Christ* (Edinburgh: T. & T. Clark, 1992), 78, and *Divine Meaning*, 7.

anthropological statements, its testimony to God's salvific acts as expressions of the self-consciousness or existential experience of the communities that produced the biblical texts. In the past century, Karl Barth has once again called the church away from ancient and modern forms of dualism to recognize the presence of God's very being in his acts of revelation and redemption in Christ. Barth thereby serves as the most recent hopeful episode in Torrance's narrative of hermeneutical history.

Certain figures in this story serve as dualist "villains" for Torrance (Origen, Augustine, Schleiermacher, and Bultmann). Some he sees as offering both help and harm (Anselm, Aquinas, and Luther). Realism, however, has three clear "heros": Athanasius, Calvin, and Barth. The point to be grasped is that this larger narrative of the historical struggle between dualism and realism contextualizes Torrance's task in any given study of a particular theologian's hermeneutics. He is not seeking to isolate that figure's historical situation and assess their contributions within it according to that person's central interests—at least not primarily. He is identifying the contributions, both positive and negative, that that thinker has made to the historical drama of dualist and realist biblical hermeneutics. Seeing these essays in this way will help explain why Torrance's handling of these figures' hermeneutics seems preoccupied with a fairly narrow set of issues: he is tracing these issues across the church's whole history and any particular figure is but one stop on the tour.

Another way of approaching Torrance's agenda is to ask the question *how do we properly narrate the church's history? Who is the proper subject of that history?* If, as with Torrance, we are more narrowly concerned with the history of the church's understanding of the place of Scripture in the divine economy of revelation, we may still ask the same question: *who is the proper subject of that history?* Torrance's history of hermeneutics project indicates how God himself has progressively pressed upon the church through the whole course of its history, and continues to press upon it, a recognition of the manner of his active presence in the world as Word and Spirit. That is why Torrance is not especially interested in attending to any given thinker's self-understanding, placing, for example, greater emphasis on the *homoousion* in Athanasius's teaching than Athanasius himself may have. Torrance is convinced that God was doing something in the development of the *homoousion* and Athanasius' promotion of it that is more important than (though certainly informed by) Athanasius's motivations in his own context. Similar to the Acts of the Apostles, then, where the primary focus is

Introduction

not the psyches or intentions of Peter, Philip, or Paul (about which so much is unsatisfyingly left out) but Christ himself at work by his Spirit to grow and guide his church, Torrance has an eye for how Christ has continued throughout the church's subsequent history to guide its understanding in opposition to alien habits of thinking that have led it astray.

This book is divided into two parts. The first, "Foundations for the History of Hermeneutics," establishes foundational concepts in Torrance's hermeneutical vocabulary, including the beginning of the conflict that has driven the history of hermeneutics, and provides an overarching historical narrative within which the individual pieces of the second part of the book can be understood. Chapter 1, "Biblical Hermeneutics and General Hermeneutics," originally written for the history of hermeneutics project (as were all other included essays except where noted), offers Torrance's own vision for a hermeneutic built on an articulation of what Scripture is in God's hands, its ontology as determined by its place in God's revelatory and redemptive work. This constructive statement on the nature of Scripture, then, supports the following essays on how Scripture should be read.

Chapter 2, "The Complex Background of Biblical Interpretation," begins the more detailed narrative by examining how Platonic thinking in general and allegorical biblical interpretation in particular made their way into the church at an early stage.

Chapter 3, "Karl Barth and the Latin Heresy," was not originally written for Torrance's planned history of hermeneutics project, but is nonetheless valuable for understanding it, being the clearest, most direct, and most succinct expression in Torrance's own words of the larger historical picture the essays of part 2 will go on to fill out in more detail.

Part 2, "Medieval and Modern Hermeneutics," advances the story from the patristic period, as treated in *Divine Meaning*, into the Middle Ages and beyond. While there is an advantage in having read *Divine Meaning*, the essays of part 1 provide enough background to understand these essays. Chapter 4, "The Place of Word and Truth in Theological Inquiry According to St Anselm," does not center explicitly on the incarnate Christ, but Torrance finds Anselm's hermeneutic to be strongly realist in the sense of locating the truth of words in the realities to which they refer rather than in the words themselves—an anomaly in the Augustinian medieval scene (pre-Thomas) whose insights are left mostly unheeded until the Reformation.

In chapter 5, "Scientific Hermeneutics According to St Thomas Aquinas," Torrance sees Aquinas setting theology on a positive new course toward greater scientific rigor and objectivity, but is more immediately critical of the way Aquinas objectifies the speculative doctrines built up over the course of the previous several centuries as authoritative divine truth. Torrance sees Aquinas finalizing the church's medieval task of assuming God's authority as its own, rather than recognizing the manner in which the authority of God is present to the church but distinct from it as Word and Spirit.

Chapters 6 and 7 discuss the hermeneutics of the biblical humanists John Reuchlin and Erasmus respectively. Both figures in these essays provide background for the Reformation and even anticipate Calvin in their distaste for the abstractions of medieval scholasticism, but their counter-proposals, Reuchlin's mysticism and Erasmus's moralism, lack the power and insight of those made by Luther and Calvin. Still, Torrance finds their work worth the consideration both are given here, at least for the background insight they offer on the humanist movement precipitating the Reformation.

Between chapters 7 and 8 stands the book, *The Hermeneutics of John Calvin*. Though that book undertakes a largely genetic task to situate Calvin as a leading Parisian humanist of his day, it also depicts Calvin pressing through the abstractions of medieval scholasticism to an appreciation of God's direct activity in his Word and Spirit in the church's hermeneutics. Moving forward from that point historically, between Calvin and the dawn of Protestant liberalism in the work of Friedrich Schleiermacher stand the intellectual histories of Protestant Orthodoxy, German Pietism, and the Enlightenment, all of which are crucial for understanding the theology of the nineteenth century and beyond. Torrance deals with this period and what he calls the "modern problem" in several places, with Immanuel Kant as its central figure.[11] Prior to Kant, the scientific advancements of Galileo and Newton had been given a philosophical interpretation by Descartes and Locke that saw the objects of knowledge imposing their truth more or less directly on the minds of knowing subjects. When Hume demonstrated that this is clearly untrue in at least the case of causality, which simply cannot be observed, Kant sought a new epistemology that accounted for a partnership of roles between knowing subjects and the objects they know, though Torrance would be quick to point out that Kant's view

---

11 Cf. Torrance, *The Ground and Grammar of Theology* (Edinburgh: T. & T. Clark, 1980), 23–27 and *Theological Science*, 88–89.

INTRODUCTION

heavily privileges subjects who impose universal categories in their acts of knowing. Schleiermacher, whose hermeneutics are the subject of chapter 8, serves as the pioneer of applying Kant's subjectivism to biblical exegesis.

Chapter 9 concludes the book with, as in chapter 1, another essay on Karl Barth that was not (apparently) originally written as a part of Torrance's history of hermeneutics project, but which nonetheless fittingly completes his narrative of that history. Barth's theology of the Word of God and the Christocentric realist biblical hermeneutic that drives it is for Torrance not only the great solution to the "modern problem," but equally and as such the modern solution to the older dualisms as well. Deeply informed by the tradition behind him but also offering uniquely modern insights, Barth's work has established itself as a turning point, changing the landscape for all that would come after it. Placing this essay at the end of this collection serves to make clear how Torrance sees the tradition preceding Barth leading to the latter's breakthrough to a realist hermeneutic that is both a recovery and an advancement.

There are profound insights to be gained in studying these essays that will enrich scholars, pastors, and laypeople seeking to serve the advancement of God's kingdom with an awareness of the church's past obediences and failures. Torrance offers us a robust and nuanced understanding of Scripture as Christ's self-announcement through the prophets and apostles by the Spirit and a hermeneutic that recognizes God's active revealing and reconciling presence to us.

Adam Nigh
March 2017

Part 1

Foundations
for the History of Hermeneutics

CHAPTER 1

Biblical Hermeneutics and General Hermeneutics[1]

The source of all our knowledge of God is his active revelation of himself. We do not know God against his will, or behind his back, as it were, but in accordance with the way in which he has elected to disclose himself and communicate his truth in the historical-theological context of the worshipping people of God, the Church of the Old and New Covenants. That is the immediate empirical fact with which the Holy Scriptures of the Old and New Testaments are bound up. They were composed under the inspiration of the Holy Spirit, and in the providence of God have been handed on to us as the written form of the Word of God. They are the Scriptures of the people of Israel, for Israel was the selected medium of God's revelation in which his Word operated prophetically in the life and understanding of a particular historical community in order to provide within mankind a place where divine revelation might be translated appropriately into human speech and where it might be assimilated and understood in a communicable form by all humanity. And they are the Scriptures of the Christian Church, for the Church was the appointed sphere in which the historical self-revelation of God through Israel, gathered up and transcended and fulfilled in Jesus Christ the Word made flesh, is given an evangelical form in the apostolic witness and tradition, *kerygma* and *didache*, through which the crucified and risen Lord Jesus Christ himself continues to meet men and women as the living Word of God and to impart himself to them as the Way, the Truth and the Life, apart from whom, as our Lord claimed, no one has access to the Father.

This means that the Church must always turn to the Holy Scriptures as the immediate source and norm of all revealed knowledge

1 This essay originally appeared as the Introduction to *Divine Meaning: Studies in Patristic Hermeneutics* (Edinburgh: T. & T. Clark, 1995), 5–13. Reprinted with permission from Bloomsbury Publishing Plc, London.

of God and of his saving purpose in Jesus Christ. Since all the doctrinal formulations of the Church take shape within the matrix of the biblical revelation where they have their kerygmatic and didactic basis, regular examination and interpretation of the Holy Scriptures are in order, so that the Church may clarify and purify its knowledge of God's self-revelation mediated through them, and put all its biblical exposition, all preaching of the Gospel, and all theological statements about its understanding of the content of God's self-revelation into question through referring them back to their divine ground. They are to be regarded as authentic theological statements, accurately related to 'the truth as it is in Jesus',[2] and thus as statements framed in obedient response to the Word of the Truth of God addressing the Church through the Scriptures, that is, in what St Paul called 'the obedience of faith' (ὑπακοὴ πίστεως).[3] This is the all-important reference that tests whether its theological statements derive from true hearing of the Word of God or are simply thought up, whether they are genuine audits corresponding to the Word of God or are no more than speculative constructs out of the Church's creative spirituality. Hence the making and testing of the doctrinal formulations in the Church involve critical inquiry into their conformity to the content of divine revelation and careful interpretation of the Holy Scriptures through which that divine revelation is mediated. That is the relevance of hermeneutics to theological activity and the relevance of theology to hermeneutical activity.

Quite clearly our understanding and interpretation of the witness and testimony of the Holy Scriptures cannot be divorced from a doctrine of Holy Scripture, for at no point may form and content be separated from one another although they may and must be distinguished. This is not the place to offer a proper account of that doctrine, but in our concern to probe into the hermeneutics of the Early Church we will not be able to avoid dealing with certain essential elements in a doctrine of Holy Scripture as they bear upon the problem of its interpretation. Hence it may be worth noting at this point, if only very briefly, several significant features of Holy Scripture in order to indicate the way in which they are to be regarded.

(a) We acknowledge the Scriptures to be the written form of the Word of God because in and through them we hear the Word of God in his divine Majesty and Grace. Admittedly, no theoretic proof can be given for this

2 Ephesians 4:21.
3 Romans 1:5; 16:26, etc.

because it is the Word of *God* with which we have to do in the Scriptures. At no point can we bring God under the compulsion of our theoretical demonstrations or constrain him to yield answers to us in accordance with our empirical stipulations. Our inquiry will necessarily take a self-critical form in which we seek to allow the Word of God to be its own evidence in declaring itself to us, and to call all our presuppositions into question before it, so that we may listen to it and seek to understand it without imposing ourselves upon it. Because it is the Word of *God* that we encounter, we approach it in humility before its divine majesty, and with receptiveness before its divine Grace, thus yielding to it as is proper precedence and ascendency over us in all our knowing and interpretation.

(b) In the Bible we hear the Word of God speaking through the mouth of men through human prophets and apostles, but above all through the mouth of his Son incarnate Jesus Christ. The Bible is a human book written by human beings, and yet in and through it, it is God's Word that we hear. Thus God's Word comes to us in a happening which is both divine and human and in such a way that we hear the divine and the human at the same time—the divine and the human belong essentially together so that while they may be distinguished they are not to be separated from one another. The pattern for our understanding of this relation between the divine and the human is supplied in the heart of divine revelation in Jesus Christ himself, who unites divine and human natures in his one Person. But whereas in Jesus Christ the divine Word and human word are united within one Person, that is, hypostatically, in the Bible the divine Word and the human word are only united through dependence upon and participation in Christ, that is, sacramentally. 'In the written word there is no such thing as a personal union, but that which is human is used by God as an instrument which remains outside his own Person.'[4] There is thus analogical unlikeness as well as likeness in the relation between the divine and the human in Christ and the relation between the divine (that is, Christ himself) and the human in the Bible. Strictly speaking then, for Christians, the real text with which we have to do in the New Testament Scriptures is the *humanity* of Jesus Christ, for it is in the humanity of the Word of God incarnate in him, that we meet and are addressed by the Word of the living God.

---

4 Darwell Stone, *Outlines of Christian Dogma* (London, 1927), 130.

(c) The Word of God does not come to us in the Bible in such a way that we meet it face to face unveiled of its divine Glory and Majesty, but only in such a way that 'we see through a glass darkly', and 'know in part'.[5] Moreover, the holy sinless Word of God incarnate in Jesus Christ comes to us veiled in *our* humanity, for it was 'in the concrete likeness of the flesh of sin' (ἐν ὁμοιώματι σαρκὸς ἁμαρτίας),[6] yet of course without sinning, which he has assumed for our sakes in order that he may communicate with us where we are in our sin, poverty and darkness and lift us up into the riches and light of the Truth of God. The written form which the Word of God has taken in the Bible is in accord with the actual way taken by the Word of God when he became incarnate in Jesus Christ in the likeness of our flesh of sin but in such a way as to condemn sin in the flesh. Just as the incarnate Son identified himself with us in our estrangement from God, entering into the depths of our ignorance and darkness, making the contradictions and questions of man in his God-forsakenness his own and struggling with them that he might bring the Truth of God to bear upon us where we are, and bring out of the depth of our lost estate under the divine judgment a true and obedient answer from man to God, so we must think of the Word of God in the Scriptures not only as accommodating himself to us in our weakness and littleness but as condescending to enter into our alienated and contradictory ways of thought and speech in order to reach us with his message and to restore us to converse with God in truth. Thus the Word of God comes to us in the Bible not nakedly and directly with clear compelling self-demonstration of the kind that we can read it off easily without the pain and struggle of self-renunciation and decision, but it comes to us in the limitation and imperfection, the ambiguities and contradictions of our fallen ways of thought and speech, seeking us in the questionable forms of our humanity where we have to let ourselves be questioned down to the roots of our being in order to hear it as God's Word. It is not a Word that we can hear by our clear-sightedness or master by our reason, but one that we can hear only through judgment of the very humanity in which it is clothed and to which it is addressed and therefore only through crucifixion and repentance. It is because the Word of God comes to us in this way that

---

5 1 Corinthians 13:12: βλέπομεν γὰρ ἄρτι δι' ἐσόπτρου ἐν αἰνίγματι ... ἄρτι γιγνώσκω ἐκ μέρους.

6 Romans 8:3. The expression ἐν ὁμοιώματι here has to be understood in the same realist, non-docetic, way as the ἐν ὁμοιώματι of Philippians 2:7.

either we are offended at it and reject it in order to cling to ourselves, or we believe in it through a decision against ourselves and so hear it by committing ourselves to its action upon us.[7] Therefore the hearing of the Word of God does not necessarily follow when linguistic and historical and psychological or other necessary examination and interpretation of the text are completed.

(d) The Word of God comes to us in the Bible and can be heard as such only within our experience of God's saving activity in the Lord Jesus Christ. He has come to redeem the very humanity to which he addresses himself. Therefore the act of his revelation is inseparable from the act of his reconciliation, and the act of his self-impartation is inseparable from the act of his atoning propitiation. We may draw near to God through the Cross of Christ because it is through the Cross that God himself has drawn near to us.[8] Correspondingly we cannot hear the Word without being reconciled to God or receive the Word without receiving the atonement set forth in the blood of Christ. It is not otherwise in the activity of the Word in the human speech of the Bible. Just as Christ laid hold of our disobedient and self-willed humanity and throughout the whole course of his earthly life bent it back in obedience to the will of God, bringing it to acquiesce in the judgments of God, and thereby presented our humanity in himself to the divine judgment in order to expiate sin and reconcile us to the Father and thus to be the one Mediator between God and man, so in the Holy Scriptures of the Old and New Testaments the Word of God has laid hold of our wayward and recalcitrant human speech in order to struggle with it and bend it back into obedience to God's Truth that it may be restored as a vehicle of genuine communication between God and man.

The extraordinary fact about the Bible is that in the hands of God it is the instrument he uses to convey to us his revelation and reconciliation and yet it belongs to the very sphere where redemption is necessary. The Bible stands above us speaking to us the Word of God and yet the Bible belongs to history which comes under the judgment of God and requires the cleansing and atoning activity of the Cross.[9] When we hear the Word of God in the Bible, therefore, we hear it in such a way that the human word of

---

7 See E. Gaugler, *Was ist uns die Bibel?* (Basel, 1942), 3; and H. Vogel, *Gott in Christo* (Berlin, 1951), 110f.

8 Ephesians 2:12–22.

9 Thus, according to the Epistle to the Hebrews, even *the book* itself, that is, the *Torah*, was not exempt from being cleansed by the atoning blood of the covenant (9:19f.).

Holy Scripture bows under the divine judgment, for that is part of its function in the communication of divine revelation and reconciliation. Considered merely in itself it is imperfect and inadequate and its text may be faulty and errant, but it is precisely in its imperfection and inadequacy and faultiness and errancy that God's inerrant Holy Word has laid hold of it that it may serve his reconciling revelation and the inerrant communication of his Truth. Therefore, the Bible has to be heard as Word of God within the ambiguity of its poverty and riches, its weakness and power, and heard in such a way that we acknowledge that in itself in its human expression, the Bible comprises the word of man with all the limitations and imperfection of human flesh, in order to allow the human expression to fulfil its divinely appointed and holy function for us, in pointing beyond itself, to what it is not in itself, but to what God has marvellously made it to be in the adoption of his Grace.[10] The Bible itself will pass away with this world, but the Word of God which it has been inspired to convey to us does not pass away but endures forever.

We can go no further in indicating the lineaments of a doctrine of Holy Scripture, but it will be apparent that if it is really the Word of God which we hear in and through the Bible we will be unable to ensure hearing of that Word through bringing to it some hermeneutical method, as if all we had to do were to apply its rules carefully in order to hear it. But if the Word of God does come to us through the medium of these documents and Scriptures then it is absolutely necessary that we learn to read what actually lies in front of us—which is not at all easy—in order that we may listen to what it says. Therefore we must not neglect the requirement for a disciplined and controlled interpretation of the Bible, that is, for scientific hermeneutics. That is of course a universal requirement whenever human communication, oral or written, is involved.

There are therefore general principles of hermeneutics that are universally applicable and equally relevant to the tragedies of Aeschylus and the songs of Deutero-Isaiah. A scientific hermeneutics will take into account differences in history and race and language and worship and thought in order to provide careful interpretation of some piece of writing in its actual context,[11] but if we hear the Word of the living God in and

---

10 See *Essays in Christology for Karl Barth*, ed. T. H. L. Parker (London, 1956), 21–27.

11 For the intimate relation of language and its structure to thought and the formation of concepts see the instructive studies by Otto Neugebauer, *The Exact Sciences in Antiquity* (2nd ed. Providence, 1957), 29ff; and of Friedrich Waismann, *Introduction to Mathematical Thinking* (New York, 1959), 49ff.

through the writings of the Old and New Testaments it will not be scientific to neglect the bearing of that fact upon the speech that is used or the documents that are composed and employed for that communication. Thus within the field of general hermeneutics there arises biblical hermeneutics which is concerned with the interpretation of texts related to the Word of God. On the other hand, in these very texts where we are concerned with God's Word to *man*, we are also confronted with sheer humanity in a way unparalleled for its range and depth and stark realism, and therefore we are the more deeply concerned with the issues of human communication, of speaking and hearing and reading and translating. No documents in all history have been or continue to be subjected to such searching examination and historico-critical inquiry as the Holy Scriptures. It is for this reason that biblical hermeneutics has exercised a powerful impact on the general science of hermeneutics so that the histories of general and biblical hermeneutics inevitably run together.

But there is also a theological reason for this. It is in the Bible where we are summoned by God to hear his Word that we learn what hearing really means. God's Word comes to us penetrating into the depths of human life, cutting through all our shams and hypocrisies, through all our passions and self-will, finding its way through the defences which we build up in our selfishness over against one another, and against God, and stands us face to face with God where we learn to listen in humility without interjecting ourselves and mixing our own speaking into our hearing, where we learn to be really open to the Other and to receive what he communicates by letting ourselves be told what we cannot tell ourselves and without pretending that we can tell it to ourselves. It is in this openness toward God's self-communication that we learn to be open toward others, to speak to them not for our sakes, for the sake of displaying ourselves, but for their sake to communicate with them, and to listen to what they want to say to us as a real communication without interpreting it as an act of self-display on their part. Really to listen to others and honestly to speak to others in respect for their humanity, is not easy for human beings, for they make themselves into walls of partition and will only hear one another through the screen of their own self-understanding and self-expression. Now it is because in the Bible we hear a Word that cuts through all those screens and pretences, and so may learn what pure hearing is, that the interpretation of the Bible has something fundamental to offer to every human attempt to listen or interpret the communication of another.

We may express this in a more theological way. Christian theology holds that God has made man for communion with himself, and that it belongs to man's proper nature, in distinction from all other creatures, to be the creature whom God addresses personally in his creative Word and enables to respond personally to him. It is on that ground that man is made to be the creature who communicates personally with his fellow man in the reciprocal relation of speaking and hearing, and therefore we fail to communicate properly with one another when our basic and constitutive communication with God is damaged or perverted. *Et ipsi dediscimus bene loqui ubi cum deo loqui desinimus.*[12]

On the other hand, to be schooled in communication with God, to be opened in love and truth by that communication, will have its profound effect in every sphere where we have communication with one another. It is on this ground that Karl Barth has claimed that there is no such thing as 'special hermeneutics',[13] for in biblical hermeneutics we are concerned with something basic that is valid for the exposition of every human word, and can therefore lay claim to universal recognition. 'It is not at all that the word of man in the Bible has an abnormal significance and function. We see from the Bible what its normal significance and function is. It is from the word of man in the Bible that we must learn what has to be learned concerning the word of man in general.'[14] Barth admits that because we are concerned in the Bible with God's revelation, which is distinguished from everything else by a majesty belonging to it and lacking in other human communication, we may speak of biblical hermeneutics as a special form of a universally valid hermeneutics. And yet, he says, if we are to deal with it in this way, as a hermeneutics prescribed by revelation as the content of the biblical word, we must remember that 'we are not dealing with a mysterious thing apart which applies only to the Bible'.[15] In other words, in the Bible we are concerned with human speech that is assimilated to the communication of God's Word that reconciles and renews, and therefore in our interpretation of it we are concerned with a basic form of communication that has healing and redemptive significance. Hence, Barth concludes, if biblical

---

12   John Calvin, *Institutio*, III.23.5.
13   Karl Barth, *Church Dogmatics*, I.2 (Edinburgh, 1956), 466.
14   Ibid., 466.
15   Ibid., 472.

hermeneutics dares to be a special hermeneutics this is for the sake of a better general hermeneutics.[16]

However, we must not forget what Schleiermacher called 'the language-moulding power of Christianity'[17] and the sheer impact of divine revelation upon the forms of thought and speech in the Old Testament as well as the New Testament, which gives biblical hermeneutics a special place with *idiomata* of its own that have to be studied and interpreted. This does not mean—and in this Barth is surely right—that the human word in the Bible is in any way less than human or somehow superhuman, but rather that it is even more fully human inasmuch as it is in touch with the Word which creates and moulds the human and is essentially humanising Word. It is after all in Jesus Christ alone that true humanity is to be found, humanity that is not dehumanised by sin or perverted by estrangement. The word that is assimilated to his human life and history and serves the communication of his Word is as such redeemed from our inhumanity and restored to human fullness.[18]

---

16 Ibid.

17 'Die sprachbildendende kraft des Christentums', *Hermeneutik und Kritik mit besondever Beziehung auf das Neue Testaments* (*Sammtliche Werke*, 1.7) (Berlin, 1938), 68.

18 [The original essay concluded with the following paragraph indicating Torrance's intentions for the chapters that were to follow in his book *Divine Meaning*:] My concern in the following studies in the field of patristic hermeneutics is not with actual exegetical interpretation of the Holy Scriptures, but rather with the epistemological ingredients and implications of hermeneutics, and therefore with the thought-world in which it is pursued. No attempt is made in this book to examine the writings of all the Greek Fathers in the early centuries of the Church, far less to develop a systematic account of their hermeneutical theory and practice. The different chapters represent no more than soundings taken in the first three centuries, but it is hoped that precisely as soundings they may serve to open up the field for further study in a more theological way than has been done before. My concern has been to bring to light the functioning of what Athenagoras of Athens called 'the real theological *logos* (φυσικὸς καὶ θεολογικὸς λόγος)'* and thus to disclose something of the way in which biblical hermeneutics is essentially a theological pursuit, for the only adequate and appropriate interpretation of the divine revelation mediated to us, as the great Greek Fathers realised, is *theological*, and cannot but be under the impact of the dynamic Word of the living God. (*Athenagoras, *An Intercession on Behalf of Christians* (Πρεσβεῖα τῶν Χριστιανῶν), 13.1. For the double meaning of the terms φυσικός and λόγος in this expression, see Torrance, '*Phusikos Kai Theologikos Logos*: St Paul and Athenagoras at Athens' in *Divine Meaning*.

CHAPTER 2

The Complex Background of Biblical Interpretation[1]

In the Christian era hermeneutics in all fields of literature has been greatly influenced by the traditional biblical emphasis upon *word* (λόγος). Because the Word of God has primary place in all constitutive relations between God, the world, and man, *word* came to have a principal role in the realm of biblical life and thought. It is not surprising, therefore, that right from the start it is the primacy of *word* that characterises biblical hermeneutics, nor is it surprising that when this biblical way of life was rediscovered at the Reformation, renewed concentration upon the Word of God should leave its mark upon the basic structures of life and thought in the West, and should affect the whole subsequent tradition of hermeneutical theory and activity.

Nevertheless, there is another side to this story: even biblical hermeneutics does not merely go back to the biblical tradition. Other influences were contributed from the outside, notably from Hellenism. That is apparent even in the hermeneutics of Judaism. After the 'sealing up' or cessation of the prophetic activity which characterised some of the later Hebrew Scriptures and the Apocrypha, and involved the reconstruction and redaction of the whole tradition, Judaism was faced with the question of formal interpretation of the Scriptures, as we can see in the institution of the Scribes as interpreters of the law.

Jewish interpretation of the Old Testament was carried out in two ways designed to transmit the practical and the theoretical teaching of the Hebrew Scriptures and to bridge the gulf, as it were, between the ancient times and the present. This was done by providing expository material elucidating and supplementing the old records through *Haggadah*

1 This essay originally appeared in *Divine Meaning: Studies in Patristic Hermeneutics*, (Edinburgh: T. & T. Clark, 1995), 15–39. Reprinted with permission from Bloomsbury Publishing Plc, London.

and *Halakah*.² *Haggadah* took the form of narrative, often largely cultic and dramatic, designed for inspiration and edification. One of the most important of these is the *Passover Haggadah* in which the Passover is vividly interpreted as a participation in the original events of redemption of Israel out of Egypt and is made to point ahead to its messianic fulfilment at the end.³

Halakah, on the other hand, was concerned with the interpretation of the *Torah* and in providing on that basis or even apart from it precepts for action and conduct in order to ensure translation into historical happening and conduct in the present of the Law once for all given in the historical events of the past. *Halakah* came to be more highly prized in Judaism than *Haggadah*, and with the overthrow of the Temple and the diminishing significance of the cult, *Halakah* became rather severely ethical, laying down accepted decisions for a way of life. If *Haggadah* can be said to correspond to the kerygmatic material in the Old Testament, *Halakah* can be said to correspond to its didactic material, but in Judaism they are more sharply divided, and the Halakhic teaching carries within itself a distinction between the ethical and the theoretical. This is due, however, to an ingredient in traditional Judaism that derives not from the Old Testament itself, but from Hellenic sources, especially from the dualism between body and spirit which unbiblical though it was came to characterise Pharisaic Judaism even in New Testament times. It was under the influence of this Hellenic influence that the ethic of Judaism changed into a form that has ever since characterised Rabbinic teaching.

Judaism added a third method of interpreting the Old Testament when again under the influence of Hellenism it adopted the use of allegory. Taken up by Aristobulus this was developed by Philo of Alexandria which enabled him not only to give a more ethico-mystical interpretation of the Old Testament but to relate its teaching to Greek philosophy, and especially to interpret the Old Testament *logos* more in line with its significance in the Platonic tradition, as 'rationality'. In other words, Philo makes a transition toward Hellenic thought in his association of *images* and *ideas* through allegorical interpretation of events.

---

2 See Emil Schürer, *History of the Jewish People in the Time of Christ* (Edinburgh, 1908), I.i, pp. 117ff; II, pp. 327ff; Herbert Danby, *The Mishnah* (Oxford, 1933), Introduction, xxixff.

3 See the new edition of the *Passover Haggadah* by Cecil Roth (London: Soncino Press, 1934).

Divine Interpretation

Hellenism had an even stronger influence in Christian hermeneutics, supplying it not only with its terminology but with many of its basic philosophical questions that communication of thought from one person to another, from one language to another, and not least from one world of thought to another, always raises. Different as the Hellenic tradition and the biblical tradition (especially in its Hebraic roots) were, it was through the conflation of these two traditions that what may be called the science of hermeneutics arose.

It is from Hellenism that we derive our term *hermeneutics*, from the word ἑρμηνεύειν, meaning, first, to bring news or to convey a message, and, then, to interpret or explain or to translate from one language to another. Hence it came also to denote translation from one way of speaking or thinking into another and more understandable form, yet without losing altogether the original sense of conveying information. In the religious realm the question of hermeneutics arose very early in connection with the understanding of the poets who were sometimes spoken of as interpreters (ἑρμηνῆς) of the gods, or in connection with the meaning of prophetic oracles.[4] An attempt was made to distinguish the mythical stories told about them and some hidden meaning or underlying sense (ὑπόνοια). Because the mystery rites were held to hold concealed significance interpretation was also required to bring it into the open, but the word used was ἐξηγεῖσθαι from which we get our familiar 'exegesis'.

Something similar to this is found in the works of Plato who used myth (μῦθος) to suggest in a narrative form a speculative notion that could not be reduced to exact statement; it was a dramatic image in temporal form of a timeless or eternal idea. Plato's interest lay not in the interpretation of poetical texts but in the understanding and knowledge of the truth. He distinguished real knowledge which is dependent on thinking from opinion or belief for which we are dependent on the reports of our senses. The object of knowledge in the proper sense is what is eternal and wholly intelligible, that is, 'ideas' or 'forms'; but the objects of sense-experience such as natural events or actual facts, which cannot be considered fully real, must be treated outwith the range of scientific knowledge or ἐπιστήμη. True knowledge, however, if it begins with sense-experience must reach beyond

---

4 See, for example, Plato, *Ion* 534E; *Symposium* 202E; *Epinomis* 975O. In this last passage, as Ebeling remarks (*Die Religion in Geschichte und Gegenwart* [3rd ed. Tübingen, 1959], Bd. I.ii, 243), we have the first occurrence of the expression ἑρμηνευτικὴ τέχνη.

it into the realm where thinking is by the mind itself apart from sense-experience. It is only of the noumenal world that we can have knowledge, whereas of the world of phenomena we can offer only opinion or conjecture.

These views were set out in many of Plato's dialogues but they are also found in the *Timaeus*, a work in which he expounded his cosmological theory, and one that fascinated and influenced countless people for centuries, and not least the world of gnostic and Neo-Platonic thought in the early centuries of the Christian era when the Hellenic mind was struggling with the biblical doctrines of creation and incarnation. In this work Plato drew a momentous distinction by asking: 'What is that which always is and has no becoming (τί τὸ ὂν ἀεί, γένεσιν δὲ οὐκ ἔχον) and what is that which is always becoming and never is (τί τὸ γιγνόμενον μὲν ἀεί, ὂν δὲ οὐδέποτε)? That which is apprehended rationally by the mind (νοήσει μετὰ λόγου) is always in the same state, but that which is conjectured through opinion by sense without reason (μετ'αἰσθήσεως ἀλόγου) is ever becoming and perishing and never really is (ὄντως δὲ οὐδέποτε ὄν).'[5] This was a distinction between the real world of noetic realities (τὸ νοητά) or rationality (τὸ λογιστικόν) and the visible world of what has become (τὸ γεγονός) or sense-objects (τὰ αἰσθητά). This tangible, sensible world has been formed by a good craftsman (ὁ δημιουργὸς), assumed to be God, to become a moving image (εἰκών) of an eternal model (παράδειγμα), assumed to be different from God himself. In making the visible cosmos (κόσμος) God put mind (νοῦς) into it, and as mind can exist only in a soul he gave it a soul (ψυχή) and it became a 'living being truly endowed with soul and mind by the providence of God' (ζῷον ἔμψυχον ἔννουν τε τῇ ἀληθείᾳ διὰ τὴν τοῦ θεοῦ γενέσθαι πρόνοιαν).[6]

This cosmological theory contained serious problems that drew to them a great deal of speculation down the ages, but in the early centuries of the Christian era, the theory took two basic forms, a Stoic form in which God came to be thought of in terms of a cosmic soul informing a cosmic body, and a Neo-Platonic form in which the distinction between the two realms was thrown into a sharp χωρισμός [chasm] between the κόσμος αἰσθητός [world of sense perception] and the κόσμος νοητός [world of thought]. And this was certainly in line with Plato's original intention in differentiating so absolutely between the world of sense or becoming which is visible and changing, and the world of mind or being which is invisible and unchangeable.

---

5 *Timaeus*, 27D-28A.
6 *Timaeus*, 30B; also see 28B-30B, 37A-C, 48E, 51D, etc.

Divine Interpretation

The meaning Plato gave to λόγος was in line with his whole outlook.[7] Because man stands between the two worlds, the intelligible and the sensible, as one who thinks and acts, who forms opinions and speaks, *logos* refers to the inner speech or conversation which he holds with himself, asking questions of himself and answering them, and refers also to the external speech or utterance of his opinion in audible words or sentences addressed to others. *Logos* is both thought and spoken. Thus conceived, the inner word (διάλογος) and the outer word (λόγος εἰρημένος) are closely related, but related in such a way that Plato distinguishes sharply between them, for the inner *logos* is purely noetic (διάνοια) and is directed to the world of being and intelligible forms, to the εἶδος of things, whereas external speech is merely a sort of image (ὥσπερ εἴδωλον) of thought that is uttered in the sensible realm and is only a passing phenomenal event. No doubt it does have a sort of participation (μέθεξις) in the realm of external forms but only as a transient sign or suggestion from which the thought passes in order to contemplate the world of being or reality. Thus in spite of the fact that speech is used metaphorically to describe thought, it is clear that in the intelligible world *logos* is ultimately concerned with the ineffable (ἄρρητον) reality which can be contemplated only in vision (θεωρία), and can be spoken of only indirectly by way of myth (μῦθος). Hence in the Platonic tradition λόγος was taken to refer to the eternal reason, the supreme mind immanent in all things, from which all rationality derives, and through participation in which alone man can have knowledge of intelligible and eternal realities. But a *logos* of God in the other sense, of speech, a λόγος θεῖος, is wanting to us.[8]

This Platonic distinction between a realm of sense and a realm of pure thought has had an immense influence upon the history of hermeneutics, for even when one is concerned with the meaning of a text it tends to carry the whole activity of interpretation beyond to the understanding of a supersensible and purely intelligible reality. In other words, it tends to lead straight into a sharp distinction between a crude literal sense and an underlying spiritual or philosophical meaning (ὑπόνοια). Because of the auditive element which is so powerful in the Hebrew, *word* plays little part in this thought, the visual image or figure represented in the latter was often regarded as mere shadow (σκιά) quite disparate from the reality that casts

---

7 See especially *Theaitetos*, 189ff, and *Sophistes*, 268ff.
8 *Phaedo*, 85C-D.

it, and therefore once it has played its part it is regarded as something to be left behind in the attainment of knowledge of the real.

Hellenism had another important contribution to make to the history of hermeneutics, through the teaching of Aristotle, notably in his work περὶ ἑρμηνείας or *de interpretatione* which later had a considerable influence upon mediaeval thought. Under the direction of Aristotle attention was given more to form and method, and because form and matter may not be divorced from one another, there resulted a more realistic form of exegesis with serious consideration of the straightforward sense interpreted according to the rules of grammar and logic.

One of the most lasting fruits of this teaching was the emphasis laid upon formal analysis of the text, in which the individual statements were to be interpreted in relation to the whole, and the whole was interpreted as gathering up the particulars. It was through this analytic and synthetic examination that meaning was determined. At the same time attention came to be paid also to the author himself in his use of speech, that is, to questions of rhetoric and philology, and it was realised that interpretation or translation from one language to another, or from one thought-world to another thought-world, required some knowledge of the historical and ideological background. Thus, in order to bridge the gap between the reader and the letter of older documents some attention to historical matters and philosophical developments was unavoidable.

We cannot follow through in detail the development and pursuit of this instruction in the schools of Athens and Alexandria, but it may be sufficient to say that while the Platonic distinction between sense and thought was dominant and ultimately determinative, attention was given to methodological scrutiny of the text, and rules for correct procedure according to grammar, rhetoric and logic became the common equipment of the schools throughout the Graeco-Roman world. Thus, observation and analytical thinking went together on the one hand, but on the other hand when the mind passed beyond the realm of sense it continued to think in visual terms through the relations of images to ideas, while the relation of images to events and the emphasis upon the auditive mode of thinking so characteristic of the Hebraic tradition had little place in it.

When hermeneutics of this sort was directed to the venerated texts of Hellenism such as the poetical works of Hesiod or Homer, it looked for hidden meanings secreted in them by the inspiration of the gods, that is, for a 'mystical' sense.⁹ It was in this connection that the study of the ancient myths was cultivated and through them Orphic and Pythagorean mysticism gained a powerful place in Hellenistic culture. The crudities of the 'stories' of the gods came under severe attack from the philosophers of the Academy, but it was always possible to seek an allegorical meaning cloaked under the garment of narrative. Moreover in the mystery rites and people's dreams, as the ancients seem to have been aware, one idea or one set of ideas might stand for others. To interpret them was regarded as an esoteric gift, so that understanding and interpretation of them was held to be accessible only to the few.

Three developments in this direction were of special significance for the rise of hermeneutics in the Early Church.

1. The Spread of Stoic Allegorical Thought

'Platonism', as Edwyn Bevan has said,

> had banished God from the material world, had left it a dark mass from which the soul must detach itself if it would find him, and yet this is the world which encloses us on every side, with which we have primarily to do. Zeno came, as it were, to men asking where they could find God, struck his hand upon the solid earth and answered 'here.' There was nothing that was not, in its ultimate origin, God; it was he in whom man lived and moved and had his being.[10]

This was not a view of the universe that can be described as *materialist* in the modern sense of that term, but one which held the *nature of things* everywhere to be inherently rational, and therefore thought of the whole material world to be constituted in accordance with a rational purpose (πρόνοια). Hence the close connections posited by the Stoics between *physics*, *ethics* and *logic*. In line with their cosmological outlook, in which they thought of a world-soul permeating the whole world-body, they could use vivid, pictorial language to express their philosophical ideas. Thus in comparing philosophy to an animal, they spoke of ethics as the flesh, logic as the bones and sinews, and physics as the soul. On the other hand they applied this in reverse, so to speak, to interpret the crude patterns

---

9 See the interesting chapter on 'Homère chez les Pères de l'Èglise', in Jean Daniélou, *Message évangélique et Culture hellénistique* (Tournai, 1961), 73ff.

10 E. R. Bevan, *Stoics and Sceptics* (Cambridge, 1959), 41.

and mythical stories of the gods in such a way as to make them yield a 'real' or 'natural' (φυσικός) meaning which was their scientific truth, that is, what was in accordance with the nature (φύσις) of the realities intended. This is discerned, however, only through tracing the reference (ἀναφορά) of sensible signs to intelligible or 'natural' signs (σημεῖα), that is, the mental facts expressed by the sensible signs, for it is they that are true or false. This was the purpose of allegorical interpretation, to make μῦθος yield ἀλήθεια, and so to show that the crudities of Classical literature were often only mythological ways of conveying philosophical truth.

Behind this lay an interesting semantic theory in which the Stoics distinguished, not two things, but three things: (i) that which signifies (τὸ σημαῖνον), the sensible or corporeal sign such as the spoken or written word; (ii) that which is signified or meant (τὸ σημαινόμενον or τὸ λεκτόν), the idea in the mind that subsists with our thought of something; and (iii) the external object (τὸ πρᾶγμα, or τὸ τυγχανόν). This had the effect not only of positing a screen of ideas in the middle between the speaker, or thinker, and the external realities, but of erecting a highly intellectualist view of truth. As far as interpretation was concerned it had the effect of concentrating attention upon linguistic expressions (λέξεις) since the significates (λεκτά) which carried truth or falsehood were abstracted from them, rather than upon things (πράγματα). On the other hand, since the external realities signified, whether sensible or noetic, were regarded as corporeal like the things signifying, allegorical interpretation, through a rationalising process, was tied down to a rather material outlook on reality.[11] Although allegorical interpretation of this kind went back to the great Stoic philosophers like Zeno, Cleanthes and Chrysippus, the centuries immediately before and after the birth of Christ saw a widespread application of Stoic allegorism to pagan literature along cosmological and ethical lines (φυσικῶς and ἐθικῶς) which laid the basis for much that was to follow.

2. The Rise of Jewish Allegorical Exegesis

The important centre for this was Alexandria. There for some time Stoic, Platonic and Pythagorean thought had been brought together, for example, by Poseidonius, and on this basis attempts were made to work out a symbolic interpretation of Egyptian mythology, for example, by Plutarch. But in

---

11 For the Stoic view of meaning and truth, see W. and M. Kneale, *The Development of Logic* (Oxford, 1962), 138ff.

Divine Interpretation

Alexandria there was also a Jewish allegorising tradition going back to the *Letter of Aristeas* and to Aristobulus, and even earlier sources, but reaching its height in the influential work of Philo in the earlier part of the first century AD.[12] Philo had behind him the older work of Palestinian Jewish scholars who expounded the Scriptures with the aid of *midrashim* through which they extended the Old Testament concept of the parable or *mashal* in order to set forth the more recondite meaning behind the sacred texts.[13] Their purpose was to make interpretation of the Old Testament books consistent with the doctrine of the transcendence of God by searching out the real ethical basis behind the laws and rituals and resolving the difficulties for belief in God which a merely literal understanding of many biblical passages appeared to create, but also to draw out the predictive elements in the Scriptures and to relate them to historical and eschatological fulfilment. It would be surprising if this interest in searching out the secrets and mysteries of the Law kept itself entirely distinct from the hermeneutical devices of Stoic and Pythagorean philosophers wherever Judaism made effective contact with Hellenism, but, as Wolfson has pointed out, 'no direct conscious attempt to interpret Scripture in terms of philosophy is to be found in these midrashic interpretations, though some of them...reflect certain philosophic concepts which have infiltrated into Judaism'.[14]

It was quite otherwise with Philo, who was a philosopher in the Greek sense as well as an interpreter of the Old Testament writings. What is distinctive of his work is that he not only brought together the earlier midrashic interpretation and Stoic allegorisation, but combined them with the philosophical theory of the χωρισμός between the κόσμος αἰσθητός and the κόσμος νοητός.[15] Philo made considerable use of this distinction to guard the utter transcendence of God from corruption through Stoic notions of the 'corporeality' of God and through a literal interpretation of Scriptural anthropomorphisms, but it had the effect of altering the essential cast of his thought by throwing it into an epistemological framework that was alien to the biblical and Judaic tradition.[16] In fact, Philo's thought absorbed into it

---

12 See H. A. A. Kennedy, *Philo's Contribution to Religion* (London, 1919), 32ff.

13 See A. S. Herbert, 'The Parable (*MĀŠĀL*) in the Old Testament.' *Scottish Journal of Theology* 7.2 (1954) 180ff.

14 H. A. Wolfson, *The Philosophy of the Church Fathers* (Cambridge, MA, 1964), 29.

15 See *De Abrahamo*, 68, 88; *De gigantibus*, 54; *De opificio mundi*, 10, 12, 15ff, *Quaestiones in Exodum*, II, 90; *Quis rerum divinarum heres sit*, III; *De somniis*, I, 185ff, etc. And cf. H. A. A. Kennedy, op.cit., 63ff.

16 Cf. H. A. A. Kennedy, op.cit., 40: 'Without realising what had happened, Philo,

The Complex Background of Biblical Interpretation

the profound change in cosmological outlook which under the impact of Platonic thought and the new astronomy yielded the Ptolemaic view of the universe. In Philo's writings this is apparent in his conception of the sensible world of time and space as imaging in transient shadows a heavenly world of timeless ideas and paradigmatic essences which God first formed as the instrument of his creation of all things and their providential ordering in accordance with his will. The true meaning of human life within this world is to be found in a 'migration' of the soul from the phenomenal world of sense and time to the noumenal world of intelligible realities. In his exposition of this Philo offers extended allegorical interpretation of the migration of Abraham and the exodus of Israel out of Egypt into the promised land or the entry of the high priest into the Holy of Holies.[17]

Philo's understanding of the Scripture was part and parcel of his religious philosophy, for he distinguished in it a literal or external meaning which he referred to as the 'body' (σῶμα) and an inner meaning which he referred to as the 'soul' (ψύχη), the literal meaning being related like 'shadows' to 'the things that really exist'.[18] To speak of this inner or hidden or intelligible meaning of the text he could use the technical terms ὑπόνοια and ἀλληγορία, but thought of these as describing the 'real' truth, the 'natural' meaning that was actually in accordance with the nature of the realities indicated, that is, the nature of God.[19] Hence Philo speaks of allegorists as φυσικοὶ ἄνδρες.[20] How Philo actually thought of the relation of the literal to the allegorical meaning is not always clear, for sometimes the literal sense seems to be left behind altogether, but we may defer to the judgment of two scholars who have subjected Philo's views to careful examination. 'The allegorical method as applied by Philo to the Old Testament is thus a special type of midrashic method, which has two characteristics. First, it must be an interpretation in which a term is changed from its literal meaning to something else, though the literal meaning is not always necessarily rejected. Second,

---

by his adoption of the allegorical method, had emptied his basal doctrine of all genuine value.'

17 See especially the *De Abrahamo, De migratione Abrahami, De vita Mosis*; and cf. the recent account of this by S. G. Sowers, *The Hermeneutics of Philo and Hebrews* (Zürich, 1965), 29ff, 62f.

18 See *De Abrahamo* 36, 200; 41, 236; *De migratione Abrahami* 2, 12; 16, 93; *De confusione linguarum*, 38, 190.

19 *De Abr.* 20, 99; *De somniis*, I.120; *De posteritate Caini*, 2.7.

20 *De Abr.* 20, 99; *De vita Mosis*, 2, 103.

that something else which the term is made to mean must be of what is described by him as philosophical.'[21] 'So Philo occupies a middle position in Alexandrian Judaism, defending the legitimacy of allegory against its literalist objectors as an indispensable apologetic and hermeneutical tool on the one hand, and on the other hand pleading for respect of the literal meaning of Scripture against left-wing allegorists.'[22] Certainly Philo himself can say: 'Both elements demand attention, the most diligent search for hidden meanings, and the preservation of those on the surface which cannot be challenged.'[23]

Nevertheless, the extent to which Philo developed the contrast between the sensible world and the intelligible world meant that the real truth could not be found through an allegorical exegesis that supplemented the literal meaning in order to make it point beyond itself altogether, or that left it behind as the understanding penetrated through it into the intelligible world, for only in that world may we know things that really are in accordance with the truth of their natures. This implied that reality in this world of sense and time can only take on a form of meaning that is symbolic, or that the sensible world is to be regarded as real only in so far as it is symbolic.[24] Thus, the purpose of allegorical interpretation of the Scriptures, as far as Philo was concerned, was to establish their ἀλήθεια over against all mythology,[25] and this meant for him the reality of God as God over against all anthropomorphic and geomorphic conceptions of him.[26]

3. The Influence of Gnosticism

Gnosticism was a syncretistic movement intensely interested in the cosmic drama of creation and redemption that broke out among (very imperfect) Christian converts of the second generation who had not properly broken free from pagan religious ideas or mythological and astrological speculation. Alexandrian gnosticism (following Basilides and Valentinus) seems to have

21 H. A. Wolfson, op.cit., 36.
22 S. G. Sowers, op. cit., 22.
23 *De migr. Abr.* 20.89.
24 *De migr. Abr.* 12; *De mutatione nominum* 62-65; *De somn.* I.185ff.
25 *De praemiis et poenis*, 2.8; *De fuga et inventione*, 179; *De agricultura*, 96ff; *Legum allegoriarum, Lib.* II.19.
26 *De confusione linguarum*, 21, 98; *De migr. Abr.* 23, 113; *Quod Deus sit immutabilis*, 53, 59-68; *Quaestiones in Genesim*, I.55; II.54; *De sacrificiis Abelis et Caini*, 91-101; *De somn.* I.40, 237.

been influenced by Egyptian and Philonic conceptions reposing upon a philosophical syncretism. Although the gnostics soon divided up into different sects elaborating various theomorphic and mythological systems, they all appear to have been concerned with the entanglement of human beings in the tension between light and darkness, spirit and matter, order and disorder, good and evil, and to have been obsessed with an esoteric and non-rational knowledge of the way of salvation.[27] This was the *gnosis* (γνῶσις) that gave them their name. Through initiation into it freedom from Fate (εἱμαρμένη) was attained, and the deep secrets of existence and destiny revealed: 'Who we are and what we become, where we have come from and where we are going, where we are hastening to and whereby we are redeemed, and what the meaning of our birth is and the meaning of rebirth.'[28]

Basic to the whole outlook of gnosticism was the Pythagorean and Platonic, Posidonian and Philonic gulf between the κόσμος νοητός and the κόσμος αἰσθητός, although this was infinitely widened,[29] and in certain aspects deeply affected by oriental dualism particularly apparent in Mandaean and Marcionite gnosticism. In Valentinian gnosticism, which was widely influential, the two worlds were differentiated as the πλήρωμα of Light and noumenal essences, and the κένωμα of shadow and privation. *Pleroma* was the fullness of that which is, or true being, whereas *kenoma* was the realism of emptiness and non-being, the shadowy and evanescent counterpart of the world of ideas and essences above, but beyond both worlds was the *Monad* or Universal Being, exalted and remote, supreme over all and unknowable.[30] According to the more philosophically minded Basilides we cannot know what God is but only what he is not, for he is absolutely ineffable and inaccessible. Hence we cannot properly think of him as existing (οὐκ ὢν θεός) so much as altogether nothing (οὐδέν). It is in accordance with the predetermination of this 'non-existent' God that all things have their existence, but in a non-existent way for he formed

---

27 Cf. the teaching of Poseidonius 'that the soul might receive direct enlightenment from beings not in the body, apart from all process of reason' (E. Bevan, *Stoics and Sceptics*, 117). This idea was prevalent in the Hermetic literature.

28 *Excerpta ex Theodoto*, 78.2. See also Epiphanius, *Pan. haer.* 26.3, 10, 13; *The Gospel of Truth*, 22.16ff; 25.10ff; *The Gospel of Thomas*, 1–4, 50.

29 Cf. R. Maclaren Wilson, *Studies in the Gospel of Thomas* (London, 1968), 211.

30 Irenaeus, *Adv. haer.* 3.1ff, especially 4.1ff; 6.1ff, 8.1ff, 14.1ff; Hippolytus, *Refutatio omnium haeresium*, 7.21–24.

DIVINE INTERPRETATION

them out of non-existents.[31] This is difficult to conceive rationally but the difficulty arises out of the epistemological dualism imposed upon thought by the vast gulf between the sensible and the intelligible worlds, and the complete transcendence of God over the world of intelligible realities.[32] In the nature of the case the gnostics had to have recourse to imaginative and mythological construction. The situation was somewhat different with Marcion who sought to avoid mythological speculation, while working within the same dichotomy, but only at the expense of positing the myth of an ultimate dualism between two supreme Beings, the Creator God of the Old Testament and the Redeemer God of the New Testament.[33] Thus, in one way or another a vast gulf, a fundamental χωρισμός, was characteristic of the various forms of gnostic thought.[34]

The gnostics differed also in their views of creation. For the most part they did not attribute it to the God of the New Testament but to one whom they called *Demiurge* (ὁ δημιουργός) who through some kind of disturbance and disorder in the supramundane world became the creator and ruler of the visible and material world which was therefore regarded as existing in tension and conflict with the invisible and spiritual world above. In Valentinian gnosticism the antithesis between the eternity and permanence of the upper world and the temporality and transience of the creaturely world is put down to the unsuccessful attempt of the Demiurge to imitate the limitless, eternal, infinite and timeless nature of the former by extension in time, ages and immense numbers of years in the latter, imagining that he could represent infinity by quantity. Time and history thus belong to fallen existence and must pass away with it.[35] Some gnostics identified this creator with the God of the Old Testament who seeks to subject man to himself, but others identified him with the pre-existent Christ or an emanation from the pre-existent *Logos*.[36] Moreover, throughout the various systems human beings were regarded (as in Orphism and Stoicism) as fallen seeds of light or sparks of the divine that had become entangled in matter and

---

31 Hippolytus, *Ref. omn. haer.* 7.8-9; 10. Cf. *Apocryphon Ioannis*, 22.19ff; *The Gospel of Truth*, 17.8, 22; 18.32.

32 Cf. Philo, *De opif. Mund.* 7, 29; 10, 36; 21, 66; 44, 129f; 46, 134.

33 Irenaeus, *Adv. Haer.* 1.16; 27.1f; 2.1, 4; Hippolytus, *Ref. omn. haer.* 7.17.1ff; 10.15; Tertullian, *Adv. haer.* 1.2f.

34 Thus, Hans Jonas, *The Gnostic Religion* (Boston, 1963), 250f.

35 Irenaeus, *Adv. haer.* 1.17.2; 2.5.1f; 7.1f.

36 Irenaeus, *Adv. haer.* 1.4f, 7f, 11; 2.3-8, 13f; Hippolytus, *Ref. omn. haer.* 5.17.1ff, 19.1ff; 6.13, 14, 35; 7.23-25; Origen, *In Ioannis Evangelium* 2.8.

evil and darkness, but yearn for redemption out of non-existence back into the *pleroma* of true being and for restoration from self-estrangement in this sensible world back into the divine world to which they properly belong. The great drama of redemption (ἀπολύτρωσις) was carried out through emission or prolation from God of an intermediate but supramundane being, that is, *Aeon* or *Nous*, called Christ, and through a movement on his part of descent into the *kenoma* and of ascent again into the *pleroma*, in the course of which he united himself temporally to Jesus imparting to men through him the gift of *gnosis* and the *Paraclete* by means of which they could win free from subjection to the material world and be gathered back into union with God.[37]

Behind this lay a more complicated conception of the relation of redemption to the creation which we may give in its Basilidean form. Basilides related the saving descent and ascent of Christ to the primordial act of creation in which the world of non-existence came into being through the depositing of a cosmic Germ or Seed that contained in itself a conglomeration of cosmic seeds, thus constituting the multitude of forms and substances. But this Seed is also a three-fold Sonship (υἱότης) of the same substance with the non-existent God (ὁμοούσιος τῷ οὐκ ὄντι θεῷ). The first sonship was more rarified (λεπτομερές) and soon after being deposited in creation flowered and returned to the non-existent God, while the second sonship, which was more dense (παχυμερεστέρα) ascended only to an intermediate sphere of being (ὂν μεθόριον), these two corresponding apparently to the Son and the Holy Spirit respectively. The third sonship, however, was left behind in the world of non-existents where it receives and imparts benefits among the formless mass of men, and corresponds to the multiplicity of the sons of God, imprisoned for a while in the material world, over whom the whole creation groans and travails until people, formed and purified by the following of Jesus, attain manifestation and ascent to the blessed Sonship of divine Light. The world will endure until all the sons of light are gathered up and the whole sonship attains to the non-existent God.[38] There is no salvation for the world itself, and so no

---

37 Irenaeus, *Adv. haer.* 1.4f, 2.14.

38 Hippolytus, *Ref. omn. haer.* 7, 10–15; 10.10. Valentinus had a more elaborate mythological counterpart to these three sonships, Hippolytus, op. cit. 6.24ff, 10.9; Irenaeus, *Adv. haer.* 1.1–8; 2.18f. For succinct accounts of these mythologies see R. Macl. Wilson, *The Gnostic Problem* (London, 1958), 125–36, and for a selection of the relevant literature, see. R. M. Grant, *Gnosticism, An Anthology* (London, 1961), 143ff.

salvation can be actualised within creation, for the created world is alien to God and must finally perish altogether.[39]

Because of the radical dualism that ran throughout the whole multiform system of gnostic thought the attitude to Christ could only be docetic. His historical 'corporeal' nature fell not only within the realm of non-existence but of phantasmal appearance, his spiritual nature alone being real, the one passible, the other impassible. According to Valentinus four natures are to be ascribed to Christ, or, apart from his nature as Saviour, three natures which he called the psychical (ψυχικός, *animalis*), the corporeal (σωματικός, *corporealis*), and the spiritual (πωεθματικός, *spiritualis*). In line with his view that the flesh is not saved but cast aside like a leather tunic, Valentinus claimed that the corporeal nature was possessed only out of economy (ἐκ τῆς οἰκονομίας), that is, merely for a temporary dispensational purpose, but there was nothing material about it for it was constructed 'economically' (κατ' οἰκονομίαν) out of the psychical.[40] A somewhat similar distinction obtained among men themselves, for they were divided into three kinds, those who are merely earthly, carnal or material (χοϊκοί, σαρκικοί, ὑλικοί), those who are psychical or animal (ψυχικοί), and others again who are spiritual (πνευματικοί). The 'hulics' (or 'blockheads') who are engrossed in material existence are the unbelievers who go into corruption and perdition. The 'psychics' refer to ordinary believers such as are found in the Church (the ἐκκλησιαστικοί) who may advance to an intermediate position with the Demiurge through faith and good works, although they may fall back into perdition if they choose evil; but the 'pneumatics' are those who are impregnated with seeds of divine light, and it is especially for them that the Saviour came.[41] It was his function to bring the hidden knowledge of God and of the origin and destiny of mankind, that is, supersensible gnosis which when mediated to the 'pneumatics' enables the spiritual element in them to partake of redemption.

The gnostics held that they were the πνεθματικοί or spiritual élite of the race (ἡ ἐκλογή)[42] who in virtue of their spiritual nature and mystic knowledge of the deep things of God (τὰ βάθη τοῦ θεοῦ) were capable of

39 Irenaeus, *Adv. haer.* 1.17.2.

40 Irenaeus, *Adv. haer.* 1.6.2, 7.2f, 21.2; Hippolytus, *Ref. omn. haer.* 10.9; Tertullian, *Adversus Valentimanos* 26. A similar view was held by Basilides, Hippolytus, *Ref. omn. haer.* 7.27.

41 Irenaeus, *Adv. haer.* 1.6.1ff, 7.5, 8.3, 13, 6, 21.1ff; 3.15.2; Hippolytus, *Ref. omn. haer.* 5.1.

42 Clement of Alexandria, *Stromateis*, 4.26, 165.3.

divine enlightenment, rebirth into the *pleroma* and ultimate union with God. Owing to the dualistic and docetic character of this outlook the emphasis fell naturally upon the 'pneumatic' and 'spiritual' side of things, so that the gnostics operated with sharp distinctions,[43] for example, in their separation between Christ and Jesus, water-baptism and spirit-baptism, or between mere faith (ψιλὴ πίστις) and perfect knowledge (τελεία γνῶσις), arrogating the latter exclusively to themselves, and concentrating upon graduated initiation into higher and higher spheres of *gnosis*. Although this knowledge of the depths is available to gnostics in this world, by its very nature it involves a movement that carries them beyond it, for it cannot be actualised in what is material or temporal. To partake of it is at the same time to engage in ascent out of the material world. This is how Irenaeus described the gnostic concept of redemption:

> The mystery of the inexpressible and invisible power must not be performed by means of visible and corruptible creaturely things, nor must the mystery of unthinkable and incorporeal realities be performed by means of sensible and corporeal things. Knowledge (*gnosis*) of the ineffable Greatness is itself perfect redemption, for since both defect and passion came through lack of knowledge, the whole system of what was thus formed is destroyed by knowledge. Thus knowledge is the redemption of the inner man. This is not corporeal, for the body is corruptible, nor is it psychical for the psyche is the fruit of defect and is but the lodging of the spirit. Redemption must therefore be of a spiritual kind, for the gnostics affirm that the inner and spiritual man is redeemed through knowledge, and as they reach knowledge of Universal Being they need nothing else, for that is true redemption.[44]

As far as hermeneutics is concerned, gnosticism presents intractable difficulties, indeed inherent self-contradictions. If the hiatus between the lower and the upper world is extended so far that not only is this world the sphere of the non-existents, but God himself of whom we think in correlativity with ourselves is God-non-existent (οὐκ ὢν θεός) and Nothing (οὐδεν), then what kind of thinking is this? This is as much a problem in Valentinian as in Basilidean gnosticism, for the 'God' of the Valentinians is by definition unthinkable and incomprehensible, as it says in *The Gospel of Truth*.[45] However, if we can think and speak only within *kenoma* or the

---

43 Cf. Jude 19: οὗτοί εἰσιν οἱ ἀποδιορίζοντες, ψυχικοί, πνεῦμα μὴ ἔχοντες.

44 Irenaeus, *Adv. haer.* 1.21.4; cf. 2.18.6.

45 *The Gospel of Truth*, 17.4–9, 22; 128, 32; cf. *The Apocryphon of John*, 17.7ff.

emptiness of non-existence, then how can we offer any account at all of the things that really are, since our relation to them can be only through a sort of vast vacuum or blank? If we say that this may be done through a special knowledge or *gnosis*, then how do we even know this, for either we know it somehow already, or if we do not, we do not even know what it is we are to know. In other words, if we seek to know God by pushing abstraction of him to the limit of an infinite discrepancy between what he is and what we can think or say of him, then our thoughts and statements can only be about nothing, and we are simply engaged in empty movements of thought and speech within the *kenoma*. These are in fact some of the arguments that Irenaeus brought against the gnostics in the second book of his work *Against the Heresies*.[46]

But Irenaeus goes further in his critique. He argues that within the shadowy existence of this sensible world where we make use of transient and temporal images, or within the vacuum of non-existence where we can only make use of forms that partake of non-existence, it is not possible to give any account of real things, things that really are, and so are shut up to offering a purely imaginary or mythological account of them. But even this would not be possible unless the shadows and images (σκιαί and εἰκόνες) that have to be taken from the sensible world for this purpose are somehow correlated to the realities (even if they are οὐκ ὄντα) of the supersensible and intelligible world. Moreover, if they on their part are regarded as images and shadows of what is beyond in the Father himself and are presumably correlated to him, then again problems arise.[47] God must have in himself some likeness of the shadows and the images, and indeed some of the emptiness that reflects him, or of the defect with which all that is sensible and creaturely is bound up, which it would be impiety to think. But in any case, asks Irenaeus, how do shadows cast shadows, and how can shadow and vacuum be related rationally together?[48]

Now in order to get out of this difficulty the gnostics claim that although knowledge of the truth comes to us in the form of these images and types,[49] they are actually superior to the sensible and material world, for far from being derived from it the whole world of creation was formed

---

46 Irenaeus, *Adv. haer.* 2, 3ff, 7f, 10, 13f. Even Valentinus himself, the actual producer of this vacuity, Irenaeus says, becomes a vacuum, 2.4.1.

47 Irenaeus, *Adv. haer.* 2.14.3; cf. Hippolytus, *Ref. omn. haer.* 5.19.1ff.

48 Irenaeus, *Adv. haer.* 2.4, 1–3, 7.1–7, 8.1–3, 15.1f, 16.1f, 17.2.

49 Cf. *The Gospel of Philip*, 115.67, 69; 133, 12–16; 134, 12f.

for them. In this way, argues Irenaeus, they convert these images into archetypes and then make the upper world of God conform to them; thus in fact they project upon God the patterns of their own creaturely thinking. But this can be regarded in another way. If shadows cannot cast shadows, then the ἰδέαι and the παραδείγματα in the intelligible world are substantial essences or 'bodies', and as such they cast shadows and are imaged in the lower world. But is that not to make them into supramundane beings and gods? That is just what the gnostics did do, and Irenaeus shows that they have in this way lapsed back into heathen pluralism. Thus it becomes apparent that *gnosis* by its very nature operates through mythological hypostatisations and objectifying modes of thought that project into God human forms and feelings, and human, mental, psychological and even physiological processes.[50] Such people, Irenaeus insists, will be compelled continually to find out types of types and images of images and will never be able to fix their mind on the one and true God. They throw their thoughts beyond God, surmounting the Master himself in their own hearts, being indeed elated in their own assumptions, but in reality turning away from the true God.[51]

This progressive mythologisation is very evident in the development of Valentinian gnosticism from its original form evident in documents such as *The Gospel of Truth*. In it Christian teaching is already extrapolated from the New Testament setting into an alien mythical framework, but in the teaching of Valentinus, as set out by Irenaeus, Hippolytus and Tertullian, we find that incipient mythology is greatly elaborated with the help of cruder and more popular mythology such as we find in the *Apocryphon of John* and in the Ophite gnostic tradition, but all this undergoes further elaboration in the thought of Ptolemaeus, a pupil of Valentinus.[52] The same process can be seen at work when we compare the teaching of Valentinus with that of the earlier Basilides as he replaces the latter's God-non-existent with the *Propator* (προπάτωρ) of Depth (βύθος) and Silence (σιγή) out of whom there evolve tiers of supramundane beings which in spite of their philosophical and theological names are little more than an ingenious sophistication of heathen astrology and Egyptian mythology.

Yet all this, and this is our concern with it, is held to be 'justified' through allegorical variations upon biblical texts and themes. This is *allegorising in*

---

50 Irenaeus, *Adv. haer.* 2.13, 3f, 8; 18, 3ff.

51 Irenaeus, *Adv. haer.* 4.19, 1.

52 See Tertullian, *Adv. Valent.* I.14, 33; Irenaeus, *Adv. haer., praef.* and 1.1.1f. Cf. also R. M. Grant, *Gnosticism, An Anthology* (London, 1961), 163ff.

reverse, for the biblical accounts of events in the life of the Lord and other New Testament figures, and the sayings and parables and sentences that are taken from the Scriptures, are reinterpreted as allegorical presentations of mythical aeons and processes that crowd the intermediate realm between the incomprehensible God and the material world. In this way the gnostics brought to the Scriptures their own preconceived framework of hypotheses and quarried at random from biblical passages, forming them into strange new patterns of their own in order to find support for their notions, thus, as Irenaeus declared, twisting the natural sense of the Scriptures to a non-natural sense, and breaking up the order and connection of things inherent in the Scriptures themselves.[53] This same point was made by Tertullian,[54] who was no less emphatic in his condemnation of the methods of Valentinus. If he did not, like Marcion, cut out of the Scriptures only what suited his own subject matter, he was even more cunning in his use of interpolation and distortion in doing violence to the truth. 'Valentinus abstained from excision, since he did not invent Scriptures to square with his own subject-matter, but invented matter that could be adapted to the Scriptures. Nevertheless he took away more, and added more, by taking away the proper meaning of the particular words, and by adding fantastic arrangements of things that bore no relation to the facts.'[55]

What Tertullian means here can be seen not only in the twisting of the evangelical *kerygma* and economy into unreasonable patterns, but in the progressive displacement of Jesus by a mythological system even from the place that he was given in *The Gospel of Truth*. Gnosticism was not interested in Christology but only in cosmological orientation and the kind of self-knowledge that went with it.[56] Behind it all there lay, as Irenaeus

---

53 Irenaeus, *Adv. haer.* 1.8, 1–2, 9.4; see further 1.3, 18ff; 2.10, 13f, 14, 20f, etc.

54 Tertullian, *De praescriptione haereticorum*, 9: 'No divine saying is so unconnected and diffuse that its words are only to be insisted on, and their connection left undetermined.' And ibid., 14: 'so long as its form exists in its proper order, you may investigate and discuss, and indulge all your passion for curiosity into what appears doubtful and obscure.'

55 Tertullian, *De praescr. haer.* 38. Cf. also 17: 'Truth is just as much opposed by an adulteration of its meaning as by corruption of the text.' Tertullian notes the Valentinian alteration of the text of John 1:13 from the original singular to the plural, to avoid reference to the Virgin Birth of Jesus and so distorts the meaning out of a docetic interest, *De carne Christi*, 19, 24.

56 *The Gospel of Thomas*, 1–4, 50, 67. This is very evident in the various formulae gnostics used in ritual restoration from alienation, see Irenaeus, *Adv. haer.* 1.21, 5; Epiphanius, *Pan. haer.* 13, etc.

The Complex Background of Biblical Interpretation

saw so clearly, the epistemological dualism which by positing an infinite discrepancy between God and human knowing of him, takes away all ground for positive control of man's thinking about God, and throws him back upon himself and the fancies of his own imagination. Thus, by the *very gnosis* which they think they have discovered about God, they change the conception of God himself, and exalt their own opinions above the greatness of the Creator—which is only to make man himself in his own imagination and self-understanding the measure of God.[57]

As we look back over these various developments of thought that arise from the cleavage between the sensible and the intelligible worlds, we can see that there are two different, though related, forms of allegorical interpretation. One is designed as a means of demythologising biblical statements of the acts of God in history or the presence of God in space and time, which can be conceived only mythologically within a framework that assumes an abstraction between idea and phenomenon, timeless reality and contingent happening. Another makes this abstraction so complete that it must assume that God is so utterly unknowable and unspeakable that we can have no conceptual knowledge of him, formed within the limits of our creaturely existence and yet objectively grounded in what he is in himself or in his self-revelation, but in spite of that assumes that we may have some kind of symbolic knowledge of God gained in hidden ways.[58] Although related to his incomprehensible, non-existent Being, this can be thought out only through correlation with forms of thought drawn from other areas of experience where formal or conceptual knowledge arises. The former method of allegorical interpretation strips off myth, by detaching from it all reference to space and time, leaving us with only a symbolical relation to the other world. The latter method of allegorical interpretation sublimates mythology by developing mytho-poetic thinking in a semi-philosophical manner, lifting it above space and time into a realm of the imagination. Yet both of these forms of allegorical interpretation appear to pass over into each other, for both of them operate with a mode of thinking in which the forms of thought used are detachable and changeable, and can be rationalised only when assimilated to other forms of thought that do not arise on the same ground and are not necessarily related to the subject-matter in question. Thus

---

57 Irenaeus, *Adv. haer.* 2.14, 3f, 16.1–3.

58 This is very clear in the *Apocryphon of John* 22.19–26. For the hidden nature of this knowledge see Irenaeus, *Adv. haer.* 1.3.2, 30.4; *The Gospel of Truth*, 18.10f; *The Gospel of Thomas*, 1f (cf. the comments by B. Gärtner, *The Theology of the Gospel of Thomas* [London, 1961], 95f, 101f, 114f).

Divine Interpretation

like the ebionite and docetic heresies in the Early Church, they presuppose a conception of God who is infinitely separated from us in the lower world of sense and time, who does not interact with creation, and is inaccessible to any kind of objective knowledge operating with forms of thought deriving from him. By definition this God cannot really involve himself by word or act in our mundane existence except by way of some sort of paradoxical relation of the non-existent Being to non-existents.[59] The basic presupposition of all this way of thinking is a doctrine of the complete abstraction of God, Creator or Redeemer, from creaturely and human being. Given that as an axiomatic assumption, every statement is bound to be interpreted in a different light and to be accorded a different meaning.[60] Thus even one like Valentinus, as Tertullian said, can employ biblical statements and formally adapt his matter to them, yet in such a way that the real substance of the Gospel is taken away and its proper meaning altered.

There is a further issue arising out of the χωρισμός between the κόσμος αἰσθητός and the κόσμος νοητός that demands our consideration: its hidden challenge to the rationality of the universe. Stoic thought was no doubt an attempt to overcome this threat, but in many ways it went too far, for it brought together the visible and invisible worlds in such a way as more or less to make them the obverse of one another, spirit being but the insideness of things, as it were. This had the effect of yielding a notion of universal law in the realm of spirit as well as in the realm of matter, and tended (especially when blended with Pythagorean elements) to the identification of πρόνοια with εἱμαρμένη, of providence with fate. In so doing, however, it overlooked the irrational character of evil and could only proclaim a merciless gospel of 'courage to be' to men and women caught in the toils of the necessity of things or subjected to a harsh lot in life. In the face of this, the gnostic movement appears as a widespread revolt in the longing for emancipation from the shackles of fate and in the conviction that man is not at home in a materialist and pitiless existence. But if the Stoics stood for a dogmatic philosophy of the inevitable nature of things which corresponded to a rational science of nature, then the gnostics stood for a reaction against the scientific logic that tied ethics and physics ineluctably together on the ground of the rationality of the universal system of being. What helped

---

59 Cf. Irenaeus, *Adv. haer.* 1.18.2, 21.4.

60 This shift in meaning is apparent in the gnostic use of not only theological terms but of traditional philosophical and cosmological terms such as *cosmos*—see H. Jonas, *The Gnostic Religion* (Boston, 1958), 252f.

The Complex Background of Biblical Interpretation

gnosticism in many ways was the kind of thought fostered by Philo and new trends in Ptolemaic cosmology that seemed to lift the heavens high up from the earth and to promise the human spirit detachment from its slavery in a deterministic material existence. But gnosticism carried this further, for it pushed the idea of redemption out of the created world altogether, in the belief that the world of space and time was alien to God and that God was alien to it, and that so long as man is imprisoned in material existence he is estranged from himself as well as from God. Hence he must achieve liberation from creaturely being, detachment from matter, transcendence over space and time, and all that ties him down to earthiness, if he is to be saved from final estrangement, but this involves taking off into a empyrean realm on the wing of super-terrestrial forms of knowledge unobstructed by this-worldly objectivities and earth-bound rationalities.

The reaction to gnosticism was very sharp, not only on the part of the Church but on the part of the champions of Classical Hellenism, as we can see in the critique of men like Celsus, Plotinus, Victorinus or Porphyry. They interpreted it as a flight from science, a repudiation of the rationality of the universe, a disruption of the cosmic harmony, and indeed a sort of blasphemy. There were powerful speculative tendencies in gnostic thought not unlike elements in Neo-Platonic philosophy, but Plotinus felt that the *contradiction* introduced by the gnostics into the relation between the visible and the invisible worlds would only result in confusion and darkness, and foster impiety. That was one of the main points felt so deeply by Irenaeus. By separating the creation from God and by making it alien to him, they made it impossible for people to know God within the range of our knowledge in the world with which we are connected in the scheme of things, and then they threw their thought speculatively above and beyond the Creator himself, which is at once irrational and impious (*irrational est et impium*). The root problem lies in the contradiction the gnostics posited between the two worlds. How can things below be the images of things above if they are contrary to them and have nothing in common with them? (*Unde autem et haec illorum imagines, cum sint illis contraria, et in nullo possunt eis communicare?*)[61]

That problem was brought to its sharpest point by Cerdo and Marcion, who not only separated the two worlds, the visible and the invisible, completely from one another, but assigned to each a God of its own, with 'an immense interval separating one from another', and so turned

---

61   Irenaeus, *Adv. haer.* 2.7, 6f; 8.1–3; 10.1f; 25.36; 26.1f; 27.1; 28.2–9.

the difference between them into an *ultimate antithesis* dividing the two supreme Beings from each other.[62] Such a bitheism (even when shorn of mythology) was of course inherently self-contradictory, as the Church Fathers were not slow to point out, but it gave the Church a serious problem because Marcion backed it up on the one hand with a forceful presentation of the evangelical message of free grace, especially in its Pauline form, and on the other hand with a shrewd discernment of evil as a dark irrational power from which we can be delivered by the sheer act of an alien but merciful God. Salvation was therefore by *faith*, not by esoteric *knowledge*. There were elements of truth here that the Church of the second century still had to grasp properly, and conflict with Marcion served to deepen its understanding of the Gospel. But Marcionism had two far-reaching doctrines which left their mark upon the Church for centuries even when Marcionism itself was utterly rejected. These were the aspects which, together with the continuation of gnostic tendencies, were to affect interpretation of the Scriptures.

The first was Marcion's antithesis between creation and redemption. That was latent in all gnosticism but in Marcion's thought it was part of an ultimate dualism which severed the creation from the activity and concern of the Father. This made Marcion's theology essentially contradictory, as both Tertullian and Irenaeus showed.[63] Marcion's dualism implied an ultimate monism while denying it, and was inherently irrational. But if the true God is separated from creation then he is utterly *unknowable* in any circumstances by creaturely beings, although what Marcion taught was that he was quite unknown (ὁ ἄγνωστος θεός) until Christ came.[64] On the other hand, Marcion's dualism made impossible anything but a thoroughly docetic view of Jesus Christ, which undermined the actuality and therefore the reality of his revelation of God. But it meant also that redemption is not and cannot be actualised within the sphere of our creaturely being in space and time.[65] This implied that all biblical passages that spoke of divine

---

62 Irenaeus, *Adv. haer.* 1.27.1f; 2.1, 4; 3.12, 12; 25.3; Hippolytus, *Ref. omn. haer.* 7.37.1f, 10.19.1f; Epiphanius, *Pan. haer.* 41.1, and especially Tertullian, *Adv. Marcionem*, 1.1–6; cf. *Con. Noetum*, 11. See E. C. Blackman, *Marcion and His Influence* (London, 1948), 66f.

63 Tertullian, *Adv. Marc*, 1.1f; Irenaeus, *Adv. haer.* 1.27.1.

64 This was generally held by the gnostics, cf. Irenaeus, *Adv. haer.* 1.11.1; 2.1; Tertullian, *Adversus Marcionem* l.24f. Cf. Norden, *Agnostos Theos* (Leipzig, 1913), 65ff, and Blackman, *op. cit.*, 54f.

65 Irenaeus, *Adv. haer.* 2.31.1; Tertullian, *Adv. Marc.* 1.13, and in detail, bk. 2, regarding the Creator and bk. 3, regarding the Incarnation.

acts of salvation within our visible and sensible world had to be cut away, or be radically reinterpreted. The history of the effects of this is to be seen both in the monophysite tendencies in Christology and in the penchant for allegorical exegesis.

The second was Marcion's antithesis between the Law and the Gospel, and between the Old Testament and the New Testament, which Tertullian called Marcion's 'special and principal work'.[66] This was consistent with the separation between the two supreme Beings, for according to Marcion, 'the God of the Old Testament' was 'the God of creation', and 'the God of the New Testament' was 'the God of the Gospel'. This was to throw 'mercy' into antithesis with 'justice', to disengage the saving truth of the Gospel from all providential fulfilment of God's purpose within history and indeed to remove the divine 'goodness' from any essential involvement with time. Hermeneutically it demanded an exegesis of the New Testament that cut its statements away from the Old Testament and translated them out of their Judaic background into a very different world of timeless ideas. F. C. Burkitt pointed out that to understand Valentinus and Basilides rightly one must 'consider them as Christians who were striving to set forth the living essence of their religion in a form uncontaminated by the Jewish envelope in which they had received it',[67] but this anti-Judaic element was far stronger in Marcion. It brought to the surface the difficulty which those reared in the old Classical traditions had in assimilating the Old Testament into a philosophical framework that was, at certain essential points, quite alien to it. That marks, although in an extreme form, the damaging cleavage between the Gentile Church and Israel which has sadly persisted throughout the centuries and has constantly tempted the Church to distort the image of Christ by forcing upon him a Gentile mask and so to make of him a baffling and bewildering figure. But it was a Jew who contributed to this, Philo of Alexandria, who offered the Church an interpretation of the Old Testament which, as we have seen, allegorised its basic message and expounded it in a form to make it acceptable within the Hellenic disjunction between the κόσμος αἰσθητός and the κόσμος νοητός.[68]

---

66 Tertullian, *Adv. Marc.* 1.22, and in detail in books 4 and 5.

67 F. C. Burkitt, *Church and Gnosis* (Cambridge, 1932), 27f.

68 Cf. E. Bevan, *Stoics and Sceptics* (Cambridge, 1959), 94: 'The Philosophy which Philo expounds is essentially the popular Greek philosophy, a blend of Platonism, Pythagoreanism, and Stoicism, slightly modified by the Hebrew belief in God.' See also W. W. Harvey, in his edition of Irenaeus, *Adv. haer.* vol. I (Cambridge, 1957), 288.

CHAPTER 3

Karl Barth and the Latin Heresy[1]

It was a fundamental principle of the great Athanasius that to approach God through the Son and call him Father is a more devout and accurate way of knowing him than to approach him only through his works by tracing them back to him as their uncreated Source. To know the Father through his incarnate Son who is of one and the same being as God is to know him strictly in accordance with what he is in his own being and nature as Father and Son, and as Holy Spirit, which is the godly and the theologically precise way.[2] On the other hand, to seek knowledge of God from what he has created out of nothing, would be to operate only from the infinite distance of the creature to the Creator, where we can think and speak of God only in vague, imprecise and negative terms, for what God has created out of nothing does not tell us anything about who God is or what he is like in his own being. It is through God alone that we may know God in accordance with his nature. We may know God in truth only as we are given access to him as Father through Jesus Christ his incarnate Son and in his one Spirit, an access opened to us as we are brought near to God and are reconciled to him through the cross.[3]

Athanasius could never conceal the awe he felt over the fact that, through God's astonishing condescension in the incarnation to be one of us and one with us, he has disclosed to mankind the ineffable mystery of his Godhead as Father, Son and Holy Spirit, yet in such a way that his transcendent holiness sets a limit to what we may apprehend—there the cherubim spread the covering of their wings. Frail creatures though we are,

---

1 This essay originally appeared in *Scottish Journal of Theology* 39.4 (1986) 461–82. It also appeared in slightly edited and expanded form in *Karl Barth: Biblical and Evangelical Theologian* (Edinburgh: T. & T. Clark, 1990), 213–40. The version here is taken from the latter, with permission from Bloomsbury Publishing.

2 Athanasius, *Contra Arianos*, 1; *De decretis*, 31. See my discussion of this, *The Trinitarian Faith: The Evangelical Theology of the Ancient Catholic Church* (Edinburgh, 1988), 49ff.

3 Ephesians 2:14–18.

through the Spirit given to us by Christ we may participate in some real measure in the knowing of the Son by the Father and of the Father by the Son of which our Lord spoke in the Gospel: 'All things have been delivered to me by my Father; and no one knows the Son except the Father, and no one knows the Father except the Son and anyone to whom the Son chooses to reveal him.'[4] This was a favourite passage with the Greek Fathers ever since it was first given theological prominence by Irenaeus.[5] Knowledge of God takes place through a movement of divine revelation from the Father through the Son in the Spirit and an answering movement of faith in the Spirit through the Son to the Father. Since this is a way of knowing God through *internal*, not external, relations, it is essentially trinitarian in content and structure. At the same time it is and must be thoroughly Christocentric, for it is only through Jesus Christ that we know the Father and only through him that we receive the Holy Spirit. Everything depends on the indivisible inner relation in being of the Son and the Spirit to the Father—that is why Athanasius gave increasing attention throughout his life to explaining and defending the Nicene *homoousion*, not only in the doctrine of the Son but in the doctrine of the Spirit as well.

Barth's Classical Evangelical Position

It was in this classical evangelical tradition of the Early Church that Karl Barth took up his own position early in his theological career. His road into it was through his struggle, begun in his Swiss parish, over the nature and content of divine Revelation, as he sought to expound the Holy Scriptures and proclaim the Word of God. He soon realised that his own struggle was, at its roots, very much the same as that of both the Nicene Fathers and the Reformers, over the identity and primacy of God's Revelation in Jesus Christ. In the fourth century, the question at issue was the supreme truth of the Deity of Christ and the Holy Spirit, for if they were divided in being and act from God the Father, the Gospel would be empty of any divine content, and there would be no substance to the doctrine of the Holy Trinity. In the sixteenth century the very same issue arose in another form over the doctrine of Grace, for if the gift of Grace were not identical with the Giver, then there could be no real *Self*-giving of God through Jesus Christ and in the Holy Spirit, and the Word of the Gospel would be empty of any divine

---

4 Matthew 11:27; Luke 10:22.
5 Irenaeus, *Adversus Haereses*, 2.4.3; 2.18.6; 4.11.1, 4, 14.

reality. Here, too, the doctrine of the Trinity was at stake, and with it the very foundation of Christian theology. Thus Karl Barth found himself compelled to contend once again for the truth of the Nicene Creed that the incarnate Son is of one and the same being as God the Father and that the Holy Spirit is 'the Lord and Giver of life'. This was the essential import of the *homoousion* which gave dogmatic expression to the indivisible oneness in being and agency between the Father, the Son and the Holy Spirit, and thus to the fact that precisely by believing in divine Revelation the Church believes in God himself. As Barth liked to express it: 'God reveals himself as Lord', 'God himself is the content of his Revelation'.

What Karl Barth found to be at stake in the twentieth century was nothing less than the downright Godness of God in his revelation, for the Augustinian, Cartesian and Newtonian dualism built into the general framework of Western thought and culture had the effect of cutting back into the preaching and teaching of the Church in such a way as to damage, and sometimes even to sever, the ontological bond between Jesus Christ and God the Father, and thus to introduce an oblique or symbolical relation between the Word of God and God himself. Barth's struggle for the integrity of divine Revelation opened his eyes to the underlying epistemological problems, not only in Neo-Protestantism and Roman Catholicism, but in Protestant orthodoxy as well. These were bound up with the Western habit of thinking in abstractive *formal relations*, which was greatly reinforced by Descartes in his critico-analytical method, and of thinking in *external relations* which was accentuated by Kant in his denial of the possibility of knowing things in their internal relations. This is what I have called 'the Latin heresy', for in theology at any rate its roots go back to a form of linguistic and conceptual dualism that prevailed in late patristic and mediaeval Latin theology.

Significance of 'the Latin Heresy'

Let me explain. The Council of Nicaea had been convened in 325 A.D. to deal with the crisis into which the Church had been thrown by the teaching of Arius that, while Jesus Christ was named and honoured as the Son of God, he was not very God, but only participated in God by grace. Operating with the axiomatic assumption of an epistemological and cosmological dualism which shut God out of any direct interaction with the world, he held that the Son or Word of God was actually a creature who, like all other creatures, had been made out of nothing and was therefore *external* to God, altogether unlike him, foreign and different from God in being. On hearing these ideas the Nicene Fathers covered their ears with their hands in horror, for the teaching of Arius flatly contradicted the witness of the New Testament, according to which Jesus Christ the only-begotten Son of God lived and acted out of an unbroken oneness between himself and the Father. After a careful examination of the many statements in the Scriptures about the relation of Jesus Christ to God the Father, in which it sought to distil as faithfully as possible their fundamental meaning, the Council found itself compelled to acknowledge that there is an indivisible oneness between Jesus Christ and the Father. Rejecting any idea that he is different in being or nature from God, they insisted that the incarnate Son is true God of true God, perfectly and wholly one with the Father in being and act. That was the basic belief they formulated in the *homoousios to Patri*, which constituted for them the sovereign evangelical principle at the very core of their Confession of Faith. It gave expression to the ontological substructure upon which the various New Testament presentations of the Gospel message rested and by which they were integrated. Thus the *homoousion* gave precise theological expression to the truth that, while distinct from one another, the Father and the Son eternally belong to one another in the Godhead. That is to say, the Father/Son relation disclosed in Jesus Christ inheres eternally *within* the one Being of God.

Theology of Internal Relations

There are very obvious connections between the theology of Barth and that of Athanasius. I have in mind, for example, the absolute primacy Barth assigned to knowledge of God through the Father/Son relation over the God/creature relation, which gave rise to his remarkable blend of Theocentricity and Christocentricity on the one hand, and to his rejection of any independent natural theology on the other hand. My concern here, however, is with the place which Barth, like Athanasius, gave to *internal relations* in the coherent structure of Christian theology, and of the way in which he exposed and rejected the habit of thinking in terms of *external relations* which had come to characterise so much of Western theology.

Athanasius had been quick to discern that if we recognise that the Son is eternally inherent in God, then everything else in our understanding of the Christian Faith will be governed by it. However, if we operate with the premise that there is only an external relation (i.e. *not an ontological but a moral relation*) between Christ and God, then our understanding of the Gospel and of every Christian doctrine is bound to be very different. Athanasius made that very clear in his trenchant analysis of Arianism, which in various forms and degrees rejected the Nicene realism in its application of the *homoousion* to the doctrine of the Spirit as well as the Son, substituting in its place a metaphorical or symbolical way of understanding divine Revelation, and thereby undermined the doctrine of the Holy Trinity. The problem Barth had to face was essentially the same, but in some respects at least it was rather more difficult. The Western Church, Roman Catholic and Protestant alike, had always acknowledged the Nicene-Constantinopolitan Creed and had thus officially rejected the Arian heresy. Throughout the centuries, however, it had become infected from below with subtle forms of anthropological and epistemological dualism when the habit of thinking in terms of real internal relations constantly tended to be replaced with Arian-like habits of thinking in terms of external, symbolical or merely moral relations, which resulted in a serious loss of direct contact with reality.

It is my purpose here to direct attention to Karl Barth's non-dualist and holistic way of thinking in contrast to the dualist and abstractive modes of thought that came to be built into the infrastructure of Western theology, Protestant as well as Roman Catholic. I hope that this approach will help to promote a better understanding of his theology, if only by bringing to light the epistemological grounds of disagreement between him and his critics. Consideration will have to be restricted to his doctrines of Revelation and Reconciliation.

Revelation

'God reveals himself as Lord.' In that single statement Karl Barth expressed the basic equation in his doctrine of divine Revelation. God's Revelation is God himself, for it is God in his living Being and Activity who is the content of his Revelation. It is not something divine, something like God, or some emanation of his power, that God reveals to us in the incarnation of his Son and in the sending of his Spirit, but his very Self, his own ultimate Reality as God. This was for Barth the crucial import of the Nicene-Constantinopolitan Creed: what God is in his revealing and saving activity toward us in Jesus Christ and the Holy Spirit, he is inherently and eternally in himself and what he is inherently and eternally in himself, he is toward us in Jesus Christ and the Holy Spirit. God's Self-revelation is, therefore, Barth contended, the root of the doctrine of the Trinity, for through the Son and in the Spirit we are given to know God *in his internal relations* as Father, Son and Holy Spirit.

That the *incarnate* Son of God is one in being and agency with the Father, means that Jesus Christ, God and Man, is the objective content of divine Revelation. Jesus Christ *is* God revealed to us; he *is* the Word of God made flesh. God's Revelation is hypostatically embodied in Christ, and cannot be detached from him as the *Self*-revelation of God, for that would be tantamount to disjoining what God is in his Self-revelation from what he is in his inner Being as God. That the Holy Spirit *sent* to us by the Father in the name of the Son is one in being and agency with the Father and the Son, means that he is the living Presence and Action of God in whom God's Self-revelation in Christ is mediated to us and activated among us. He *is* God's Self-revealing who cannot be detached from what God reveals, for that would be tantamount to disjoining what God is in his Self-revealing from what he is in his own inner Being as God. Thus divine Revelation is properly understood as both the living content of his once-for-all Self-revelation through the Son, and the dynamic event of his continuous Self-giving in the Spirit.

The Truth as It Is in Jesus

Revelation, to recall once more what both Athanasius and Calvin used to say of the Holy Scripture, is 'God speaking in Person'—that is, God communicating himself in Jesus Christ in the oneness of his Word, Person and Act. By its very nature divine Revelation is characterised by an intrinsic wholeness which we cannot grasp through *partitive* modes of thought in accordance with the distinctions between person, word and act found in creaturely being. God's Word and God's Truth are embodied in Jesus Christ. Hence we do not have to do with Christ apart from his Word or with the Word apart from Christ, nor with Christ apart from his Truth or with the Truth apart from Christ. According to Karl Barth it is this reality and wholeness of God's Word and Truth embodied in Jesus Christ, that Western theology regularly tended to lose. It failed to realise that the content of Revelation is anchored in the ultimate Being of God and thus eludes abstractive and analytical modes of thought; and failed to see that the wholeness of the Truth of God embodied in Jesus Christ inevitably breaks through any frame of concepts and statements which we may use to express it.

Authentic theological concepts and statements developed under the constraint of God's Self-revelation and its inherent *Logos* or intelligibility, do not have their truth in themselves but in the Truth of God in Jesus Christ into which they are locked and to which they refer. Hence if we are to be faithful to the divine content of Revelation and to the embodiment of God's Truth in Jesus Christ, we must learn to distinguish the ultimate *Datum* of God's Self-revelation from our knowledge and expression of it, and let it confer relativity upon all we say or think. That is what scientific rigour in Christian theology demands: thinking strictly in accordance with the revealed nature of God the Father in Jesus Christ his only-begotten Son. It is in Christ that we learn to let God be God, for it is God himself who through the Son and in the Spirit is the ultimate Judge of the truth or falsity of our theological concepts and statements. It is only *in him* that we are put in the right with the truth, and are thereby shown that before God we ourselves are always in the wrong. For Karl Barth that was the sharp epistemological relevance, the critical force, of justification by grace alone: 'Let God be true, and every man a liar', as St Paul wrote.

It was thus that Karl Barth sought to develop a distinctive kind of dogmatics in which constant account is taken of the fact that it is none other than the Lord God himself who meets us in Revelation. By his very nature revealed to us in Jesus Christ God encounters us as he who is infinitely greater than we can ever conceive, who transcends all our theological formulations, but who nevertheless actually gives himself as the object of our knowledge in Christ. This is not to say that our knowledge of God is false because it is inadequate to his nature, but rather that inadequacy of this kind belongs to its essential truth in pointing away from itself to the ultimate Truth of God. Hence, in order to be really faithful to God as he has revealed himself, dogmatics must build recognition of its own inadequacy into its basic structure. It must never lose sight of the fact that even when God makes himself known to us, his Truth retains its own boundless mystery, majesty and wholeness, in virtue of which it far outreaches the creaturely limits of human thought and speech. This is why Barth felt constrained to draw a clear distinction between *dogma* and *dogmas*. In *dogma* the theologian is concerned with the fundamental *Datum* of divine Revelation, the one source and norm of all our knowledge of God, to which it points and by which it is judged. *Dogma* is not itself the Truth of God's

Revelation, but the unformalisable intuitive recognition of it evoked in us by Revelation, and which implicitly exercises a regulative force in all faithful attempts to give our understanding of Revelation explicit formulation in *dogmas*. In this sense *dogma* constitutes the informal base upon which all formal accounts of our knowledge of God rest, and from which they cannot be cut off without becoming theologically empty and meaningless. Everything would go wrong, however, if it were thought that *dogma* could be reduced to explicit formalisation in *dogmas*, for that would imply that dogmatic formulations of the faith are to be regarded as transcriptions or even constitutions of its essential substance. It was in rejecting any such idea that Karl Barth insisted that dogmatics is the *science of dogma*, not the science of dogmas.

Propositional Truth

The Latin heresy, as I have called it, has to do with the strange dialectic in which knowledge of God is abstracted from its objective ground in his self-revelation, and is then formalised in dogmatic propositions which are identified with the Truth as it is in God. This dialectic may be traced back to Tertullian: to his concept of the Word of God on the one hand, and to his concept of the Rule of Faith on the other hand. Although Tertullian certainly rejected the teaching of Arius, he operated with an Arian-like dualist mode of thought which led him to think of the Word of God, not as eternally generated in him, but as an emanation from his Mind which became Word only when God spoke it in creating the world. At the same time, Tertullian identified the Deposit of Faith with a fixed formula, the *regula fidei*, which he claimed had been instituted by Christ himself and handed down entire and unchanged from the Apostles. This Rule of Faith was a compendium of 'irreformable truths' formulated in definitive statements regarded as identical with the truths which they were meant to express. In fact, they constituted a set of doctrinal propositions abstracted from the substance of the Faith or logically deduced from divine Revelation and systematically connected together to form a prescriptive instrument in regulating belief and teaching in the Church.

This conception of the Word as semi-detached from God was taken up by St Augustine in terms of a distinction between 'the internal mental Word', or 'vision' in the Mind of God, which as Word is 'formable but not yet formed', and 'the external Word' which assumed definite form as Word when uttered in the incarnation and was thus Word in the proper sense. Through Peter Lombard this conception of the *Word*, along with the Augustinian dualism between the intelligible and sensible worlds, passed into the central stream of mediaeval theology where it was given a basic place in the teaching of St Thomas Aquinas.[6] He held, for example, that God and the angels or the blessed departed converse 'wordlessly' with one another through 'the vision of thought' for there is no Word *as word* in God. When God's Word is communicated to us, however, it comes in forms alien to its essential form in God. That is to say, as John Reuchlin argued at the end of the Middle Ages, latent in the heart of Latin Christianity there was a rejection of the consubstantiality of the Word, a denial that what God is to us as *Word* incarnate, and as he communicates it to us in the Holy Scriptures, he is antecedently and eternally in his own Being as God.[7] It is to that dualist conception of the Word that the mediaeval Latin tradition in oblique, tropological or symbolic interpretation of the Bible must be traced.

Augustinian and Thomist Dualism

In line with this development mediaeval Latin theology took its distinctive shape when the Augustinian dualism with which it was informed was combined with Aristotelian abstractive processes of thought which operated by prescinding rational content from reality. This gave rise to the view that thought and reality, sign and thing signified, were related, not through any direct act of cognition, but only in an external and indirect way through the intermedium of grace indwelling the Church. Thus, St Thomas held that we have no direct conceptual or evidential relation to God, for he does not communicate himself to us in his own intelligible relations but only in an indirect way through the Church.[8]

---

6 Cf. 'Scientific Hermeneutics according to St Thomas Aquinas', which I contributed to *The Journal of Theological Studies* XIII.2 (1962) 259-89 [included in this volume as Chapter 5, 'The Hermeneutics of St Thomas Aquinas'].

7 See further my essay 'The Hermeneutics of John Reuchlin, 1455-1522,' in *Church, Word, and Spirit, Historical and Theological Essays in Honor of Geoffrey W. Bromiley*, eds. E. Bradley and R. A. Muller (Grand Rapids, 1987), 107-21 [included in this volume as Chapter 8, 'The Hermeneutics of John Reuchlin'].

8 For this way of thinking see Edward Schillebeeckx, *Revelation and Theology*, and *Concept of Truth and Theological Renewal*, Theological Soundings 1.1 and 1.2, (London, 1967-68). See my analysis of 'non-evidential' and 'non-conceptual' relation to God in the essay 'Theological Realism' contributed to *The Philosophical Frontiers of Christianity:*

In this event the human mind requires some kind of infused grace or faith enabling it to assent to the truth of God in spite of its non-evidence. Along with this, Latin theology elaborated a Tertullian-like method of deriving theological ideas and doctrines by treating the Sacred Scriptures like Aristotelian first principles. Thus through processes of reasoning from first principles to conclusions, it sifted out the ideas deduced from the Scriptures and built them into a logico-deductive system of propositional truths and definitive articles of belief. These two cognate trends in Latin theology were coordinated within the Church which as a mystical body was held to be the depository of divine grace and which as a juridical society was held to be endowed with divine authority to dispense and administer grace. It was in virtue of this double capacity that the Church was regarded as spanning the gap between the sensible and the intelligible, the human and the divine, the temporal and the eternal.

In the fifteenth and sixteenth centuries, however, these two strands in Latin theology held together by canon law began to fall apart, while in Reformation theology the Nicene struggle was renewed for the ontological and dynamic wholeness of God's Self-revelation through Christ and in the Holy Spirit. There took place, on the one hand, a powerful recovery of belief in the consubstantiality and objectivity of the Word of God, and with it the conviction that we are given direct cognition of God in and through the Holy Scriptures. On the other hand, there took place a revival of the understanding of the Truth of God as embodied in Christ clothed with his Gospel, in which the damaging effects of dualist and abstractive modes of thought began to be overcome. It is through union with Christ *first*, Calvin taught, that we partake of all his benefits, and not the other way round. He laid great stress upon the doctrine of the *Testimonium internum Spiritus Sancti*. By that he referred, not as in the Augustinian or pietist tradition to some inner illumination in believers, but to the Spirit of Truth who inheres in the very Being of God and through whom God bears witness to himself. It is that Self-witness of God which he makes to echo within us as through union with Christ we partake of the Spirit whom he sends to us, and hear the living Word of God addressing us directly in the Holy Scriptures.

Essays Presented to D. M. Mackinnon, eds. Brian Hebblethwaite and Stewart Sutherland (Cambridge, 1982), 176ff.

Protestant Dualism

After the Reformation this unified understanding of God in his revelation and of Christ clothed with his Gospel broke up, when the underlying Augustinian dualism which the Reformation inherited from the Roman Catholic Church, and along with it much of the intellectual apparatus of mediaeval Latin thought, reappeared.[9] Now in one stream of thought there developed a pietist-liberal tradition, heavily influenced by the Renaissance, in which the Word of God was identified with an inner word or light in the soul which could not be distinguished from subjective structures in man's religious self-consciousness. Where is that more evident than in the widely-influential *Glaubenslehre* of Schleiermacher? And in another stream of thought there developed a Protestant scholasticism or orthodoxy which, with the help of Aristotle once again, gave rise to systems of dogmatics built out of logically derived propositional truths and statements. Where is this more evident in the Reformed Church than in the *Westminster Confession of Faith* which was so heavily indebted to Latin scholasticism for its logico-causal structure, and which as such constituted a closed system of doctrinal propositions formalised in such a way that they were equated with the divine truths they were intended to express?[10] Thus it is understandable that Charles Hodge, in his defence of the *Westminster Confession*, objected to a distinction being drawn, not only between 'the substance of faith' and 'the system of doctrine', but between the substance of the faith and the essential form in which it was expressed in that system! Hence there emerged within Protestant theology, especially within the dualist framework of Augustinian-Newtonian thought, basically the same problems and heretical ideas that had emerged centuries earlier in Latin theology within the dualist framework of Augustinian-Aristotelian thought which left such a permanent mark on the Roman Catholic Church.

Thus we find deeply embedded in the Reformed Church 'the Latin heresy', as I have called it, to which Karl Barth objected so strongly, in his conviction that it was high time for the Church to renew the struggle of the Council of Nicaea and the Reformation for the old truth that 'God's Revelation is God himself, the one ever present, eternal and living God'. He set himself to engage in that struggle on a double front.

9 Thus Barth in his Foreword to H. Heppe, *Reformed Dogmatics* (London, 1950), vi.

10 See my articles 'The Deposit of Faith.' *SJT* 36.1 (1986) 1–28; and '"The Substance of the Faith": A Clarification of the Concept in the Church of Scotland., *SJT* 36.3 (1986) 327–38.

Karl Barth's Attack

On one front, Barth attacked the idea that there is no inherent *logos* or rationality in divine Revelation, and that theology must therefore borrow it from secular philosophy and culture, or have recourse to some preconceived conceptual system of natural theology, in order to give it rational expression. That was Barth's quarrel with Liberal and Neo-Protestant theology: it had lost its sense of the Godness of God, by stumbling at the unique nature or singularity of divine Revelation due to the identity between its content and God himself. This was evident not only in its denial of the Deity of Christ but in its assimilation of the Spirit of God to the human spirit and thus to the equation of the Word of God with mythological projections of the religious self-consciousness. The ontological detachment of Christ from God that this implied inevitably led to a detachment of Christianity from Christ, and its assimilation to the religious patterns of a pluralist society and fragmented culture. That was the end-result of nineteenth-century Protestant theology which became so apparent in the secularisation of the Church in the twentieth century.

On the other front, Barth reacted strongly against so-called Orthodoxy, in which objective descriptions of the truth were confounded with or mistaken for the truth itself, so that they were not subjected to its critical questioning or judgment, but inevitably fell under the control of some intellectual system or philosophy used in defence of evangelical belief. This he found to be particularly evident in rationalist Fundamentalism which manifests so clearly the other side of the Latin heresy in its interpretation of divine revelation in terms of propositional truths which it deduces from Holy Scripture and elaborates into rigid articles of belief and doctrine. As Barth saw it, the heresy of Fundamentalism is not so much that it rejects the consubstantiality of the incarnate Son of God as that it disregards the consubstantial relation between God's Self-revealing and Self-giving and the objective content of what he communicates in his Word. That is to say, Fundamentalism is found to sin against the consubstantiality of the Holy Spirit, and to substitute a static for a dynamic view of divine Revelation. It clearly operates with an epistemological dualism which cuts off God's Revelation in the Bible from the living dynamic Being of God himself and his continual Self-giving through Christ and in the Spirit, and therefore treats the Bible as a fixed corpus of revealed propositional truths which can be arranged logically into rigid systems of belief. Behind the fundamentalist refusal to recognise that the Bible under divine inspiration refers to Truth independent of itself, there is evidently a failure to acknowledge the unique reality of God in his *Self*-revelation and *Self*-communication to mankind, which corresponds rather closely to the failure of Liberalism to acknowledge the singularity of divine Revelation. Behind both, however, there is surely an evangelical failure to appreciate the profound inner relation between Revelation and Reconciliation.

Reconciliation

If the supreme truth for which the Church struggled at the Council of Nicaea and at the Reformation was that God himself is the living content of his Revelation, that must be understood quite concretely as Jesus Christ, for the *homoousios to Patri* was asserted of the *incarnate Son*: 'who for us men and for our salvation came down from heaven, and was made flesh from the Holy Spirit and the Virgin Mary, and was made man, and was crucified for us under Pontius Pilate'. Thus the oneness in being and agency between Christ and God must be understood from a *soteriological* perspective. This is something that Karl Barth never allowed himself to forget. Reconciliation is not just a truth which God has made known to us; it is what God has done and accomplished for us, the very Truth of God who freely gives himself to us in his Revelation. 'Revelation is Reconciliation, as certainly as it is God himself: God with us, God beside us, and chiefly and decisively, God for us.' How could God actually reveal and give *himself* to us across the chasm, not only of our creaturely distance but of our sinful alienation from him, except through a movement of atoning reconciliation? Along with Athanasius, therefore, Barth could only think of the actualisation of divine revelation as taking place in the saving and atoning life of Jesus Christ as God become one of us in order to expiate our sin and guilt by acting in our place and on our behalf, and thus to reconcile us to himself. 'For there is one God, and one Mediator between God and man, the man Christ Jesus, who gave himself a ransom for all.'[11] Jesus Christ is himself the content of God's Self-revelation precisely and only as he is God with us as we are, God become what we are, in order to reconcile us to God and actualise from the side of man as well as from the side of God his Self-revealing and Self-giving in one indivisible movement of propitiation through the Son and in the Spirit.

---

11 1 Timothy 2:5.

Rejection of External Relations

It was made very clear in Athanasius' long debates with Arians and semi-Arians that if we operate only with an *external* relation between the Son and the Father, we are unable to give any saving significance to the human life and activity of Christ in the form of a servant, for it rules out of account any direct personal intervention by God himself in our lost and damned human condition. All that might then be offered would be a merely moral interpretation of what the Gospels and Epistles of the New Testament have to tell us about the redemption of mankind. For Karl Barth that was the decisive issue over which sides had to be taken in the doctrine of atoning reconciliation. It was over this issue that his criticism of Western theology was so sharp, for it had allowed an epistemological and ontological dualism to cut between the Person of Christ as God incarnate and his saving work, with the result that it has constantly offered an interpretation of the sacrifice of Christ on the cross in *external* moral or juridical terms. Barth set himself to think out, therefore, as consistently as possible the implications for atoning reconciliation of the unity between the incarnate Son and the Father, and between the Person and Work of Christ.

Since the Father/Son or Son/Father relation falls within the one Being of God, the incarnate life and activity of the Son must be understood in terms of their *internal* relation to God the Father Almighty, Creator of heaven and earth and of all things visible and invisible. It is none other than God himself who has 'come down from heaven' and is personally and directly present and active in Jesus Christ, *not for his own sake, but for our sakes*. That is the Godness of God in divine Reconciliation, without which the whole life and work of the Lord Jesus Christ from his birth of the Virgin Mary to his crucifixion under Pontius Pilate and his resurrection from the grave would be empty of saving reality.

Moreover, since he who became incarnate in Jesus Christ is 'of one being with the Father, through whom all things were made', since it was the Creator Word made flesh who was the Lamb of God consecrated to bear away the sins of the world, the doctrines of redemption and creation cannot be torn apart but must be allowed to interpenetrate each other. Reconciliation was a creative as well as an atoning act of God accomplished in the ontological depths of human existence and its desperate condition under divine judgment, in order to redeem mankind from bondage and misery, sin and guilt, and to regenerate human nature, raising it up from its lost and corrupt condition into union with the divine Life embodied in

Jesus Christ and exhibited in his resurrection from the dead. This means that the mighty act of God in the resurrection belongs to the very essence of atonement, but it also means that it is in the reconciliation of all things in heaven and earth, visible and invisible, that the whole creation is brought to its fulfilment in the Love of God.

Mutual Relation of Incarnation and Atonement

It is entirely consistent with this that the incarnation and the atonement are to be understood in their mutual relations with each other. The incarnation includes the whole life and activity of Jesus Christ culminating in his resurrection and ascension, while the atonement begins from his very conception and birth when he put on the form of a servant and began to pay the price of our redemption. As the one Mediator between God and man, the Man Christ Jesus is not only God *with us*, but God *for us*, God who has crossed the chasm of alienation between us and himself, God who has taken our rebellious and corrupt human nature upon himself, God who has made our sin and guilt, our misery and death, our condemnation and godlessness, his very own, in order to intercede for us, to substitute himself in our place, bearing the just punishment of our sin, and offering and making restitution by suffering what we could not suffer and where we could make no restitution at all.

That is the doctrine of Jesus Christ as Mediator who is God of God and Man of man in one Person, and who as such reconciles God to man and man to God in the hypostatic union of his divine and human natures. This hypostatic union, however, was the atoning union in Christ between the Holy One of God and our sinful humanity which he made his own but which, while making it his own, he healed and sanctified in his own sinless life. That is to say, we must think of atoning reconciliation as accomplished *within* the incarnate constitution of the Mediator and not in some *external* transactional way between himself and mankind. Thus there took place in Christ as Mediator an agonising union between God the Judge and man under judgment in a continuous movement of atoning reconciliation running throughout all his obedient and sinless life and passion into the resurrection and ascension when he presented himself to the Father on our behalf and presented us in himself as those he had redeemed and consecrated to be his brethren.

Jesus Christ does not mediate a reconciliation (any more than a revelation) other than what he is in himself, as though he were merely the intermediary or instrument of divine reconciliation. He embodies what he mediates in himself, for what he mediates and what he is are one and the same. He himself in the wholeness of his Person, Word and Act is the content and reality of divine Reconciliation. He *is* the propitiation for our sins; he *is* our redemption; he *is* our justification. It is in this identity between Mediator and mediation that the living heart of the Gospel is to be found. If we let go the intrinsic oneness between Jesus Christ and God, or between the Person and the Work of Christ, then our grasp of the Gospel of salvation is bound to disintegrate and we will inevitably lose its substance.

Karl Barth's objection to most Western doctrines of the atonement was that they had resiled from this soteriological emphasis on the inner connection between incarnation and atonement found in the early centuries of the Church, and that consequently they kept interpreting the sacrifice of Christ on the Cross mainly as an external transference of penalty between sinners and God, rather than as the culmination of God's incarnational penetration into the alienated roots of humanity in order to bear upon himself our judgment, to cancel sin and guilt and undo the past, and to effect within it once for all atoning reconciliation between the world and himself.

The Unassumed is the Unhealed

From Irenaeus to Cyril of Alexandria the Church had everywhere taught that in becoming one with us and one of us in Jesus Christ, God had humbled himself to take our lost cause upon himself by assuming our fallen human nature, our humanity diseased in mind and soul, our actual human existence enslaved to sin and subjected to judgment and death, precisely in order to save us in the very heart of our depraved condition in body and mind where we are at enmity with God. Particular stress was laid upon the fact that it was our alienated *mind* that God had laid hold of in becoming what we are, in order to effect reconciliation with himself deep within the rational hegemony of human being for it was there that sin had entrenched itself inextricably in human existence. It was held, of course, that in his very appropriation of our sinful humanity the incarnate Son of God healed and sanctified it in himself; instead of sinning like all other human beings, he condemned sin in our flesh by living a life of perfect holiness within it, and through his obedient Sonship he converted our disobedient human being back into true filial relation to the heavenly Father.

From the fifth century onwards, however, there developed in Latin theology, an increasing rejection of this teaching in favour of another, according to which it was not our fallen humanity that Jesus took from the Virgin Mary, but humanity in its perfect original state. That idea led in due course to the Roman doctrine of the immaculate conception of Mary herself, which has ever since divided the Latin from the Greek Church. In this way, Latin theology (with some notable exceptions such as Peter Lombard) rejected the cardinal soteriological principle of the ecumenical Church that 'the unassumed is the unhealed', that 'what Christ has not taken from us has not been saved'. Strange to say, almost all Protestant theology, not least in its evangelical forms, has followed Latin theology down this road—although here too there have been notable exceptions such as Martin Luther and H. R. Mackintosh.

This particular form of the Latin heresy may be traced back to the famous *Tome* of Leo the Great sent to the Council of Chalcedon early in the fifth century, in which a dualist approach to the understanding of the Person and Work of Christ, as God and Man, was set out, which provided the West with its paradigm for a formulation of a doctrine of salvation in terms of external relations. It was on that basis that there developed in the Middle Ages a moral-influence conception of atonement through contemplation of the wounds of Jesus, very evident in the *Stabat Mater*, and in the teaching of Peter Abelard, or a severely juridical conception of atonement as an external penal transaction between God and sinful humanity, as in the teaching of St Anselm (at least as usually interpreted!). At best, however, those doctrines of atonement, together with the idea of ransom from the devil, had to do with what Romans call 'actual sin', and not with *original* sin and guilt lodged in the roots of individual and social human being—salvation was through the healing medicine of grace merited by Christ and dispensed through the sacraments. In Roman theology this way of interpreting atoning reconciliation in terms of moral or juridical relations and transferable grace also opened up the possibility for a codification of the means of saving grace and its administration by the Church through the elaboration of canon law—a development which had a dominant impact on high mediaeval theology in its formative period, when it was coordinated with the logico-causal structure of scholastic systems of thought.

In contrast to this distinctly legalist slant in the understanding of saving grace, the Reformers strove to recover in their doctrine of reconciliation the same truth for which they contended in their doctrine of revelation, namely, the identity between the content of God's Self-communication in Jesus Christ and what he is in himself. Hence in their account of saving grace they contended for the identity of the Gift of God in Grace with God the Giver. The central focus naturally fell on the justification of the sinner by free grace, for it was there that the conflict between an evangelical and a legalist understanding of atoning reconciliation was sharpest. While this was generally referred to as justification by faith, that must not be construed to mean that faith contributes anything to our salvation, for, as Calvin insisted, no faith on our part can 'conciliate the grace of God'. In line with this, Reformation theology laid great stress on the all-sufficiency of the atoning sacrifice of Christ and its absolutely decisive and unrepeatable nature, not least in reaction to the Roman notion of propitiatory sacrifice as reflected in the sacrifice of the Mass which was celebrated to conciliate the grace of God. We also find in Reformed theology the old Greek patristic emphasis upon reconciliation as 'the blessed exchange' in which God in Christ took our place that we might be given his place, but on the whole this still tended to be formulated within the parameters of the Latin conception of the incarnation.

Here once again, unfortunately, the dualism inherited from the Augustinian-Aristotelian framework of mediaeval theology had the effect of undermining and fragmenting the wholeness of the doctrine of atoning reconciliation. As the conceptions of incarnation and atonement began to be torn apart there appeared in Protestant theology obvious counterparts to the two main strands in mediaeval Roman doctrines of atonement mentioned above, and even various forms of the idea of ransom from the devil. It was characteristic of the development of Protestant theology that there emerged different 'theories of the atonement', all of which in one way or another operated with an external way of relating theory and event in the interpretation of the death of Christ.

It is hardly surprising, therefore, that Karl Barth, in his reappropriation of the Nicene *homoousion* in the saving as well as in the revealing acts of Christ, should charge Western theology, Protestant as well as Roman, with a damaging disintegration of the wholeness of God's reconciling work in the incarnate life and passion of our Lord. Thus the great question he has posed to us is whether we are ready to take with full seriousness once again the unity of the incarnation and the atonement, and the soteriological fact that in making himself one of us in Jesus Christ, God became what we *actually* are in order to redeem us and reconcile us to himself.

Barth's Doctrine of Atoning Reconciliation

In bringing this discussion to a close let me now focus attention upon two prominent features in Barth's doctrine of reconciliation where, it seems to me, criticism of his thought reveals how subtly and deeply evangelical theology is still entangled in the Latin heresy.

a) *The Total Nature of Christ's Substitutionary Life and Death*

If in the incarnation God came to be one of us and as one of us to act in our place, in our stead, and on our behalf, then that must be understood in the fullest way of the *Man* Christ Jesus. As we have seen, Barth fully agreed with Athanasius that unless it was God himself who was personally and directly active in Jesus, nothing that he did was really of any saving significance. But Barth also agreed with Athanasius that in effecting reconciliation in Christ Jesus, the one Mediator between God and man, God acted from the side of man as man as well as from the side of God as God, all for our sake. That is to say, Barth stressed the *Godward* movement as well as the *manward* movement of Christ's reconciling life and passion, for his human activity was not merely instrumental but integral and essential to its vicarious nature. Although atonement was certainly the Act of God himself, it was the Act of God *as Man*, and thus act of God translated into our human existence and made to issue out of it as a fully human act in the obedient self-offering of man in holiness and filial love to God the Father and in unbroken fellowship with him. Thus the substitutionary as well as the representative role of Christ in the wholeness and integrity of his humanity must be recognised as occupying a central place in a proper doctrine of atoning reconciliation. This was Barth's stress upon the vicarious humanity of the Lord Jesus Christ. Now if it was as Man as well as God that Jesus Christ took our place, he must be recognised as acting in our place in *all* the basic acts of Man's response to God: in faith and repentance, in obedience and prayer, in receiving God's blessing and in thanksgiving for it. It is at this very point, however, that both liberal and evangelical theologians object, for they feel that the inner citadel of human freedom is being threatened. God may have done everything else for us, but there is something he does not and cannot do for us, in the personal decision of faith and repentance which each person must make for himself or herself. Thus they will have nothing to do with the concept of *total substitution* in what Jesus Christ does for us and our salvation.

This objection to the teaching of Karl Barth is very evident in the criticism of his insistence that salvation is all of grace from beginning to end. But to accuse Barth of saying that since in grace God is everything, therefore man is nothing, betrays that both Liberals and Evangelicals can only juxtapose God and man, divine grace and human freedom, in a *logical* way, in which 'all of God' logically excludes 'anything of man'. It is just here that one discerns how deeply the Latin heresy in construing the Gospel in dualist and abstractive terms is embedded even in evangelical theology. Behind it there is evidently a rejection of the principle that the unassumed is the unhealed, and in particular a rejection of the truth that it is our alienated mind that the Son of God assumed in the incarnation in order to heal it from its deep-seated distortion through being turned in upon itself. The Latin heresy operates with a form of the autonomous reason which has not been allowed to come under the judgment of the Cross, in which Christ wholly took our place, substituting himself for us in mind as well as in body. In refusing to agree that our minds need to be redeemed, liberal and evangelical thinkers evidently allow an unreconciled and unregenerated human reason to become lodged in the heart of their theologies. It is an unbaptised rationalism of this kind that so often characterises fundamentalist theology, especially in its apologetics and polemics. It was precisely because Karl Barth took the total nature of Christ's substitutionary life and death so seriously, that he set himself to think out afresh the nature of reason, intelligibility and objectivity in the light of God's self-revelation and the reconciliation of the human mind with the Word and Truth of God in Jesus Christ, and so also the nature of the remarkable rationality with which God has endowed the universe in its created correspondence to the uncreated and transcendent Rationality of God.

b) *The Wholeness of the New Creation in Jesus Christ*

If in Jesus Christ the Word of God, by whom all things are made and in whom they have their creaturely being, became incarnate, died on the Cross and rose again, then we must think of the whole creation as having been redeemed. If in Jesus Christ the Creator himself became a human creature, without of course ceasing to be Creator, and if in him divine nature and human natures are not separable, as Nestorian heresy would have it, then we must think of the being of every man, whether he believes or not, as grounded in Christ and ontologically bound to his humanity. It is precisely in *Jesus*, as St Paul taught, that every human being (and indeed the whole creation) consists. It was as such that he died and rose again, so that we cannot but hold that the whole creation has been redeemed and sanctified in him, including the whole human race. But at this point some evangelical theology in particular objects and charges Barth with what they call 'universal salvation'.

What is really going on here? Is it just another form of 'the Latin heresy' which we have just found conflicting with salvation by grace alone? Behind the charge of universalism against Barth there lies a controlling frame of thought which operates with a notion of external logico-causal connections. If Christ died for all men, then, it is argued, all men must be saved, whether they believe or not; but if all men are not saved, and some, as seems very evident, do go to hell, then Christ did not die for all men. Behind both of these alternatives, however, there are two very serious mistakes. On the one hand, there is evidently a disjunction between the divine and human natures of Christ, and between the incarnation and the atonement, and therefore between the being of Christ himself and his atoning activity. On this view the humanity of Christ is not believed to be inseparably united in one Person with his Deity. Hence his humanity is not regarded as having any inner ontological connection with those for whom he died, but is regarded only as an external instrument used by God as he wills, in effecting salvation for all those whom God chooses and/or for those who choose to accept Christ as their personal Saviour. Thus a separation is projected between the universal power and range of the kingdom of Christ and the limited efficacy and range of his atoning sacrifice.

It was high mediaeval theology, following St Augustine, that taught that while the death of Christ may be sufficient for all, it is efficient only for some, i.e. 'the elect'. While this was a conception promulgated by Alexander of Hales, the teacher of both Bonaventura and Thomas Aquinas, Calvin himself repudiated it,[12] but Calvinist 'orthodoxy' sadly brought it back. What is this erroneous notion of limited atonement but a sad breach in the biblical and apostolic doctrine of the primacy and completeness of

---

12 *Concerning the Eternal Predestination of God*, tr. J. K. S. Reid (London, 1961), IX.5, 148.

Christ? To refer to St Paul again: 'He is the image of the invisible God, the first-born of all creation in whom all things were created in heaven and on earth, visible and invisible, whether thrones or dominions or principalities or authorities—all things were created through him and for him. He is before all things and in him all things hold together. He is the head of the body, the Church; he is the beginning, the first-born from the dead, that in everything he might be preeminent. For in him all the fullness of God was pleased to dwell, and through him to reconcile to himself all things, whether on earth or in heaven, making peace by the blood of his cross.'[13]

On the other hand, account must also be taken of an associate form of this aberration lurking beneath the charge of 'universalism' sometimes laid against Barth, namely a way of construing the efficacy of the atonement in terms of a logico-causal relation between the death of Christ and the forgiveness of our sins. Here these critics appear to substitute an operation of causal grace in the Cross in place of the ineffable activity of God the Holy Spirit so wonderfully revealed in Jesus' birth of the Virgin Mary and his bodily resurrection from the dead. This damaging intrusion of logico-causalism into post-Reformation theology was considerably reinforced first through Lutheran and Calvinist scholasticism which brought back Aristotelian metaphysics into dogmatics, and then through the triumphant advance of the Newtonian 'system of the world' governed throughout by external causal connections, which inevitably encouraged deterministic ways of thought. It is a logico-causalism of this kind, with Augustinian-Thomist, Protestant scholastic and Newtonian roots, that appears to supply the deterministic paradigm within which there arise the twin errors of limited atonement and universalism both of which, although in different ways, are rationalistic constructions of the saving act of God incarnate in the life, death and resurrection of the Lord Jesus Christ. It is that root error which we must beware of, namely, the replacing in our thought of the unique activity of God exhibited in the Virgin birth of Jesus and his resurrection from the dead with an activity of another kind which we can construe, in terms of necessary relations—which would surely come rather near to sinning against the Holy Spirit.

Let me repeat, the problem of universalism versus limited atonement is itself a manifestation of 'the Latin heresy' at work within Protestant and Evangelical thought. If Karl Barth is still misunderstood or criticised over his approach to the efficacious nature and range of redemption, it must be

13 Colossians 1:15ff.

through mistaken opposition to his faithfulness in thinking out as far as possible the implications of the oneness of the Person and Work of Christ, or of the inseparability of incarnation and atonement. It is because atoning reconciliation falls within the incarnate constitution of Christ's Person as Mediator, that it is atoning reconciliation which embraces all mankind and is freely available to all in the unconditional grace of God's Self-giving. Why some people believe and why others do not believe we cannot explain, any more than we can explain why evil came into the world. The Gospel does not offer us a logical or causal explanation of the origin or presence of evil, or of precisely how it is vanquished in the Cross of Christ. But it does tell us what the Lord God has done to deal with evil. It tells us that in his unlimited love God himself, incarnate in Jesus Christ, has entered into the dark and fearful depths of our depraved and lost existence subjected to death and judgment, in order to make our sin and guilt, our wickedness and shame, our misery and fate, our godlessness and violence, his own, thereby substituting himself for us, and making atonement for sin, so that he might redeem us from our alienation and restore us to fellowship with the Father, the Son and the Holy Spirit. The saving act of God in the blood of Christ is an unfathomable mystery before which the angels veil their faces and into which we dare not and cannot intrude, but before which our minds bow in wonder, worship and praise. However, of this we can be perfectly certain: the blood of Christ, the incarnate Son of God who is perfectly and inseparably one in being and act with God the Father, means that God will never act toward any one in mercy and judgment at any time or in any other way than he has already acted in the Lord Jesus. There is no God behind the back of Jesus Christ, and no God but he who has shown us his face in the face of Jesus Christ, for Jesus Christ and the Father are one. What the Father is and does, Jesus Christ is and does; what Jesus Christ is and does the Father is and does.

It has been the great mission of Karl Barth to call the universal Church back to its original foundation in God's unique and exclusive Self-revelation in the one Mediator between God and man, the man Christ Jesus. In so doing he has taught us to develop an appropriate Christocentric mode of thinking, at once dynamical and ontological, that is, one governed throughout by the distinctive activity of God embodied and exhibited in the birth, life, death, and resurrection of Christ and in the sending of the Holy Spirit in his name. It is only through the Son and in one Spirit that we have access to the Father.[14] As Barth has demonstrated throughout his *Church Dogmatics*, this is essentially a trinitarian mode of knowing and thinking in the Spirit which moves through the Son to the Father, and which is grounded in and answers to God's own revealing and saving activity, from the Father, through the Son and in the Holy Spirit.

14 Ephesians 2:18.

Part 2

Medieval and Modern Hermeneutics

CHAPTER 4

The Place of Word and Truth in Theological Inquiry according to St Anselm[1]

In order to get our orientation in St Anselm's thought we can hardly do better than start with the little epistemological preface which he inserted into the *Epistola de incarnatione Verbi*. There he has in view the case of those who reject some Christian belief because they cannot grasp it by their understanding, foolishly judging that what they are incapable of comprehending themselves simply cannot be. Anselm rejoins that

> no Christian ought to dispute with respect to what the Catholic Church believes with its heart and confesses with its mouth, how it is not the case (*quomodo . . . non sit*); but by holding indubitably to the unchanging faith, by loving and living according to it, he ought, as far as he is able, humbly to inquire into the reason why it is the case (*quaerere rationem quomodo sit*).[2]

That is to say, Anselm rejects as irrational any attempt to judge the truth or falsity of some belief merely by reference to the alleged limits of the understanding itself, or to reject it for some reason external to the belief in question. The only right and wise thing to do is to probe into the ground on which faith arises and claims to rest with the question *quomodo sit*—How far is it really the case? To what extent is reality as the Christian believes it to be?[3] This is to ask for some inner reason resting upon the *esse* of what is believed and being questioned, through which it may become evident whether there is a necessary relation between the knowledge of faith and

---

1 This essay originally appeared in Roberto Zavalloni (ed.), *Studia medievalia et mariologica, P. Carolo Balic OFM septuagesimum explenti annum dicata* (Rome: Editrice Antonianum, 1971), 131–60.

2 St Anselm, *Ep. de Inc. Verbi* (= *E.I.V.*), I (ed. F. S. Schmitt, *S. Anselmi Opera omnia*, II, 6, 10f., 7, 1f).

3 Cf. St Anselm, *Monologion* (= *Mon.*), 64 (I, 75, 1ff); *Cur Deus homo* (= *C.D.h.*) I, 25 (II, 95, 18f. 96, 2f); also Barth, K., *Fides quaerens intellectum* (Eng. tr.), 26ff.

the inherent rationality of what is believed.[4] That is the rational way in which to test a belief for its truth or falsity.

What Anselm is challenging is an abstraction of the understanding or the structure of the reason from the object of knowledge and then a deployment of it in a speculative argumentation outside the field of empirical relations with reality.[5] True knowledge arises where the understanding and experience are coordinated, but that is why faith plays such a basic role in our knowledge of God, for it is in the movement of faith that that coordination takes place. Hence there is nothing strange in saying 'he who does not believe will not understand': 'For he who does not believe will have no experience, and he who does not have experience will not know (*qui non crediderit, non experietar; et qui expertus non fuerit, non cognoscet*).'[6]

To the unbeliever, then, Anselm insists that as direct experience of the object is a necessary condition of knowledge, so experiential faith is a necessary condition for any understanding of what the Church confesses and for any judgment as to its truth; but to the believer he points out that it is not sufficient to rest content with faith as it arises from the hearing of God's Word, for the understanding already embedded in faith invites him to inquire into the truth of what is experienced and believed so that his knowledge may be grounded solidly upon it—indeed, unless he develops the understanding immanent in faith, it may perish and faith along with it:[7] 'The knowledge of the man with experience (*experientis scientia*) surpasses the knowledge of the man who hears (*audientis cognitionem*) by the extent to which experience exceeds the hearing of a thing.'[8]

Since it is in the experience of faith that we grasp the reality of God, the initial knowledge of faith (*audientis cognitio*) matures into rigorous and tested knowledge (*experientis scientia*) as we clarify and develop our understanding of what is grasped and believed. This is the procedure which Anselm elsewhere speaks of as *fides quaerens intellectum*.[9]

Two comments may be offered about this. *Fides quaerens intellectum* is not an inquiry in which faith seeks to understand itself as such but one

---

4 *E.I.V.*, I (II, 20, 18f); *C.D.h.*, I, 25 (II, 96, 2); *Mon.*, prol (I, 7, 10).

5 *E.I.V.*, I (II, 7, 5ff. 8, 1ff).

6 *E.I.V.*, I (II, 9, 5-6).

7 *E.I.V.*, I (II, 9, 9ff)

8 *E.I.V.*, I (II, 9, 7-8): *Quantum enim rei auditum superat experientin, tantum vincit audientis cognitionem experientis scientia.*

9 St Anselm, *Proslogion* (= *Prosl.*), prooemiun (I, 94, 7).

in which attention is directed upon the objective reality with which the knowledge of faith is actually in touch in order to let it disclose itself to the understanding in a firmer grasp of its truth. This results in a clarification and strengthening of faith, for then faith does not rest on ecclesiastical authority or even on biblical authority as such but on the solid truth that underlies all the teaching of the Holy Scripture. Hence, far from leaving the realm of divine revelation or renouncing the source of knowledge in the testimonies of God, inquiry of this kind brings the mind directly under the compulsion of the divine Truth and the impress of its rationality, and so enables faith to enunciate its theological statements with greater clarity and precision.[10] In the second place it must be noted that while *experientis scientia* is distinguished from *audientis cognitio* and is ascendent over it, it cannot do without it or leave it behind, for it is precisely through faith which comes *ex auditu* that *experientis scientia* acquires its basic conceptuality or rational structure. That is why Anselm does not envisage any ascent from *scientia* to *sapientia*, to a vision of God that ultimately transcends audition of His Word, for it is the Word heard by faith that is the source of our ability to conceive of God and it is in the obedience of faith that our conceiving of God takes place—*fides esse nequit sine conceptione*.[11] Hence while theological inquiry probes through the hearing of faith into clear and firm *scientia* of what is experienced in faith, it can do so only through the conceptual act in the heart of faith itself, and therefore only in the constant exercise of faith and never apart from the word of Holy Scripture, as read or proclaimed in the Church. In this conceptual act, however, the mind is concerned not merely with words or conceptions as such but with the reality cognised through them, for it is an act in which the mind is so adapted to the disclosure of God through His Word that God Himself in His own Truth (*veritas*) and Rationality (*ratio*) is communicated to it. That is why Anselm casts himself upon God in prayer, that under the impact of God's own activity his mind may be brought to know Him as it must know Him in accordance with His divine reality and nature.[12]

Our task is now to investigate the place of word (*verbum*) and truth (*veritas*) in St Anselm's thought in the hope that this will help us to understand what theological inquiry, as he conceived it, is about.[13]

---

10 *C.D.h.* II, 19 (II, 131, 7 ff).
11 St Anselm, *De concordia*, (= *De conc.*), q. 3 (6) (II, 271, 7f).
12 See here the opening chapters of the *Proslogion*, 1–4 (I, 97–104).
13 Cf. here the valuable essay of V. Warnach, *Wort und Wirklichkeit bei Anselm von*

I. *Word*

Anselm defines word (*verbum* or *nomen*) as *vox significans rem*—vocable signifying a reality.[14] That definition is of decisive importance, for it insists that the function of word (primarily, at any rate) is not to express some inward or spiritual condition, that is, to be the instrument whereby the speaker expresses himself, but to be the sign through which attention is directed to some objective reality or event. Words are what they are through relation to their referents:[15] 'Every word is a word corresponding to some object...For what has not been, and is not, and will not be, there can be no corresponding word.'[16]

Anselm distinguishes words considered merely in themselves (*voces significativae*), from the realities or objects (*res*) they are employed to denote,[17] and defines their meaning in the fulfilment of that denotation or rather in the realities themselves as they are perceived by the eye or thought or expressed in speech.[18] Words are rightly understood, therefore, not through a thinking of the signifying words but through a thinking of the things signified, for they are interpreted not as if they contained or exhausted the meaning in themselves, but as adapted for and pointing to realities beyond themselves. Thus the closer we get to the realities they signify, the more they are adapted to them and the more definitely they point to them, the truer they are.[19] Word that corresponds to reality in this way Anselm speaks of as *proprium et principale rei verbum*.[20]

His views become clearer when we note several of the distinctions he draws. There are, he says, three ways in which we can speak the same thing (*unam rem loqui*): 'We speak things either by using sensibly sensible signs, i.e. signs which can be perceived by the bodily senses; or by thinking the things inwardly in our mind, whether through the imagination of material

---

Canterbury, in *Salzburger Jahrbuch für Philosophie*, Bd. V-VI, 196–2, 157ff.

14   St Anselm, *De Grammatico* (= *De Gram.*), 17 (I, 162, 25–26); cf. 18 (163, 21ff. 164, 1ff); *Prosl.* 4 (I, 103, 18f.).

15   *Mon.*, 10 (I, 24, 27ff. 25, 10ff).

16   *Mon.*, 32 (I, 50, 20f): Nempe omne verbum alicuius rei verbum est . . . Eius enim quod nec fuit nec est nec futurum est, nullum verbum esse potest.

17   *Mon.*, 10 (I, 24, 27f) *Mon.*, 65 (I, 76, 24f).

18   *Mon.*, 10 (I, 24, 24ff).

19   *Mon.*, 33 (I, 52, 18f.).

20   *Mon.*, 10 (I, 25, 22).

entities or through the discernment of the reason, in accordance with the diversity of things in themselves.'[21]

This is very different from the threefold word of Augustine, for it does not involve the radical dichotomy between the intelligible and sensible worlds since the inward thinking and speaking are directed immediately to the concrete reality and not to some purely spiritual event that leaves it behind. Even when thought, word is *verbum rei*, for it is thought in accordance with the nature of the thing itself.

Hence Anselm draws another distinction between *esse in re* and *esse in intellectu*. That had far-reaching importance for his argument in the *Proslogion* where it was stated in the form of a distinction between having something in the understanding and understanding that it actually exists.[22] For our purpose it is another statement of the same point that is more relevant: 'There is more than one way in which something is said or thought in the heart. For a thing is thought in one way when the word signifying it is thought, and in another way when the entity, which the thing is, is understood.'[23] Thus words signifying things do their work in vain when we fail to understand the things they actually signify, and try to understand them in accordance with what they are in themselves.[24]

In this relation between speech and the things thought or spoken of Anselm does not have in mind the individual words by themselves, for words have their meaning in denoting realities independent of themselves and they function properly only when employed in sentences or propositions that involve judgments in their acts of signification.[25] Of course a word is often a compressed sentence in itself, and stands for a whole concept, that is for a line of thought involving a judgment, but just because it is realities independent of our words that we think and speak, such words can only be regarded as linguistic short-hand for significant statements about realities. This raises another important distinction which Anselm makes, between the truth of signification and the truth of things,[26] but meantime we must

---

21 *Mon.*, 10 (I, 24, 31f. 25, 1ff).

22 *Prosl.*, 2 (I, 101, 9–10): *Aliud est rem esse in intellectu, aliud intelligere rem esse.*

23 *Prosl.*, 4 (I, 103, 17ff): *Non uno tantum modo dicitur aliquid in corde vel cogitatur. Aliter enim cogitatur res cum vox eam significans cogitatur, aliter cum id ipsum quod res est intelligitur.*

24 Cf. Barth, op. cit., 163f.

25 *De Gram.*, 4 (I, 149, 11ff); *De veritate* (= *De ver.*), 2 (I, 179, 1ff), 13 (p. 197, 1ff. 198, 1ff).

26 *De ver.*, 2 (I, 177, 6ff. 178, 1ff. 179, 1ff). See my essay, 'The Ethical Implications

try to see more clearly that for Anselm *verbum rei* is the essential word formed in accordance with the nature of what is thought or spoken.[27]

In the three-fold way of speaking mentioned above Anselm points out that while the first three *varieties* are concerned with the contrast between the external and the internal sense, the *sensus* and the *intellectus*,[28] that is, with the words and lexical equivalents which vary from language to language, the third is the form of speech as it is objectively determined by the reality denoted, and approximate to it. It does not vary but is the primary and proper word that underlies all variations in different languages. Anselm speaks of this word as 'natural' for it derives ultimately from the *locutio rerum* of the supreme Being through which the realities denoted were created, and therefore does not arise by convention so much as through the impress of those realities upon the mind:[29] 'Since all words are invented on the ground of these, where these are, no other word is necessary for the recognition of a thing, but where these cannot be, no other word is of use for pointing the thing out.'[30]

It is in and through the *verbum rei* that speech really does its work in ostensive acts that lead to the recognition of the objects concerned. It is so related to the reality denoted that in and through it the reality itself comes to view. It is the primary function of words, then, to be as it were, the transparent medium through which we think or speak things directly. The realism of this *cogitatio rerum* or *locutio rerum* is one of the most outstanding features of Anselm's thought.[31] Indirect speaking or thinking is normally necessary only when the object is not present, and we have to rely on memory and the images it conjures up.[32] It is at this point, as Fr Warnach has pointed out,[33] that Anselm's view is sharply differentiated

---

of Anselm's *De veritate*', *Theologische Zeitschrift* 24 (1968) 309ff.

27 *De Gram.*, 17–18 (I, 162–164).

28 *De Gram.*, 4 (I, 149, 13).

29 *Mon.*, 10 (I, 24–25), and *De ver.*, 2 (I, 177ff). The distinction between natural and conventional is similar to, but not quite identical with another, between *significatio substantialis* and *significatio accidentalis*. *De. Gram.*, 12 (I, 156, 22ff. 157, 1ff), 15 (p. 161, 6ff) and *De ver.*, 2 (I, 179, 10ff).

30 *Mon.*, 10 (I, 25, 12ff): *Et quoniam alia omnia verba propter haec sunt inventa: ubi ista sunt, nullum aliud verbum est necessarium ad rem cognoscendam; et ubi ista esse non possunt, nullum aliud est utile ad rem ostendendam.*

31 See *Prosl.*, 4 (I, 103, 16f) *Mon.*, 32 (I, 50, 16ff), 33 (p. 52, 15ff).

32 *Mon.*, 31 (I, 48, 17ff), 33 (p. 52, 20f), 62 (p. 72, 14f).

33 Warnach, op. cit., 165f.

from Augustine's, for according to Augustine the word is always formed out of the memory; memory always plays the role of an intermediary.[34] Anselm is no less conscious of the importance of memory, as we can see from his discussion of the Trinity, in which he owes not a little to Augustine, but unlike Augustine he does not explain the place of what we may call 'tacit knowledge' by calling in some form of Plato's doctrine of reminiscence, but recognises that we are always able to know more than we can express in words or define in concepts. That applies above all to our knowledge of God and the statements we make about Him,[35] but in all knowledge we employ forms of thought and speech that approximate to their objects.[36]

According to Anselm, every real word (*verbum rei*) by which some reality is spoken mentally is in some degree the likeness or image of that reality: 'All words of this kind by which we speak any realities in the mind, that is, think them, are likenesses and images of the realities to which they correspond as words; and every likeness or image is more or less true according as it more or less closely intimates the reality of which it is the likeness.'[37] The *verbum rei* is something formed in the mind. It is not to be confounded with the *res* itself, but is an *expression* formed in the mind as the result of the *impress* of something other than it, as the person responds to it, intuits it, or listens to it, as the case may be.[38] It is in the propriety of the expression to the reality that meaning and truth lie. Hence the *verba rerum*

> may be said, without absurdity, to be truer the more they resemble the realities to which as words they correspond and the more expressly they stand as signs for them. For (with the exception of those entities which we employ as their names in order to signify them like certain sounds such as the vowel *a*) no other word seems to resemble a reality so much as the word which corresponds to it, or which expresses it, so much as that likeness which is expressed in the eye of the mind as it thinks the thing itself. Rightly, therefore, must that be called the supremely proper and primary '*rei verbum*.'[39]

---

34 St Augustine, *De Trinitate*, XV, c. 10, n. 15.

35 *Mon.*, 64ff (I, 74ff).

36 *Mon.*, 10 (I, 25, 24), 31 (p. 50, 13) etc.

37 *Mon.*, 31 (I, 48, 18–21).

38 *Mon.*, 33 (I, 52, 8ff), 38 (p. 56, 24f); cf. 68 (p. 78, 14f).

39 *Mon.*, 10 (I, 25, 15–22): *Null aliud verbum sic videtur rei simile cuius est verbum, aut sic eam exprimit, quomodo illa similitudo, quae in acie mentis rem ipsam cogitantis*

Or, as Anselm puts it in another passage: 'Whatever reality the mind, either through the imagination of the body or through the reason, seeks to think truly, it tries to express its likeness, so far as it is possible, in its own thought. The more truly it does this, the more truly does it think the thing itself.'[40]

It will be apparent from these citations that when Anselm uses the terms 'expression' and 'express', he is not using them in the subjective sense which predominates today, but in their old objective sense. Only in the case of self-reflection or in the case of an absent object not in the vision of the mind, will speech involve an expression of a subjective state of the speaker, but even then it will be the result of an impression from something other than itself.[41]

At this point, however, a critical question arises, which Anselm brings up. Every word is a word corresponding to some object or reality. If it did not have a relation to something other than itself of which it was the word or image, it would not be the word or image of anything—it would be empty and non-sensical. There can be no doubt, however, that objects, even creaturely objects, are *very different in themselves from what they are in our knowledge of them*, for in themselves they exist by virtue of their own essence, while what is in our knowledge is not their essence but their likeness.[42] That would be quite disastrous if the words or images themselves were the immediate objects of knowledge, or if we cognised the realities they express only by the inspection of the images in our minds. But that is not Anselm's view: rather do we inspect the realities through the images that arise in the mind, so that through them we think and speak the realities themselves. *Rem cogitare, rem dicere, rem exprimere*, are characteristic Anselmic expressions. All-important is Anselm's insistence that we are able to distinguish between a thing and the likeness of a thing—if we could not make that distinction there would be no ground for distinguishing truth from falsity.[43]

By their very nature, then, the words, expressions and images we employ correspond to realities other than themselves, realities that are what they are independently and not through the words, expressions and

---

exprimitur. Illud igitur iure dicendum est maxime proprium et principale rei verbum.

40 *Mon.*, 33 (I, 52, 15–19).
41 *Mon.*, 33 (I, 52, 20f), 62 (p. 72, 14ff).
42 *Mon.*, 36 (I, 54, 18f. 55, 1ff).
43 *De ver.*, 6–9 (I, 183–89).

images that denote them. Unless there were these realities there would be no words, expressions or images of them. Anselm does not attempt to offer any account of how these words, expressions and images are related to the realities they indicate, for that in the nature of the case is not expressible in words, but he remains convinced that those realities show through in their distinctness and independence, which has the effect of revealing the measure of their unlikeness or disparity between our words, expressions and images and the realities themselves. This is where one of the most persistent of our problems lies, for man is a creature who, unlike God, fails to express adequately what he perceives, and the fault lies with him, and not with what he perceives. Hence to get at the truth he must strive to uncover his own falsifications.[44]

It is because our words, images, and expressions correspond to what is other than themselves, and function denotatively by pointing away from themselves, that we need not be alarmed by the measure of their disparity or unlikeness to the realities they indicate, for it is precisely that unlikeness or disparity that helps us not to confound them with the realities they indicate, and thus serves their denotative purpose. That is why Anselm can insist that our theological statements, even if they fall short of the Truth they intimate, are not therefore necessarily false.[45]

Since words are of this kind and function in this way, we use them rightly when we do not let our understanding stop short at the words themselves, but pass through them to think and speak the things or realities to which they direct our understanding. Indeed unless we do that we do not properly understand the words as signifying vocables even when they are considered in the continuity of their grammatical and logical connections. Hence in discussion with his pupils Anselm warns them not to be content with understanding what he says but to consider the things themselves about which he speaks:[46] 'Since words (*voces*) do not signify unless they signify things, in order to say what the words signify, it is necessary to say what the things are.'[47] To understand propositions or statements we have to listen in to the truth to which they refer. Anselm's term to describe that all-important concomitant act is *subauditio*.[48] Truth resides not primarily

---

44 *De Gram.*, 8 (I, 152, 21f) *De ver.*, 6–7 (pp. 183–86); cf. *Mon.*, 29 (p. 47, 22).
45 *Mon.*, 65 (I, 77, 1–3).
46 *De Gram.*, 8 (I, 152, 9f), 18 (p. 164, 7ff).
47 *De Gram.*, 17 (I, 162, 23f).
48 *De Gram.*, 7 (I, 152, 1f).

in statements or propositions but in the essence of things, so that unless we give ear to the latter we have not really understood the former even if we have listened to it.[49] This involves the distinction between *veritas significationis* or *enuntiationis*, and the *veritas essentiae rerum* which we must now go on to consider.

II. *Truth*

Anselm supplies the best examples of the *subauditio* in action, especially in the *Monologion* and in the *Cur Deus homo*.[50] In both of them he begins with the actual knowledge he has, which has been acquired through faith and the understanding that is embedded in it, that is through understanding and believing what has been communicated through the Scriptures and the Church. But in both of them he is determined to penetrate through the truth of biblical and ecclesiastical statements to the *solida veritas* upon which they rest,[51] in order that everything may be expounded directly in the light of the truth and under its guidance,[52] and so under the necessary structures of the reason which it acquires when it listens to the truth and submits to its compulsion.[53] This is not to resist or impugn the authority of the Scriptures, or of the doctrines of the faith that arise out of them, but on the contrary to establish them all the more firmly through this critical activity upon their true foundations.[54]

By *truth* Anselm clearly means the reality of things as they actually are, and therefore as they ought to be known and expressed by us. Everything is what it actually is and not something else, and cannot be other than it is. Therefore it must be discerned and known in accordance with the necessity of its being what it is.[55] That is what Anselm called the *veritas rei*, or 'the rational solidity of the truth, i.e. its necessity'.[56] To that truth or

---

49 *De ver.*, 9 (I, 188, 27ff. 189, 1ff).

50 *Mon.*, prol. (I, 7, 5ff. 8, 21ff); *C.D.h.*, praef. (II, 42, 11ff), I, 1 (pp. 48, 25f. 49, 1f), 4 (p. 52, 3f); II, 19 (p. 131, 7ff).

51 *C.D.h.*, II, 19 (II, 131, 9).

52 *Mon.*, prol. (I, 7, 5ff), 19 (p. 33, 26ff); *C.D.h.*, II, 9 (II, 106, 7f).

53 *Mon.*, 19 (I, 34, 12); *C.D.h.*, praef. (II, 42, 13f); I, 4 (p. 52, 3ff); I, 10 (pp. 66, 19ff. 67, 1ff).

54 *Mon.*, prol. (I, 7, 7ff) *C.D.h.*, II, 19 (II, 131, 7ff).

55 *Mon.*, 16–19 (I, 30–35).

56 *C.D.h.*, I, 4 (II, 53, 3ff); *Mon.*, 23 (I, 41, 21ff. 42, 1ff).

necessity in the object of knowledge there corresponds a truth or necessity in knowledge, the impossibility of conceiving the object as being other than it is. Hence, all interpretation and understanding must be critically tested through a *concomitant* or *concordant* activity in which we listen in to the truth of things, yielding to their natural necessity, for in that way we are enabled to straighten out our conceptions and statements in accordance with the nature of things as they really are.[57] Only when we are able to embody in our thinking or in our statements a rational order or necessary sequence which reflects or participates in the *ratio veritatis* have we engaged in scientific activity.[58]

To the question as to the nature of the truth Anselm devoted a special treatise, *De veritate*, in which he defined truth as rectitude or rightness (*rectitudo*).[59] The truth of things is that they are what they are and what they ought to be in accordance with their natures. When they are what they ought to be, they are rightly, and that rightness of their being remains whether we know them or not; it is immutable.[60] Hence by *rectitudo* Anselm defines the truth of a thing in terms of its *essence*, its being what it is, and its *necessity*, its inability to be other than it is. But he distinguishes this rectitude which is truth, from the rectitude or straightness which we perceive by the senses in physical bodies, as the rectitude which is perceptible by the mind alone (*rectitudo sola mente perceptibilis*).[61] That is by no means to give a purely intellectual definition of truth, but on the contrary to insist that truth is that which we perceive in the *essentia* of things, in real being.

This truth or rectitude in the essence or being of things Anselm distinguishes on the one hand from the truth of signification,[62] and on the other hand from the supreme Truth of God.[63] The truth of signification is that which must be signified of a thing in accordance with its nature. Hence the truth of signification is the effect of the truth of being or the essence of things. But because God is the source and Truth of all truth,

---

57 *Mon.*, 19 (I, 33, 26 ff. 34, 1ff), 23 (p. 41, 21ff); *C.D.h.*, I, 10 (II, 67, 1ff).

58 *C.D.h.*, II, 19 (II, 131, 7ff. 14ff); *De conc.*, I, 2 (II, 248, 5f).

59 *De ver.*, 2 (I, 178, 25. 179, 11), 3 (p. 180, 12), 4 (181, 4f), 5 (pp. 181, 25f. 182, 5ff), 10 (pp. 189, 31. 190, 1ff), 11 (p. 191, 6f. 19f), 12 (pp. 191, 27f. 192, 5ff. etc.), 13 (pp. 196, 28f. 197, 4ff. etc).

60 *De ver.*, 7 and 13 (I, 185ff, and 196ff).

61 *De ver.*, 11 (I, 191, 19f), 12 (p. 192, 7f), 13 (p. 196, 29).

62 *De ver.*, 2 (I, 177, 20f. 178, 1ff. 179, 1ff).

63 *De ver.*, 10 (I, 189f), 13 (pp. 196ff).

Divine Interpretation

as the Creator of all being, the truth of the essence of things is what they must be in accordance with their natures in dependence upon God as their Creator. Hence the truth of the essence of created things is the effect of the supreme Truth.

What do we mean when we speak of the truth of statements, then? When is a statement true (*quando est enuntiatio vera*)?[64] Anselm answers that the truth of a statement (*veritas enuntiationis*) cannot be found in the statement (*enuntiatio* or *oratio*) or in its signification as such, nor can it be identified with the thing stated (*res enuntiata*) which is rather the cause of its truth. It is found in the act of signification and in its proper fulfilment. A statement is true when it signifies that that which is, is, and signifies it as it should be in accordance with its nature. Hence the truth of a statement is its rightness. By that Anselm means an objective rightness, one that remains when the signification itself perishes, for it derives from the rightness of the thing signified, and shows through when it is signified rightly, although it is not affected by the signification itself.[65]

The truth of statement, then, is two-fold, for in signifying that that which is, is as it should be, it signifies both what it has been made to signify and what it has undertaken to signify. In other words, a true statement involves an actual conformity between the statement and the thing stated, and an intended conformity. Although the statement is enunciated under the compulsion of the reality or in accordance with its natural necessity, nevertheless there enters into it a real moment of the will in which the person making the statement fulfils what he has undertaken to signify.[66] Anselm's use of the term rectitude (*rectitudo*) is designed to cover that, and also what he calls the truth of will (*veritas voluntatis*)[67] and the truth of action (*veritas actionis*)[68] which are so apparent in moral behaviour, i.e. uprightness. Even in these realms Anselm insists that rectitude or rightness is objectively grounded, for the same *ratio veritatis* governs them as governs all significant activity in spoken or written speech.[69]

---

64 *De ver.*, 2 (I, 177f). See again my article in *Theologische Zeitschrift* 24 (1968) 309ff.

65 *De ver.*, 2 (I, 179, 10ff), 13 (pp. 198, 1ff. 199, 1ff).

66 *De ver.*, 2 (I, 179, 2ff).

67 *De ver.*, 4 (p. 180, 21f).

68 *De ver.*, 5 (p. 181, 12ff).

69 Cf. the discussion in *De ver.*, 2 (I, 177ff), and *De ver.*, 5 (pp. 181ff).

In saying that the rightness by which signification is called right remains even when the signification itself perishes, Anselm is insisting that the *veritas significationis* cannot stand by itself, but follows as effect from the very nature of the thing which is signified.[70] Hence to understand the *veritas significationis* or the *veritas enuntiationis* we have to look through the signs employed to the things signified and understand the truth or the rightness of their being. The truth of thought and the truth of discourse both depend, therefore, on the existence of things and become manifest when we think and speak as we ought about them, making our affirmations or denials in accordance with the natures of the existents themselves.[71]

Hence Anselm presses on to consider the truth of the essence of things (*veritas essentiae rerum*),[72] in which he finds a rightness of being that points beyond to the eternal Truth which is its source. Whatever there is, is truly, in so far as it is that which it is in the supreme Truth. Therefore truth is in the essence of things that are because they are what they are in the supreme Truth. But if nothing ought to be other than it is in the supreme Truth, then whenever anything is what it is in the supreme Truth it is what it ought to be, and so it is what it is, rightly. Thus Anselm also defines the truth of things as *rectitudo*. It is in that rightness that he finds the objective truth of signification, and finds indeed an objective signification in the existence of things themselves, since by the very fact that a thing is, it pronounces what it should be (*quoniam eo ipso quia est, dicit se debere esse*).[73]

Now that objective signification in the existence of things is also grounded beyond itself, in the eternal Truth of God, and indeed in the divine Rightness. The obligatory relation to the Truth of God deepens its objectivity indefinitely. However, there is a fundamental difference between the divine Rightness and all other rightness. The rightness of signification and the rightness of being are what they are obliged to be, but the supreme Truth is not Rightness because it has any obligation. Everything else is under obligation to it, but it is under obligation to nothing, nor is it what it is for any other reason than that it is. Thus, the divine *rectitudo* is the ultimate source and cause of all other truths and rightnesses, and is itself caused by nothing outside of itself. Under the supreme Truth, then, which is the Truth of all truth, some truths are only effects, while others are causes

---

70 *De ver.*, 2 (I, 177, 6ff. 178, 1ff. 179, 1ff), 9 (pp. 188, 27f. 189, 1ff).
71 *De ver.*, 3 (I, 180, 7ff), 7 (p. 185, 8ff), 13 (pp. 197, 10ff. 198, 1ff).
72 *De ver.*, 7 (I, 185, 8ff).
73 *De ver.*, 9 (I, 189, 24f).

Divine Interpretation

as well as effects. Thus the truth that is in the existence of things is both the effect of the supreme Truth and the cause of the truths of thought and of statement, but the truths of thought and statement are in no sense causes of other truths.[74] All truths point back to the one supreme Truth and it is ultimately only in the light of that Truth that one can speak of the truth of signification or the truth of being. Strictly speaking, according to Anselm, truth is improperly said to be of this or that thing, since truth does not have its being in things or out of things or through the things in which it is said to be: 'The supreme Truth which subsists in itself is the Truth of no thing, but when something is according to truth, then it is called the truth or the rightness of that thing.'[75]

Two comments may now be offered about this account of truth. Through his use of *rectitudo* Anselm intends to assert with the greatest force the objectivity of truth. Thus the truth of signification is not only the conformity of statement to the reality stated, but an obligatory conformity, for the statement is enunciated under the claim or demand that comes from the side of what is stated, and is made in acknowledgement of that claim and in accordance with the nature of the reality that stands behind it. This means that there is an irreversible relation between the sign and the thing signified, the statement and the thing stated, for the truth of human statements is the consequence of the existence of things. But the objectivity is even deeper, for the truth of the existence of things follows similarly from the Truth of God Himself, since those things are not only what they are but are what they are under the compulsion that derives from God Himself. It is indeed in this indefinite objectivity that reaches out far beyond them that the truth of true human statements is to be discerned.

Practically speaking, this means that interpretation operates with a two-fold truth, the truth of signification and the truth of being. Statements are rightly interpreted when they are understood in their compulsory reference to the things signified, and when those things signified are understood for what they are and for what by their natures they must be. But when we see that the rightness of signifying points beyond to a rightness of being, and that the rightness of being points beyond to a source of being in the supreme Being, then we see that the truer statements are, the more they are open toward the ultimate Truth. By their very nature true statements have an indefinite quality about them which they acquire

---

74 *De ver.*, 10 (I, 189, 30f. 190, 1ff).
75 *De ver.*, 13 (I, 199, 27f).

through pointing to the infinite and eternal Truth of God. That applies above all to theological statements, for they are statements about God than whom none greater can be conceived, the God who infinitely transcends our thoughts and statements about Him. Therefore statements about Him are rightly made and are rightly interpreted when we respect the rationality of the Truth that is so wide and so profound that it cannot be exhausted by mortals: *veritatis ratio tam ampla et profunda est, ut a mortalibus nequeat exhauriri*.[76]

III. *Word of the Creator and Word of the Creature*

In the light of what we have found Anselm saying about word and truth, we must now go on to ask how he thought of the relation between the human word and the divine Word. We return to the distinction Anselm draws between thinking a thing by thinking the word signifying it and thinking a thing by understanding the very entity which the thing is.[77] We think truly of a thing when through the word signifying it we think the reality itself—that is what Anselm called *cogitatio rerum*. Corresponding to this is the distinction between speaking of something *secundum formam vocum* and speaking of it *secundum rerum naturam*.[78] Since words only signify when they signify things, we understand them when we not only listen to what is being said but consider the things themselves that are being spoken about—that is, we have to pay attention to the *locutio rerum*. The *cogitatio rerum* or the *locutio rerum* describes the fundamental form of thinking or speaking that arises out of the pressure of reality itself upon us, for it is a form of thinking or speaking that is objectively rooted in reality. Anselm supplies a clear example of this basic thinking or speaking in the *Proslogion* when he develops a train of thought that forced itself upon him as he was meditating upon the grounds of faith.[79]

We now recall the important observation Anselm made when he was discussing the *proprium et principale rei verbum* with which we are concerned in basic thought and speech, that the *locutio* in which words of

---

76 C.D.h., *commendatio operis* (II, 40, 4–5).

77 *Prosl.*, 4 (I, 103, 17ff).

78 *De Gram.*, 18 (I, 164, 9f), cf. 8 (p. 152, 9f), 17 (p. 162, 25f); and *De casu diaboli*, 11 (I, 250, 21f) where the contrast is between *secundum formam vocis* and *secundum rem*.

79 *Prosl.*, prooem. (I, 93, 12ff).

this kind consist points back to a *locutio rerum* that existed in the supreme Substance (*apud summam substantiam*), before the creation of the *res* themselves, both as the means through which they were created, and as the means, once they are created, through which they may be known.[80] Behind this lies the biblical teaching that all things that are made are created through the Word of God, and they remain in existence in that they consist in and continue to be upheld by that Word of the Creator. In the Augustinian tradition, within which Anselm himself stood, this had often been given a rather Platonic interpretation, to mean that all creaturely realities owe their being to participation in the eternal forms or ideas of the divine Mind or Reason. Hence, as Anselm himself says, they exist more truly in the Word of God, in the *cogitatio* and *locutio* of God than in themselves.[81]

In Anselm's thought this is cognate to his notion that the truth of the essence of things derives from and points back to the supreme Truth as effect to its cause. But far from detracting from the reality of existence as merely phenomenal in comparison to noumenal reality, this had the effect of deepening and strengthening the objectivity of the truth of existence, for Anselm did not take over from Augustine the notion of a radical dichotomy between the *mundus sensibilis* and the *mundus intelligibilis*. That affected Augustine's understanding of the operation of the divine Word, for with him the divine *locutio* is nothing more and nothing less than the divine *cogitatio*, and so his understanding of the divine Word reaches back to the point where it is identified with the Light and Truth of the divine Being. But what is highly distinctive in Anselm's thought—and this is where he breaks decisively with the Augustinian tradition—is the seriousness and realism with which he understands the *locutio* in God, *apud summam substantiam*, to which the *intimae locutiones* in created realities go back.[82] It is that connection that gives the *locutio* or *ratio* embedded in created things a depth of objectivity in which it is revealed that what they are in themselves they are independently of our knowledge of them.

Two points of capital importance are to be considered here.

---

80 *Mon.*, 10 (I, 25, 22-27).
81 *Mon.*, 10 (I, 25, 22f), 31 (p. 49, 7ff), 36 (p. 55, 2f), etc.
82 *Mon.*, 10-12 (I, 24-26).

A) Since things are known truly through an *intima locutio* that derives from and is backed up by a *locutio* in God we may make statements about them that are genuinely objective. But we may make statements like that only when we penetrate into the *intima locutio* of created things and let it govern our speech about them. That is to say, the form that these objects take in our knowledge of them is not one which we impose upon them, but which we discern in them and express in corresponding statements about them. This is to state again the point we noted before when Anselm insisted that the rightness or truth of the essence of things is independent of the statements we make signifying them, but here the relation between the signification and the reality signified is expressly described as *locutio*, which makes it all the more clear that the truth of signification is, not something that we think up and impose upon the objects concerned, but a truth which we hear and put into our own words. In this event our own words rest upon a basic *rei verbum* which derives from a creative *locutio* in God.

When we ask how we are to think of this speech or *locutio* as embedded in created substance, i.e. in what sense they can be said to speak to us and reveal their natures, Anselm points on the one hand to the fact that they all derive their existence, and the truth they bear in their essence, from the creative activity of the Word of God, and on the other hand to the fact that they all have an internal rationality (*ratio*) which they derive from the rationality (*ratio*) of the supreme Truth. The first of these two points depends on the realism in which we think of the divine *locutio*, and the relation between *dicere* and *intelligere* in God, which we shall consider shortly, but at the moment we note only Anselm's profound sense of the fact that the speech of God 'whether separately by the utterance of separate words or all at once by the utterance of one word',[83] is that which gives not only being but *rationality* to all created things. It is the second point, however, that helps us to see more clearly how he regards the *intima locutio* of created objects, and relates it to the *intima locutio* of the Creator.

Anselm's use of *ratio* is parallel to his use of *veritas*. In all true knowledge there is a *ratio* of inquiry and of knowing,[84] which corresponds to the *ratio* of the thing investigated or known,[85] but behind both there is

---

83 *Mon.*, 12 (I. 26, 26ff).

84 *Mon.*, 1 (I, 13, 12ff); *C.D.h.*, praef. (II, 42, 13f); *E.I.V.*, 1 (II, 6, 2f. 7, 1f), 6 (pp. 20, 16ff. 21, 4ff); *De conc.*, q. 3 (6) (II, 272, 1f); *De processione Spiritus Sancti*, 11 (II, 209, 14f), etc.

85 *C.D.h.*, I, 3 (II, 50, 18f) 25 (p. 96. 1ff) II, 16 (p. 117, 20f) *Prosl.*, prooem. (I, 93f), etc.

the *summa ratio* of God Himself,[86] which he speaks of as the *ratio summae naturae*[87] and identifies with the eternal Word consubstantial with the Father.[88] Used in this way *ratio* refers to the rationality or order or mode of the truth, and therefore may be noetic or ontic depending on whether the reference is to the act of knowing or to the nature of the thing known, but used absolutely it refers to the *ratio veritatis* in God Himself.[89] As with the *veritates* so with the *rationes*, the *ratio* of knowing derives from and is the effect, but voluntary effect, of the *ratio* of the object known, and although that ontic *ratio* is the ground of the noetic *ratio*, it is itself caused or posited by the *ratio* of God in the objects of His creative activity.

According to Anselm, then, the rationality of our knowing is grounded in the object of knowledge but the rationality of the object depends not on itself but on the eternal Word and Truth, upon the Rationality, of God Himself. Hence the right use of the human *ratio* is in no sense creative and normative, and even the ontic *ratio* in the object is one conferred on it in its creation by God. Neither as noetic nor as ontic is the *ratio* higher than the Truth of God, but the Truth of God is the master of all *rationes*, the ultimate *ratio veritatis*.[90]

In view of the foregoing, the investigation of a creaturely reality must involve an activity in which we penetrate into its inner law of existence or rationality, allow our understanding to be informed and guided by it, and seek to articulate that understanding in an orderly manner, i.e. *sola ratione*.[91] We allow the truth of the reality to force itself upon us in its own inherent intelligibility, and establish our knowledge through the development of necessary reasons derived from the side of the reality investigated. But what else is this than to give ear to the *intima locutio* in the creaturely object, and to translate it into an appropriate language of our own? It is through laying bare the ontic *rationes* in things that we allow them to disclose themselves to us as they are and as they should be, i.e. in their truth. But in so doing we know them not just as they are in themselves but as they should be in the supreme Truth, that is, in a dimension of rationality and

---

86 *Mon.*, 16 (I, 31, 2ff), 34 (p. 53, 17f).

87 *Mon.*, 9 (I, 24, 15).

88 *Mon.*, 33f (I, 51ff).

89 *C.D.h.*, comm. Op. (II, 40, 4); II, 19 (pp. 130, 29. 131, 7ff); *Ad Proslogion Responsio Editoris*, 3 (I, 133, 11).

90 For a fuller account of Anselm's understanding of *ratio* see Barth, op. cit., 44ff.

91 *Mon.*, 1 (I, 13, 11); *C.D.h.*, I, 20 (II, 88, 8) II, 11 (II, 111, 28); II, 22 (II, 133, 8).

objectivity that reaches out far beyond them into God, and is backed up by His creative Word. This means that even in the knowledge of creaturely realities we operate with an objective conceptuality, or with an inner logic (*ratio* or *locutio*) in the nature of things, which forces us to call in question all objectification or conceptualisation worked up from the side of man and imposed upon what he seeks to know and interpret, and which summons us to disciplined scientific activity in which we seek to order and rectify our thinking and speaking in accordance with the nature and rationality of what we seek to know and interpret.

So far we have been speaking of the investigation of creaturely objects that are mute and determinate in their nature, but what of creaturely realities that do not only have an *intima locutio* somehow embedded in them through their creation, but are themselves *loquens* by nature, such as the objects of faith which speak to us and which we hear through the Holy Scriptures? In other words, what is the nature of the reality we investigate when we seek to understand and interpret biblical and theological statements? What is the relation between the *locutio* of man in these statements and the *locutio* of God Himself in His Word? That is the second point of capital importance in Anselm's thought which we have to consider.

B) If human statements about created realities are true in so far as they derive from and correspond to a *locutio rerum* that goes back to the creative Word of God, and indeed a *locutio apud summam substantiam*, how much more is that the case with true human statements about God! They derive their content and their truth through a *locutio* which God has provided for us in the Holy Scriptures and which is mediated through the preaching and teaching of the Church, a *locutio* that goes back to the eternal Word of God consubstantial with Himself. True human statements about God are made, therefore, in response to speech directed to man by God, so that the thinking and conceiving that these statements involve take place on the basis of a word from God that has been heard and understood by man, i.e. received through faith. However, just as the truth of signification derives from the truth in the essence of created things, although that in turn is the effect of the supreme Truth, and just as the inner rationality of our knowledge derives from an objective rationality in the nature of created realities, although that in turn is one conferred upon them with their creation and points back to its source in the *ratio summae naturae*, so the *intima locutio* of theological statements derives from and depends on the words and acts of God in revelation, yet they are the created images or similitudes of the eternal Word of God consubstantial with Himself. But this Word of God Anselm thinks of seriously as *verbum* as well as *ratio*, as a *dicere* as well as an *intelligere* and therefore as *locutio* eternally real in the divine Being Himself. It is because the *locutio* of theological statements goes back through the *locutio* in biblical statements, which is the mediate object of faith, to an eternal *locutio* in God Himself that those statements, when true, enshrine a conceptuality that is objectively rooted and grounded in God's own self-revelation, and is not just constructed out of man's own independent interpretations. That is the great contribution of St Anselm to the doctrine of the Word of God and to the nature of biblical and theological statements.

There are two problems here that require further thought and elucidation: In what sense can we speak of the *locutio* of the supreme Being as mediated to us through created realities? How can we through the use of human words, which correspond to created realities, speak truly of the supreme Being who transcends them altogether? These two questions are taken up by Anselm and discussed in sustained arguments in the *Monologion*, to which we turn only to take out of them the essential points relevant to our immediate purpose.

1) When Anselm speaks of a *locutio apud summam substantiam*,[92] he asks to be understood as using the term *substance* in a unique sense appropriate to the supreme Being who is who He is in and through Himself, who ever remains identical with Himself in His immutability and simplicity, unaffected by *accidents* of facts of any kind external to His own Being, although He is the source of all other being, creating it out of nothing.[93] As such He is to be spoken of as Spirit who exists in so wonderfully singular and so singularly wonderful a way of His own that all other beings that seem to be comparable with Him are not.[94]

Hence the kind of *locutio* that takes place in the supreme Being is one according to His nature, and must be spoken of as *locutio Spiritus*.[95]

The *locutio* in the supreme Being, however, is not something different from the supreme Spirit, nor indeed from His *intelligentia* by which He understands all things. In Him speaking and understanding are not

---

92 *Mon.*, 10 (I, 25, 26f), 11 (p. 26, 3ff), 12 (p. 26, 26ff).
93 *Mon.*, 25–26 (I, 43f).
94 *Mon.*, 27–28 (I, 45f).
95 *Mon.*, 29 (I, 47f).

separable, for He does not, like man, fail to express (*dicere*) what He understands (*intelligere*).⁹⁶ This is the *locutio* in God through which all things have been created, but the *locutio* itself is not a creature and cannot be contained within created realities (*impossibile est inter creata contineri*).⁹⁷ However, if the *locutio* is not different from the Spirit but is consubstantial with Him, then it does not consist of more words than one, but is the One Word through whom all things were created.⁹⁸

This makes it clear, therefore, that the *locutio* in God is not a sort of language, any more than the *verbum rei* belongs to this or that language, for it is the primary and proper word basic and common to them all. But words of this kind (*verba rei*) by which we mentally think or speak *things*, are the likenesses or images of the objects to which they correspond, and are more or less true according as they approximate to their objects. What are we to say then about the Word by which all things are spoken and through which they are made? It cannot be said to be the likeness of created things, for then it would not be the Word of the supreme Truth. Rather do all created things have their truth in this Word. In the strict sense it is this Word only that exists, while created things are rather to be regarded as in its likeness, for it is according to it and by it that they are anything at all. Any relation or likeness between the Word of the supreme Truth and created things, does not affect its reality, for it is itself the supreme Truth: 'Hence it follows that this Word is not more or less true according to its likeness to created things, but every created nature has a higher mode of being and dignity, the more it is seen to approach that Word.'⁹⁹

But even so a difficulty remains, Anselm says. How can what is simple Truth be the *Word* corresponding to those objects of which it is not the likeness? Every word is a word corresponding to some object, i.e. a *rei verbum*, and every *rei verbum* is the likeness of the object to which it corresponds. Does that mean that 'if there were no creature, that Word would not exist at all, although it is the supreme Being in want of nothing? Or perhaps the supreme Being which is the Word, would still be the eternal Being, but not the Word, if nothing were ever created through that Being?'¹⁰⁰ Anselm answers in the negative, for that would mean that there

---

96 Cf. also *Mon.*, 60 (I, 70f), 62 (pp. 72f).
97 *Mon.*, 29 (I, 47, 14f).
98 *Mon.*, 30 (I, 48, 8–12).
99 *Mon.*, 31 (I, 50, 10–15).
100 *Mon.*, 32 (I, 50, 22ff).

would never be a Word in God unless there were some being apart from Him. Moreover, if there were no Word in God He would say nothing to Himself, but since for God speaking is the same as understanding, it would mean that He understands nothing, which is most absurd. On the contrary, we must think of the eternal Spirit as eternally mindful of Himself and as understanding Himself after the likeness of a rational mind, or rather, not after the likeness of another, Anselm insists, for we must think of the Spirit in the first place (*principaliter*), and of the rational mind after His likeness: 'But if He understands Himself eternally, He speaks Himself eternally. If He speaks Himself eternally, His Word is eternally with Him (*At si aeterne se intelligit, aeterne se dicit. Si aeterne se dicit, aeterne est verbum eius apud ipsum*). Accordingly, whether the Spirit is thought of apart from any other existing being, or along with other existents, the Word of the Spirit must be coeternal with Him.'[101]

This argumentation makes clear that for Anselm the Word of God is to be understood as eternally Word (*verbum, locutio*) in God Himself, that in God the *Logos* remains Word and does not disappear simply into Reason (*ratio*). *Dicere* and *intelligere* are integrally related in the unity, simplicity and eternity of the divine Being; Anselm will not confuse them with one another nor separate them from one another in his understanding. He will not allow the divine *dicere* to be understood ultimately as simply the vision of the divine Mind, or the *locutio* to be dissolved, so to speak, into the divine Light. Word has eternal objectivity in God's own Being, for He eternally utters or speaks Himself, and is Himself the Reality of His Word. It is to that eternal objectivity of the Word in the infinite depth of the divine Being that every true word goes back, for it is in relation to that Word and the *locutio rerum* it posits in creation that all true and significant words have their reality.

It follows from this that God utters Himself and what He creates by a single consubstantial Word. He does not utter Himself by one Word and create the world by another Word, but utters whatever He creates by the same Word whereby He utters Himself. This is a Word that corresponds to Himself and is His own consubstantial likeness. Hence, although it is the Word through which the world is uttered it cannot be a word corresponding to the world since it is not the world's likeness but its ultimate source of being (*principalis essentia*) and its primary reality (*prima veritas*). Thus, far from being a mutable word corresponding to created or mutable realities,

---

101 *Mon.*, 32 (I, 51, 15–18).

it is immutable corresponding to the eternal Reality of God, and is itself eternally real Word, the creative source of all other realities, and the fountain of all their rationality and truth.[102]

If the Word were only a word (*verbum rei*) corresponding to the created realities of the world, a word of the world, a word that could be contained within created realities, then doubtless we could understand it and give it proper expression; but just because the relation of the Word of God to the world depends on its unique relation to the Being of God, and corresponds to His supreme Nature, it is impossible for us to grasp how it is eternally uttered within the divine Being, and therefore how God creates the world with the same Word by which He utters Himself:

> Since it is established that every created substance exists more truly in the Word, i.e. in the understanding of the Creator, than it does in itself, in the same proportion in which the creative Being exists more truly than the created, how can the human mind comprehend the mode of that speaking and that knowledge which is so vastly superior to, and truer than, created substances, if our knowledge is so vastly surpassed by those substances as their likeness differs from their being?[103]

What may be most clearly comprehended, says Anselm, is 'that how the Spirit speaks, or how He knows those things which are created, cannot be comprehended by human knowledge.'[104]

In these circumstances the only rational thing to do, as he says later, is to acknowledge that this is in the nature of the case.[105] But although we cannot grasp how the supreme Spirit through His own consubstantial Word or internal *locutio* both utters Himself and creates all things, that does not mean that we are up against something irrational, but rather something that is incomprehensible only through its own natural sublimity. Hence what this indicates for us is the limits of human inquiry beyond which we cannot go, or the limitation of our powers to put into words what is understood. But within those limits we may and indeed must probe as deeply as we may and seek to make clear the rationality of what we are given to understand.

That brings us to the next problem.

---

102 *Mon.*, 33–34 (I, 51ff).
103 *Mon.*, 36 (I, 55, 4–10).
104 *Mon.*, 36 (I, 54, 16f).
105 *Mon.*, 64 (I, 74, 30f. 75, 1–16).

Divine Interpretation

2) If the Truth is inexplicable from the side of man, but is yet to be understood and investigated, how can we through human words which correspond to created objects (*verba rerum*) speak truly of what transcends them altogether? If the supreme Being about which we have been speaking is ultimately incomprehensible and ineffable in His own nature, then what have we been doing in making our statements about Him but constructing a picture of Him, so to speak, out of images that are really alien to Him, i.e. engaging in an objectifying movement in which we have imposed upon God false conceptual forms derived from our worldly forms of thought and speech? We have already seen how Anselm met this same argument in other forms, and that his answer has consistently been the following: through the images we use, through the forms of signification our propositions entail, and even through the basic words we employ in their correspondence to created realities, there shows through an objective rationality which is independent of our images and forms of speech. Moreover, because we can distinguish it from them, we have a firm base on the ground of which we can put our images and forms of thought and speech to the test to see how far they not only correspond to the realities they point to but provide for us the medium in which our minds come under the compulsion of those realities, under their *necessitas* or *ratio veritatis*.

It is another form of the same argument that he develops here. Granted that the forms of thought and speech which we use fall far short of the transcendent Reality and in themselves have nothing in common with that Reality, nevertheless they are sufficiently relevant to be able to point beyond themselves to that Reality and so to serve our understanding and speaking of it. The problem is stated in this way;

> The supreme Being is so far above and beyond every other nature, that whenever anything is said about it in words which are shared with other natures, the sense in which they are used is by no means one which they have in common with them.[106] For what sense have I understood in all these words I have been contemplating except the common and normal sense? If therefore the normal sense of words is alien to the supreme Being whatever I have thought out does not apply to it. How then has anything true at all been found

---

106 *Quia sic est summa essentia supra et extra omnem aliam naturam, ut si quando de illa dicitur aliquid verbis, quae communia sunt aliis naturis, sensus nullatenus sit communis.* Cf. *Mon.*, 26 (I, 44, 17f): *Unde si quando illi est cum aliis nominis alicuius communio, valde procul dubio intelligenda est diversa significatio.* And see further *Mon.*, 27 (p. 45, 4ff).

concerning the supreme Being, if what has been found is so far removed from Him?[107]

Anselm asks in reply whether in some way (*quodam modo*) something has been learned about the incomprehensible Reality, and whether in some way (*quodam modo*) something has not been discerned, and goes on to argue for an analogical mode of understanding and employment of our forms of thought and speech, through which the transcendent and objective realities are allowed to impress themselves upon our minds.

He draws a distinction between a mode of speaking in which we express some reality directly in accordance with its proper nature, and another mode in which we signify through something else (*per aliud*) that which we are unwilling or unable to express properly or precisely, as when we speak *per aenigmata*: 'Often we see something not properly as it actually is in itself, but through some likeness or image, as when we look at someone's face in a mirror. In this way we express and do not express, we see and do not see, one and the same thing. We express and see it through something else; we do not express and see it through its own proper nature (*per suam proprietatem*).'[108] By this Anselm does not mean that when he conceives of the meanings of these words, such as *wisdom* and *essence*, he can somehow read the knowledge of the supreme Being off them, for when he considers their meanings like that he naturally turns to conceive the created realities rather than those that transcend all human understanding. But common terms like these may be used to intimate (*innuere*) or to point out (*designare*) a reality with which they themselves have nothing in common, and which utterly transcends them. In other words, 'they set up in my mind a signification of their own which is utterly different from any understanding that my mind can achieve through working on this shadowy signification on its own'.[109] Hence, even though the forms of thought and speech we use are inadequate in themselves, because they point utterly beyond themselves, they may well direct us to the supreme Nature, incapable though He is of description in words or in any other way. They have to be used aright, however, under the instruction of the reason (*ratione docente*) *per aliud vel aenigmate*, that is, in such a way that we allow our minds to come under the objective necessity or rationality of what forces itself upon us *indirectly through* them, then in spite of their

---

107 *Mon.*, 65 (I, 76, 2–9).
108 *Mon.*, 65 (I, 76, 14–18).
109 *Mon.*, 65 (I, 76, 14–18).

Divine Interpretation

impropriety or inadequacy they are not false analogies.[110] We may put that rather differently by saying that for Anselm all human attempts to express understanding of the supreme Being, than whom none greater can be conceived, are compromises with the truth, but they are not for that reason necessarily false, for their function is primarily denotative, and they intend a reality beyond their creaturely content by which their creaturely content is shown to be inadequate. They can succeed in fulfilling that function provided that in some way (*quodam modo*) they serve the self-revelation of the supreme Being and allow Him to impress His image upon the mind of man.[111]

That does not take place, however, without the assistance of the supreme Being or without the active will of man. God has created the human mind to know and love Him, and has made it to reflect His image. The impress of that image upon man's mind is what Anselm calls a voluntary effect (*voluntarius effectus*),[112] for it calls for the earnest devotion of man to the Truth, in which he allows it to imprint itself upon his understanding, and learns through a relation of love toward it to distinguish truth from falsehood.[113] This activity, however, takes place within the relationship of faith set up between God and man through His Word and through the obedience to Him which His Word calls forth from man.[114] The understanding that man has for God in all this activity is not one that he achieves on his own, but one that is constantly bestowed upon him through the self-revelation of God and on the ground of His grace.[115] This has to be linked up with the teaching of Anselm that we do not know anything in any way we choose, but only in the way in which it ought to be known, for that is the way that is according to its own inherent nature. We know God, the supreme Truth, therefore in a way that is in accordance with His own will to love us and communicate Himself to us, and in such a way that, as He the Creator confronts man, man's knowledge of Him is due to God's creative act within him.[116]

---

110 *Mon.*, 65 (I, 76, 14-18).

111 *Mon.*, 66-67 (I, 77f).

112 *Mon.*, 68 (I, 78, 16); cf. *De ver.*, 12 (I, 192f).

113 *Mon.*, 68ff (I, 78ff); cf. also Anselm's discussion in *Mon.*, 49 (p. 64), 65f (pp. 75f), 77 (p. 84), 79 (pp. 85f).

114 *Mon.*, 75ff (I, 83ff).

115 *De conc.*, q. 3 (6) (II, 270ff) *Prosl.*, 1f (I, 97ff), 14 (pp. 111f), 18 (pp. 113ff), etc.

116 Cf. *De ver.*, 10 (I, 190, 8ff), where Anselm speaks of the *summa veritas* as *causa veritatis quae cogitationis est*. And see *Prosl.*, 3 (I, 103, 3ff), and the exposition of this passage by Barth, op. cit., 150ff.

It is thus that there takes shape within man's mind that inner word which is assimilated to the reality it denotes, and is the similitude or expression through which he thinks or speaks it. As such it is an objectively determined expression, compellingly related to the Word or *locutio* of God mediated to man through the Holy Scriptures and the preaching of the Church.[117] Because God is He than whom none greater can be conceived, He whom we cannot conceive on our own, it is only where His Name is manifest, where He has given revelation of Himself, where through His Creator Word He has posited *similitudines* of Himself, that there can take place the thinking and understanding and speaking of Him which, in spite of all the unlikeness and inadequacy of human forms of thought and speech in themselves, may yet be successful and valid. But even when His Word is heard and He is understood He remains in that hearing and understanding essentially He than whom none greater can be conceived, and He whom we cannot conceive on our own.[118] It is for this reason that Anselm constantly conducts his theological inquiry with prayer that God may reveal Himself, may teach Him where and how to find Him, that God may renew His self-giving to Anselm, and enable him beyond any powers or capacities which his mind may have in itself to know and see Him in accordance with the rationality of the divine Truth or God's own *ratio veritatis*.[119]

What we have been concerned to show in the foregoing examination and discussion of Anselm's thought is the immense importance of the relation between God's *dicere* and His *intelligere* which, without being simply identical, are integrally connected in the supreme Truth. This is of the utmost moment for any biblical and theological inquiry, for it means that we must learn to discern behind all biblical and theological statements both the shining and the speaking of the divine Truth.[120] The Truth with which we are concerned is the Being of God which is also Word, and the Word of God which is also His personal Being. That is the nature of the transcendent Reality of God which biblical statements mediate, as they point to it through an assimilation in likeness to it which God gives them by His grace, and through the activity of His *locutio*. Everything depends ultimately upon the *creative speaking* of God which is the ground of all

---

117 *Mon.*, 77-78 (I, 84f) *De conc.* q. 3 (2ff) (pp. 264ff); *E.I.V.* I (II, 3ff), and *Prior recensio* 1f (I, 281ff).

118 *Prosl.*, 2-4 (I, 101-4), and *Resp. Ed.* 6f (pp. 136f).

119 See *Prosl*, 2-6, and 14 especially (I, 101-5, and 111f).

120 See *Prosl.*, 14ff (I, 111ff), and Warnach, op. cit., 167f.

true knowledge of Him, the source of all our ability to speak of Him, and the active guide to all our understanding and inquiry of Him in His self-revelation.[121] It is because all created realities are truer in His Word than they are in themselves, that in the employment of the Word Himself they may serve to convey to us a knowledge of God that is quite beyond us; but because these created realities which God uses as the medium of His communication are truer in His Word than they are in themselves, they are in themselves in their relation to that Word far different from what they are in our knowledge of them, so that far from trying to reach knowledge of God through speculative reasoning from created things, we must let them fulfil for us the denotative function they are given in God's Word, i.e. to point above and beyond themselves to God's own Truth.

---

121 *Mon.*, 10 (I, 24, 24f, and 25, 25f): *Illa autem rerum forma, quae in eius ratione res creandas praecedebat: quid aliud est quam rerum quaedam in ipsa ratione locutio...? Non immerito videri potest apud summam substantiam, talem rerum locutionem et fuisse antequam essent ut per eam fierent, et esse cum facta sunt ut per eam sciantur.*

CHAPTER 5

Scientific Hermeneutics according to St Thomas Aquinas[1]

The re-entry of Aristotle into the Church's dogmatics is one of the most important factors in the development of Western theology. For its beginnings we have to go back to the early sixth century to Boethius who translated several of Aristotle's works into Latin and gave them considerable circulation. Of not a little importance were his own two commentaries on Aristotle's περὶ ἑρμηνείας or *De Interpretatione*, one rather shorter and simpler than the other. However, it was only with the introduction of Aristotelianism into the theology of the Church through the medium of Arabian and Jewish scholars that its main impact was felt. The importance of this for hermeneutics in the high Middle Age is not to be looked for in the use of new methods so much as in *the close integration of language and thought* it produced. Interpretation, it was realised, cannot be isolated from the rules of thought that govern all areas of knowledge; it must be conducted scientifically, with adequate reasons given for the significations established. A fresh consideration of this may not be out of place in view of the threat to biblical theology by a new nominalism that appears to question very radically the relation of language to thought.[2]

We may speak of the impact of Aristotelian thought upon mediaeval hermeneutics in several ways.

(a) It challenged the sharp distinction between sense and thought. According to the Platonic philosophy there was a world of ordered forms above and apart from the world of sense experience; they are reflected in it, but knowledge of them is reached only through transcending sense experience. That made it possible for the late patristic and early

---

1 This essay originally appeared in *Journal of Theological Studies* 13.2 (1962) 259-89, and is reprinted with permission of Oxford University Press.

2 An outstanding example of this nominalist scepticism is James Barr, *The Semantics of Biblical Language* (London, 1961).

mediaeval ages to develop a whole world of allegory and spiritual meaning in detachment from history and event and to regard that as a realm of intercorrelated meanings on its own, as it were, above and beyond the material and the earthly. On the Aristotelian view, however, the universal ideas exist only as expressed in the individual objects of the sensible world and we know them not apart from but only through sense experience. This had a sobering effect on exegesis for it disparaged the cultivation of a world of meanings that could be correlated on its own without scientific reference to the historical sense of Scripture and careful examination of its words and concepts; rather must everything be correlated with the actual facts and particulars narrated in the text and its sequences of thought.

(b) Another way of expounding this is to say that the Aristotelian philosophy refused to separate matter and form, for they are two aspects of one thing. They are essentially correlative. Thus a particular object is a matter as it is determined according to some organic pattern or form and the form is the determinate structure according to which the object is organised. It is in this way that the soul and the body are said to be related, so that the soul informs the body and the body is the instrument for its expression and is appropriate to it. The relation of this teaching to hermeneutics is obvious. As Miss Smalley has written, 'Transferring his view of body and soul to "letter and spirit" the Aristotelian would perceive the "spirit" of Scripture as something not hidden behind or added on to, but expressed by the text. We cannot disembody a man in order to investigate his soul; neither can we understand the Bible by distinguishing letter from spirit and making a separate study of each.'[3]

(c) In the third place, we have to note the impact upon hermeneutics of the Aristotelian notion of science as that which establishes rational connections and gathers them round a centre. Scientific knowledge is thus the orderly arranging and demonstration of sequences of truths in a particular science according to the particular principles relevant to it, e.g. biological sequences within biology and geometrical argumentation within geometry. Knowledge arises through a development from sense experience by drawing out and disentangling what is implicit in it and so proceeds by abstraction to the formulation of general notions, and to explanation by testing the relation of their causes to particular effects. This does not mean that particular principles can be demonstrated any more than first principles, but that if the critical work of reasoning is done properly they

---

3 Beryl Smalley, *The Study of the Bible in the Middle Ages* (Oxford, 1941), 229.

will be pointed out to us and we will discern the truth of them in their own nature.[4] The application of this to biblical interpretation does not mean that the truths of revelation have to be demonstrated, but that the interpretation of the Scripture cannot be separated from sober analysis of propositions, for the interpretation of language is the interpretation of thought.

This had a double effect on exegesis. On the one hand, it detached the interpretation of Scripture from a realm of mystical meanings that could not be rationally related to the text and so brought theology and exegesis into closer relation to one another. On the other hand, it introduced a powerful element of inferential reasoning into interpretation, whether of the linguistic signs used in Scripture (its words and sentences) or of the things they signified. This paved the way for a new speculative theology which proceeded by way of abstraction and generalisation from the Scripture in order to draw out and supplement its lines of thought, but also by way of abstraction and generalisation from the world of sense experience. Thus under Aristotelian influence there arose a natural theology side by side with revealed theology, and because the former could only be regarded as a *praeambula fidei*, it tended to provide the general framework within which biblical interpretation and positive theology were carried on.[5] Hence everything depended upon the degree in which the metaphysical framework of natural theology was allowed not only to provide the thought-forms in which revealed theology was to be expressed, but to impose an alien form of thinking upon it and so to triumph over it.[6]

It is above all to St Thomas Aquinas that we must turn to see how these developments affected the interpretation of Holy Scripture, not only because his own biblical commentaries have such a sober and judicious quality when compared with those of many of his mediaeval predecessors and contemporaries, but because his views gathered up so much that was outstanding in the ecclesiastical tradition and exercised a formative influence upon the future. What gave St Thomas' views their rationale was their undeviating relation to the final end to which, as he saw it, all knowing on the part of man is ordained, and what gave them their force was their organic relation to the rest of his thought. In interpretation, he held, we

4 Aristotle, *Metaphysics*, iv.4.

5 Cf. Aquinas, *De Trinitate*, q. 2.22.

6 *De Trinitate*, q. 2, a. 3. Cf. here the insistence of Bonaventura that the Scriptures have to be interpreted and considered by theology in such a way that it places philosophical knowledge beneath it (*substernens sibi philosophicam cognitionem*), *Breviloquium, Proem.* 4.

Divine Interpretation

have to determine the intention of the author and discern the significant form of what he has to say, through turning our attention to the things signified, and through noting the use of his words by examining their relation to the whole of his discourse.[7] In all this, interpretation is fundamentally an act of the intellect or understanding (*intellectus*) in which the mind pierces through to see the *quid* of a thing, that is, to read the truth in the very essence of it (*interius in ipsa rei essentia rei veritatem quodammodo legere*).[8]

The etymology of *intelligere* accepted by Aquinas was from *intus legere*, to read within, to penetrate beneath the sensible surface (*sensus*) and discern the rational meaning (*intellectus*).[9] This gives us the clue to St Thomas' conception of interpretation as an act of understanding or intimate knowledge (*intellectus*).

Sensitive cognition is concerned with external sensible qualities but intellective cognition penetrates into the very essence of a thing, because the object of the understanding is that which is (*quod quid est*), as it is said. But there are many kinds of things which lie hidden within, to which man's cognition ought to penetrate from the inside, as it were. For under the accidents lies hidden the substantial nature of the thing; under words lie hidden the things signified by the words (*sub verbis latent significata verborum*); under similitudes and figures lies hidden the truth figured (*veritas figurata*) (for intelligible things are in a way interior as compared to sensible things which are externally perceived), and in causes lie hidden effects, and conversely. But since man's cognition begins with sense (*a sensu incipiat*) as from without, it is manifest that the stronger the light of the intellect is, the farther it can penetrate into the inmost depths (*ad intima penetrare*). However, the natural light of our intellect is of finite strength and hence can but reach to what is limited. Therefore man needs supernatural light, that he may penetrate farther in order to learn what he cannot learn through his natural light, and that supernatural light given to man is called the gift of understanding (*donum intellectus*).[10]

---

7 See especially *Perihermenias*, bk. 1.1–7.

8 Cf. Hans Meyer, *The Philosophy of St. Thomas Aquinas*, 190f.

9 *Summa Theol.* 1.2, q. 108, 1, ad 3: 'Intellectus dicitur, quasi intus legens; intellectus enim nomen sumitur ab intima penetratione veritatis.' Cf. 2.2, q. 8, a. 1 and q. 49, a. 5, ad 3; *De Veritate*, q. 1, a. 12: 'Nomen intellectus sumitur ex hoc quod intima rei cognoscit; est enim intelligere quasi intus legere: aenaua enim et imaginatio sola exteriora accidentia cognoscunt; solus autem intellectus ad essentiam rei pertingit.'

10 *Summa Theol.* 2.2, q. 8, a, 1.

By the supernatural light here Thomas was not referring to some special grace but to the gift of simple intuitive apprehension which Aristotle had spoken of as the divine in us and which Augustine had taken over from his Platonic sources.[11] Although he was critical of Augustine's Platonism, nevertheless Thomas held that the power of the intellect in penetrating into the essence of a thing, into its ultimate structure or spiritual content, would not be possible were it not that man has been given to share in the divine light.[12] Now in this passage we have cited Aquinas was not discussing hermeneutics but, as he indicated, the same procedure applies to interpretation of words, for we have to discern not only their sense (*sensus*) but break through to their real meaning (*intellectus*). To understand (*intelligere*) is to read the hidden meaning (*intus legere*). This does not refer to some esoteric art, but to the same sort of activity we adopt when we seek to know the quiddity of anything. Moreover, Thomas held that this intuitive apprehension of essences is limited for even though we have the illumination of divine light within us, our powers are hindered by the body.[13] Hence the application of the act of *intelligere* to the interpretation of Scripture had a sobering effect upon exegesis. At the same time the success of intuitive penetration varied in different fields according to the nature of what is to be apprehended, being greater, for example, in respect of mathematical essences. How then are we to think of it when it is applied to the interpretation of the inspired Scriptures where we are concerned with a special instrument of divine revelation, and which we can approach scientifically only if we interpret them in a mode appropriate to their nature?

Holy Scripture has two authors: the principal author is God, the Holy Spirit, but man is the instrumental author.[14] Therefore in interpreting Scripture the intellect must penetrate through the sense of the words to the meaning of the human author and to the meaning of the divine author. This does not mean that the Scripture is equivocal for God reveals himself through the literal sense intended by the human author, but it does mean

---

11 Cf. *De Veritate*, viii.15; 15.1.

12 *De Trinitate*, 2.1; 10.6; cf. Hans Meyer, *The Philosophy of St. Thomas Aquinas*, pp. 331f.

13 *De Trinitate*, q. 1, a. 7; cf. Wisdom, ix.15. No philosopher, Thomas remarks, had yet penetrated to the essence of a fly, *Devotissima exposition super symbolum apostolorum*, a. 2.

14 *Quaestiones Quodlibetales*, q. 6, a. 3; *Summa Theol.* 1, q. 1, a. 10; *Contra Gentiles*, iv; *Comm. Ad Hebraeos* 3.7, lectio 2.

that we have to penetrate to the divine intention through the literal sense and the intention lying behind it.

On the one hand, then, we have to interpret the Scriptures as divinely inspired. In them 'the Word of the eternal Father, comprehending everything by his own immensity, has willed to become little through the assumption of our littleness, yet without resigning his majesty, in order that he may recall man who had been laid low through sin, to the height of his divine glory'.[15] It is therefore in the humanity of Christ, the incarnate Word, that we are given a way to go to the Deity.[16] 'When the Word was in the Father's bosom, he was known only by the Father, but when he became a spoken and embodied Word of mouth then he was made manifest to us: "He was seen on earth and conversed with men" (Baruch 3:38). A word is heard by ear, but it is not read until set down in letters. The Word of God could both be seen and felt, being written in our flesh.'[17]

Now because it is our nature to learn intelligible truths through sensible objects, God has provided Revelation of himself according to the capacity of our nature and has put forward in the Sacred Scriptures divine and spiritual truths through comparisons with material things. That is why Christ spoke in parables. We cannot see God in his divine radiance except as his light is hidden under many veils, as Dionysius has said,[18] and therefore his Revelation comes to us under images and metaphors. It is not extinguished by the sensible imagery that veils it, for its truth remains and far from allowing our minds to rest in the similitudes it raises them up to the knowledge of intelligible realities. On the other hand, because God's Revelation makes use of figures of crude rather than noble things, it prevents us from error through confounding the sensible figures with the divine realities.[19]

Thus it is apparent that

> the divinely inspired Scripture does not come within the philosophical disciplines that have been discovered according to human reason. Accordingly, there is needed another science divinely inspired beyond philosophical disciplines . . . because

---

15 *Compendium Theologiae*, 1.1; cf. Romans 9:28: 'Verbum abbreviatum faciet Deus super terram: et hoc est verbum fidei, quod praedicamus.'

16 *Compendium Theologiae*, 1.2.

17 *Expositio in Symb. Apost.* Trans. T. Gilby, St Thomas Aquinas, *Theological Texts*, 276.

18 Pseudo-Dionysius, *De Coel. Hier.* 2, a work that had a great influence on St Thomas. Cf. *De Trinitate*, q. 6, a. 3.

19 *Summa Theol.* 1, q. 1, a. 9, ad 2 et ad 3; *De Trinitate*, q. 1, a. 2 et a. 3.

man is ordained to God, to an end that surpasses the grasp of his reason. But that end must first be known by men who are to direct their thoughts and actions toward it. The final object of life is God, who exceeds the grasp of reason: "the eye hath not seen, O God, besides thee, what thou hast prepared for those that wait upon thee." The salvation of man requires the divine revelation of truths surpassing reason.[20]

Accordingly, the science of interpreting these Scriptures needs supernatural grace and special illumination that the intellect may penetrate into the inner depth of the divine revelation, into the very heart of the truth.[21] It will not leave the literal sense behind nor depreciate it for it is only in and through it that the illuminated intellect can reach the spiritual content and reality that lie behind. Nevertheless, it is because the divine Truth comes to us through the literal sense that there is always a depth of significance that reaches out beyond what any interpreter can discover or expound. That is the fecundity of the Scripture which it has through the Holy Spirit,[22] the fact that in it the intellect apprehends an objective reality with an infinite richness of implication reaching out finally to the perfect vision of God in heaven.

Before we pursue this farther, we must look at the other side of the question, that is, at the Scriptures considered from the point of their human authorship. The fact that Aquinas distinguished the human author from the divine, as the instrumental author, means that he thinks of the human authorship of Scripture in terms of second causes. Thus, while God is the principal author or cause, the human author is given relatively free place under him as secondary cause so that what he produces must be investigated in its relative independence as a human composition. Now when the act of *intelligere* is directed to the human words of Scripture it penetrates beneath them to read them from their inner aspect (*interius legere*) and so through the *sensus* it reaches what the author intended the words to signify, the *intellectus litteralis*. In determining this we have to consider the end to which they conduce and therefore the reason for them. Therefore interpretation is concerned not only with the literal sense of the words but with the literal causes and reasons that lie behind them (*causae litterales, rationes litterales*).[23] If language and thought, words and reasons,

---

20 *Summa Theol.* 1, q. 1, a. 1.
21 Q. *Quodlibet.* 6, a. 1; *Summa Theol.* 1, q. 1, a. 10, ad 1; 2.2, q. 173, a. 2.
22 *Scriptum super Libros Sententiarum*, ii, d. 12, q. 1, a. 2, ad 7.
23 *Summa Theol.* 1.2, q. 102, a. 2.

belong so closely together, then a faithful interpretation of the text will be inseparable from an interpretation of the thought.

In the Scriptures, then, we are concerned with rational communication, so that the rational disciplines have to be used in their interpretation. It is not difficult to see here the influence upon St Thomas of Aristotle's περὶ ἑρμηνείας upon which he himself wrote a commentary.[24] In that work Aquinas remarks that if men only made natural sounds without any intention or mental image lying behind them they could no more be interpreted than the noises of animals.[25] Moreover, if man were only a naturally solitary being, animal passions would be sufficient for him to be conformed to things and have some knowledge of them, but because man is naturally a political and social animal it is necessary that the conceptions of one man should be made known to others, and that requires speech and the significant use of words if men are to have reciprocal relations with one another.[26] Thus articulated communication in which word and thought are bound up together belongs to the very nature of man as a rational being,[27] while the interpretation of this communication involves judgments as to truth and falsity just because it is concerned with whether what is said conforms to the facts or not.[28]

To return to the point then, if it is this rational communication in and through words that we have to interpret in the Scriptures then the exegetical and argumentative modes of interpretation are not to be divorced from one another. That was a point that St Thomas laid down at the beginning of his first great systematic work, his *Commentary on the Sentences of Peter Lombard*: procedure in Sacred Scripture requires an argumentative mode, in the appeal to reasons and natural comparisons, as well as to authorities, in order to avoid error and elucidate questions of truth.[29] In other words, unless we probe right into the sequence of thought a passage involves, we are unable to deal adequately and lucidly with the text. Exegesis requires problematic thinking.

It is to be noted here that when we penetrate into the literal reasons that lie behind the literal sense of Scripture we are interpreting what is intended by the divine author as well as the human author. For example,

24 Apparently only book 1 and the first two *lectiones* of book 2 are genuine.
25 *Perihermenias*, 1.1.
26 *Perihermenias*. 1.2; 1.4.
27 Cf. also *De differentia divini verbi et humani, Opusculum*, xiii.
28 *Perihermenias*, 1.1; 1.3.
29 *Scriptum super lib. Sent. Prol.* a. 5; *De Trinitate*, q. 2, a. 1.

when we consider the reasons for the ceremonial precepts in the Old Testament, we discover that there was a twofold end which must guide our interpretation: they were ordained for divine worship to commemorate certain divine benefits, but they were also ordained to foreshadow Christ. They may therefore be taken in two ways but never in such a way that they go beyond the order of literal causes (*non transcendent ordinem litteralium causarum*).[30] Thus even though we give some of these ceremonies a Christological interpretation, we can only do that if it is congruent with the literal signification and rooted in it. We shall probe into this further when we come to discuss how St Thomas handled the fourfold sense of Scripture, but before we do that we must examine his basic doctrine of the *Word*.

Like Augustine,[31] whom he follows rather closely, St Thomas distinguishes between the internal or mental word, and the external or vocal word.[32] The mental word, or what is signified inwardly in the soul, precedes the word externally pronounced by the voice as its final and efficient cause; but if we wish to find out what the interior word in the soul is, we must learn what the word externally pronounced signifies.[33] Therefore in interpretation we must be concerned with both, and must understand how one is related to the other.

Whenever anyone engages in an act of understanding (*intelligit*) from the very fact of understanding there proceeds something within him which is a conception of the thing understood, issuing from his intellective force and proceeding from his knowledge of the thing. This conception is signified by the voice and is called the word of the heart, the thing signified by the word of the voice.[34]

This statement calls for some elucidation and comment.

(a) St Thomas distinguishes between intuitive and discursive knowledge.[35] Intuitive knowledge derives from the act of the intellect or understanding

---

30 *Summa Theol.* 1.2, q. 102, a. 2, ad 1.

31 Augustine, *De Trinitate*, bks. ix, xiv, and xv. St Thomas transposes the Augustinian notion of the *verbum mentis* into an Aristotelian framework, for he disagrees with Augustine's teaching that the soul knows itself directly by looking within.

32 For the following see especially *De differentia divini verbi et humami, Opusc.* xiii; *De natura verbi intellectus, Opusc.* xiv; and *De Veritate*, q. 4.

33 *De Veritate*, q. 4, a. 1.

34 *Summa Theol.* 1, q. 27, a. 1; cf. q. 28, a. 4, ad 1, and q. 34, a. 1.

35 *De Trinitate*, q. 6, a. 1, 3; *Summa Theol.* 1, q. 79, a. 8; q. 83, a. 4, ad 2; 2.2, q. 49, a. 5, ad 3.

in which we see into the essence and nature of things, reading directly the inner structure and order. Discursive knowledge derives from the act of reasoning in which we make judgments and reach conclusions. The internal or mental word with which we are concerned here is related to intuitive knowledge; it is the *verbum intellectus* that arises out of our vision of the essence of a thing, the *quod quid est*.

But St Thomas, following the Aristotelian tradition, refuses to accept a dichotomy between intellectual knowledge and sense experience, between *intellectus* and *sensus*, for in man who is a unity of soul and body, the intellect and corporeal existence are bound together, and all his knowledge is determined by that relationship and can never transcend or leave it behind.[36] It is not the nature of man's mind to derive knowledge from hidden principles but only through the senses of the body, while the proper objects of his mind exist only in individuals and therefore can only be known as they are embodied.[37] Although all our knowledge begins with sense experience, through our intellectual faculty we rise above mere sense experience to the knowledge of intelligible realities, and yet the proper object of the human intellect is reached in the material world through penetrating to the essence or nature of things in matter.[38] Intellective knowledge is dependent upon the sensitive as the sensitive is upon the intellective.[39] In this mutual dependence the intellect is both passive and active. The sense itself is a passive potency which suffers a change in itself by the external object which it apprehends.[40] In the act of understanding, the intellect acts passively receiving from the sense what is perceived, the *species*, and in and through it apprehends the object directly, but in so doing it also acts actively giving the species an intelligible form—that activity is what St Thomas called the intellective force which lightens up the data of sense and makes them intelligible. In this activity the sense and intellect co-operate and out of that combined passion and action there is produced the conception of the thing apprehended. Now that process comes to its completion when the intellect not only forms the conception but perceives

---

36 *Summa Theol.* 1, q. 59, a. 1, ad 1; q. 79, a. 8, ad 3; 1. a, q. 5, a. I, ad 1; 1, q. 84, a. 7; *De Veritate*, 10.6.

37 *Summa Theol.* 1, q. 84, a. 4, et a. 7; *Compendium Theologiae*, 1.80 ff.

38 *Summa Theol.* 1, q. 57, a. 1: 'intellectus humani proprium objectum est quidditas rei materialis.' Cp. 1, q. 85, a. 5, ad 3.

39 *De Veritate*, 10.6.

40 *Summa Theol.* 1, q. 78, a. 3.

its relation to the external object apprehended and consciously refers it to that object—that is what Aquinas calls the formation of the *species expressiva* or *intentio* or the *verbum mentis*.⁴¹

(b) On that background we turn to what Aquinas says about the word in the important little essay *De differentia divini verbi et humani*. There are three things in the intellect, *potentia intellectus*, *species rei intellectae* which is its form and *intelligere*, the operation of the intellect.

None of these is signified by the external word uttered by the voice, for this name 'stone' does not signify the substance of the intellect, for he who names it does not mean that; nor does it signify the species by which the intellect understands, since this is not the intention of the speaker either; nor does it signify the *intelligere* itself, since *intelligere* is not an action that proceeds out of him who understands but remains in him. But word conceived inwardly is disposed (*habet se*) through an outward movement as is proved by the exterior vocal word, which is its sign, for it proceeds outwardly from the person who utters it vocally. Therefore that is properly called the interior word which he who understands forms in his act of understanding (*quod intelligens intelligendo format*). But the intellect forms two things according to its two operations, for according to its operation which is called the understanding of invisible things, it forms definition, but according to the operation by which it compounds and divides, it forms enunciation, or some such thing. And so what is thus formed and expressed by the operation of the intellect, in defining or enunciating, signifies something by the external word. Hence the Philosopher says in the fourth book of his *Metaphysics*, 'the reason of the thing (*ratio*) which the name signifies is the definition of the thing'.⁴² Therefore what is thus formed and expressed in the soul is said to be the interior word and is therefore related to the intellect not as that by which (*non sicut quo*) the intellect understands but as that in which (*sicut in quo*) it understands because in it, so expressed and formed, it sees the nature of the thing understood.⁴³ From this we can

---

41   *Compendium Theologiae*, 1.80 f.

42   Aristotle, *Metaphysics*, iv.7.391; Aquinas, *In XII Lib. Metaphysicorum*, iv.x.16.733; cp. *Summa Theol.* 1. q. 3, ad 8: '*Verbum proprie importat rationem formae exemplaris*'; and *De Veritate*, q. 4, a. 1.

43   *De Veritate*, q. 4, a. 2, ad 3: '*Conceptio intellectus est media inter intellectum et rem intellectam, quia ea mediante operatio intellectus pertingit ad rem. Et ideo conceptio intellectus non solum est id quod intellectum est, sed etiam id quo res intelligitur; ut sic id quod intelligitur, possit dici et res ipsa, et conceptio intellectus; et similiter id quod dicitur, potest dici et res quae dicitur per verbum, et verbum ipsum; ut etiam in verbo exteriori*

conclude two things about the word: that the word is always something that proceeds from the intellect and exists in the intellect, and that the word is the reason (*ratio*) and likeness of the thing understood.[44]

(c) This, in turn, calls for further comment. In accordance with St Thomas' realism, he saw the reason and meaning of things in things themselves, 'for it is the being of a thing rather than its truth that causes truth in the mind'.[45] It is not therefore a *species* or an idea that is the object of intuition but the thing that lies behind it and is represented by it, to which the intellect penetrates through the *species impressa* by which the objective nature of a thing is expressed.[46] 'In the mind we find forms of knowledge produced by the effect of things on the mind. All this activity takes place through the form, and therefore the forms in our mind are primarily and principally related to the forms of extramental things.'[47] That is why Aquinas insists that the interior word is not an intermediary idea but arises in the union between the intellective act and the object and is directly related to the object as its proper form. That relation to the word is a real relation (*realis relatio*).[48] That real relation is attested, according to Aquinas, by the way the interior word arises and is directed outward to the object and in accordance with that movement is given signification in an external word. Therefore if we are to understand the interior word, we must examine the significance of the external word, and through it penetrate to the inner word of the mind and follow through its inner relation with the thing that is known, for in that way we understand its *ratio*. That is what it means to read the *verbum intellectus* or the *verbum intimum* lying hidden behind the *sensus*, for it is that inner word upon which the act of *intelligere* terminates.[49] That is why interpretation must never leave the literal sense, although it does not terminate there; it comes to its completion only in the *verbum intellectus* in which the understanding is referred directly to the object itself.

---

patet; quia et ipsum nomen dicitur, et res significats per nomen dicitur ipso nomine.'

44 *Opusculum*, xiii.

45 *Summa Theol.* 1, q. 16, a. 1, ad 3; cp. *De Veritate* 1.1, ad 1; 1.4; 1.5; 1.9.

46 *Summa Theol.* 1, q. 78, a. 2: 'Species intellectiva secundario est id quod intelligitur sed id quod intelligitur primo est res cuius species est similitudo.'

47 *De Veritate*, 10.4, cited from H. Meyer, op. cit., 319.

48 *Summa Theol.* 1, q. 27, a. 4.

49 *De natura verbi intellectus*, Opusc. xiv; cp. *De Veritate*, q. 4, a. 1: 'unde verbum interius est ipsum interius intellectum.'

(d) Aquinas distinguishes the *verbum mentis* explicitly from reflection. This is particularly clear in the *De natura verbi intellectus*. In knowing, the subject unites himself to the object; what is in the soul is not the external object but an image or a likeness of it which is formed in the act of perception. But St Thomas repudiates the idea that this image is the proper object of our understanding, as if all that we looked at was a subjective mirror which reflected something else; we make use of the image, not as a sort of intermediary, but as something through which we enter into a real relation with the object and act upon it, not as a passing stimulus but as an enduring foundation.[50] Now the interior word is something we form within us in the act of understanding and it bears a likeness to the object, and it would appear, therefore, very like a reflexive act.[51] Actually, however, it is expressive of it, not reflexive, for what it is related to is the quiddity of the thing and not some subjective state; it is produced by the proper act (*per actum rectum*) of the intellect in union with the object and not by reflection (*per reflexionem*) on the part of the intellect, and its characteristic is to direct us straight to the thing itself.[52] This is immensely important, for it imports a sharp criticism of all subjective interpretations of the word, as if its meaning were found in some ideal realm, and not in the concrete reality to which it intends to point us.

It is interesting to note that at this point in his discussion Aquinas does not allude to Augustine's idea that the word is formed in the vision of thought (*in cogitationis vision formatum*). Augustine says:

> When we say that thoughts are locutions of the heart, we are not denying that they are also visions (*visiones*) arising when they are true from the visions of things known. In the external sphere of bodily activity, locution is one thing and vision is another; but in the inward realm of our thoughts, both are one and the same. Hearing and sight are two different functions of bodily sense, but in the mind there is no difference between seeing and hearing.

50 *De Trinitate*, q. 6, a. 2, ad 5.

51 Cp. *Contra Gentiles*, iv.11: '*Dico intentionem intellectam id quod intellectus in seipso concipit de re intellecta. Quae quidem in nobis neque est ipsa res quae intelligitur neque est ipsa substantia intellectus, sed est quaedam similitudo concepta intellectu de re intellecta, quam voces exteriores significant; unde et ipsa intentio verbum interius nominatur, quod est exteriori verbo significatum.*'

52 St Thomas constantly remarks that there is a twofold way of knowing a thing: through the *proper form* as when the eye sees a stone *through* its species or *through* some other form similar to it, i.e. reflex only, as a cause is known through the similitude of its effect, or a man is known through the form of his image. Cp. *De Trinitate* q. 1, a. 2, or *Summa Theol.* 1, q. 14, a. 5.

> That is why, although outward speech is not seen but heard, the holy Gospel can speak of the inward locutions which are thoughts as *seen* by our Lord and not heard.[53]

Again:

> all such knowledge in the mind of man, whether acquired through the mind itself, or through his bodily senses, or by the testimony of others, is preserved in the store-chamber of memory; and from it is begotten a true word, when we speak what we know. But this word exists before any sound, before any imaging of a sound. For in that state the word has the closest likeness to the thing known, of which it is offspring and image; from the vision which is knowledge there arises a vision which is thought, a word of no language, a true word born of a true thing, having nothing of its own but all from that knowledge from which it is born. It matters not what is learnt by the man who speaks what he knows: sometimes the speaking may immediately follow the hearing. It will still be true if it arises from things known.[54]

It will be apparent from these citations how much Aquinas owes to Augustine, but he hesitates to speak of the *verbum intimum*, in man at any rate, as a *visio*, although he is ready to admit that *visio* can be extended to every cognitive act of the senses or intellect[55] and does apply it to the word of God as we shall see. Of course, one reason for St Thomas' hesitation is his objection to Augustine's psychology of interior illumination, on the ground that sensitive and intellective knowledge are mutually dependent, at least for man on earth, and if hearing and seeing are distinct in the senses, then the *verbum mentis* that arises out of an auditive experience must be correspondingly distinguished. And yet St Thomas does not restrict the *verbum mentis* to knowledge arising out of hearing any more than the external or written word can be so restricted. Nevertheless, it would appear that St Thomas is seeking to make room for the word heard and will not allow it simply to be transmuted into vision. In this respect he is nearer to the biblical way of thinking than Augustine and nearer to the Reformers. At the same time the closer relation between the interior word and the word spoken or heard imports a more realist approach to biblical interpretation,

---

53 Augustine, *De Trinitate*, xv.10.18. Burnaby's translation, *Augustine: Later Works* (*Library of Christian Classics*, vol. viii).

54 *De Trinitate*, xv.12.22, trans. Burnaby.

55 *Summa Theol.* 1, q. 67, a. 1; 1.2, q. 77, a. 5, ad 3; 2.2, q. 167, a. 2, ad 1; cp. 3, q. 30, a. 3, ad 1.

and a great hesitancy to 'take off' into wordless mystical visions which were encouraged by Augustine's theory of illumination.[56] St Thomas has a strong sense of the fact that in our knowledge of God the intellect engages in an articulate activity that is direct and does not just arise out of the reflective activity of the reason, and that our knowledge of God is by God's creative will according to the condition or mode of the knowing subject as well as according to the nature of what is known.[57] Thus word, as well as vision, belongs to the essential form of human theological activity.

How then does Aquinas think of the relation between the word of man and the Word of God? To answer that we must pick up his argument from the long citation given above from the *De differentia divini verbi et humani*. He reached two conclusions: that the word comes out from the intellect and yet remains in the intellect, and that the word is the rational meaning (*ratio*) and likeness (*similitudo*) of what is understood. Then he goes on to say that when the thing understood is the same as the understanding subject, that is, when a person directs his intellectual act toward himself, the word is the rational meaning or likeness of the intellect from which it proceeds—otherwise, however, the word is not the rational meaning of the understanding subject, but of the object understood. That is a very important point to which we shall return later: the word is not expressive of the subject except where he seeks to understand and express himself.

Next, Aquinas recalls the fact that the human word is what we shape or form in the act of understanding; the word does not precede us who utter it. But when St John says, 'In the beginning was the Word', he is speaking of the divine Word that is not made; rather are all things made by that Word, the Word who precedes all making and is expressive of the Trinity. Then Aquinas goes on to note three fundamental differences between the human word and the divine Word.

'According to Augustine,[58] the first difference is that our word is formable before it is formed.' Aquinas explains that in this way: our human

---

56 Cp. *De Trinitate*, q. 6, a. 2; *Summa Theol.* 2.2, q. 173, a. 3.

57 *De Veritate*, q. 2.4; 2.6; q. 10.4; *Summa Theol.* 1, q. 12, a. 11, &c.; S. s. *Sent.* 1, d. 3, q. 1, ad 1, &c.; *De Trinitate* q. 2, a. 2.

58 *De Trinitate*, xv.16.25, 26. See also Aquinas, *Catena Aurea in Joann.* 1.1, where a citation is made from Augustine's *Serm. 38, De Verbo Domini*: 'Now the word of God is a Form, not a formation but the Form of all forms, a Form unchangeable, removed from accident, from failure, from time, from space, surpassing all things, and existing in all things as the kind of foundation underneath, and a summit above them.'

word is formed by a rational process in the mind that is only complete when we conceive the reason of a thing (*rationem rei*) for that is the meaning of the word (*ratio verbi*). The word is a product or an offspring of our thought.

In the *De Veritate*[59] Aquinas likens that to the production of a work of art in which three things are considered, the intended result, its pattern or shape, and the finished work itself. Similarly there is a threefold word: the voiceless conception or word of the heart, the pattern or exemplar of the external word (the interior word which is shaped for vocalisation), and the externally produced or vocal word. This means that our human word is bound up with our thought processes leading to the contemplation of the truth.[60]

Thus although the word is strictly the *verbum intellectus* expressing the object which we intuit, it is the product of ratiocination and as such is inseparably bound up with our human thinking or search after truth—it has its place only in the movement from confused knowledge toward perfect contemplation of the truth, from potentiality to action, and is fully formed in the completion of that movement. The human word is therefore a habit (*se habere, habitus*), the dynamic disposition in the movement between that which has and that which is had, between that which is disposed and that to which it is disposed.[61] 'And so our word is in potentiality before it is *in actu* but the divine Word is always *in actu*.'[62] God's Word does not need to be formed. His form is his own being and is not received from anything prior—it is not a habit but pure act. Thus God does not need to find out the truth or to engage in discursive reasoning as if he needed to advance from the known to the unknown, or from the partially known to the perfectly known. Hence, it is strictly improper, says Aquinas, citing Augustine again,[63] to talk of the thought of the Word of God. There is nothing of potentiality in God. He is *actus purus*. He understands not *successive* or *discursive* but *simpliciter* and *simul*. We must think of the *verbum Dei* accordingly.[64]

---

59 *De Veritate*, q. 4, a. 1; cp. S. s. Sent. 1, d. 27, q. 2, a. 1 and a. 2, ad 4.

60 Therefore, in St Thomas' terminology, it may be *incomplex* or *complex* according as it corresponds to the work of the intellect in intuitive or in analytic activity; cp. *De Veritate*, q. 4, a. 2; Q. Quodlibet. 5, q. 5, a. 2.

61 For St Thomas' notion of *habit* see the *Expos, in XII lib. Meta. Arist.* v.1.20.

62 *De differentia divini verbi et humani*. Cp. *Summa Theol*. 1, q. 14, a. 1–3.

63 Augustine, *De Trinitate*, xv.16.26: 'Therefore we speak of the Word of God and not of the Thought of God, lest we believe that in God there is something unstable, now assuming the form of Word, now putting off that form and remaining latent and as it were formless.'

64 *Summa Theol*. 1, q. 34, a. 1, ad 2 et 3; *Compendium Theol*. 1.28f.

Aquinas on Scientific Hermeneutics

An interesting point arises here in a criticism Aquinas has to offer (mistakenly, I believe) of Anselm's alleged confusion between *cogitare* and *intelligere* and between *dicere* and *intelligere*,[65] but the argument is better put in the *Summa Theologica*, where he agrees with Anselm, that 'we may explain to speak (*dicere*) in God as seeing by thought (*cogitando intueri*), inasmuch as the word of God is conceived by the intuition of the divine thought (*inquantum intuitu cogitationis divinae concipitur verbum Dei*). Still the term "thought" does not properly apply to the Word of God.'[66] Then he goes on to point out that we cannot equate *dicere* and *intelligere*, because while God's understanding and his being are identical,[67] speaking in God refers to the uttering of the word (*proferre verbum*) which is related to him as speaker *personaliter*. This appears to import that in our reception and understanding of God's Word we cannot simply transmute hearing into thinking, or the Word of God into thoughts and ideas. *Idea* relates to the *essence* of God but word to his *person* and therefore to convert the Word of God into ideas would be to ignore his person.[68] Does this mean that St Thomas is found resisting the complete primacy of vision in theology and wishes to make room for the distinctive place of the *Word* of God in our understanding as something that is already articulated as word by God's speaking of it? On the other hand, by approaching this whole question from the side of psychology,[69] from our understanding of the interior word of the soul behind the exterior word of the mouth in human experience, Aquinas must say that the word is not a habit in God but only pure act. God's form is his own being, and as such is neither received from anything prior nor communicated to anything posterior. Therefore his Word is not communicated in its own essential form to us, but only in forms alien to it and therefore indirectly in the form of what we mean by word or speech.

But there is another question which arises here. There is no multiplicity in God,[70] and therefore just as we cannot speak of *cogitationes* in him so we must be careful about speaking of *verba* in him. This carries us to the next

---

65 Anselm, *Monologion*, 60–63.

66 *Summa Theol.* 1, q. 34, a. 1, ad 2; cp. also *De Veritate*, q. 4, a. 2, ad 2, 4, 5; *S. s. Sent.* 1, d. 27, q. 2, a. 2, ad 3.

67 *Summa Theol.* 1, q. 14, a. 4 et 5; *Compendium Theol.* 1.29.

68 *De Veritate*, q. 4, a. 4, ad 4 et 5.

69 Cp. *Expositio in libros de Anima*. The third book of Aristotle's *De Anima* had an immense influence on Aquinas.

70 *S. s. Sent.* 1, d. 24, q. 2, a. 1; *Summa Theol.* 1, q. 14. a. 1 et 4.

point Aquinas makes in the argument of the *De differentia divini verbi et humani*.

The second difference between our word and God's is that ours is imperfect, but God's Word is most perfect, for we cannot express all the things that are in our soul by one word, and so there must be many imperfect words through which we express separately (*divisim*) all the things that are in our knowledge. But in God it is not so.[71] For since he understands and understands himself and whatever he understands, by his own essence, by one act, one unique Word of God is expressive of all that is in God, not only of the Father but of creatures as well; otherwise it would be imperfect.[72]

Thus it is by one Word that God not only reveals himself but relates all creatures to himself, and the content of that Word is the fullness of his divine knowledge. With us human beings our words convey less than we know and are defective instruments, but that is not the case with God's Word for the whole of his wisdom is contained in it. Hence there is an element of impropriety in speaking about the words of God, for that is a way of speaking assimilated to our human imperfection. Thus behind all the words of Holy Scripture, behind all the commands and utterances of God in them, there stands the reality of the *unum unicum verbum Dei*.[73] The many words of God are figuratively words because they signify this one Word.

'The third difference is that our word is not of the same nature with ourselves, but the divine word is of the same nature with God and subsists in the divine nature.' The words we speak have an accidental not an essential relation to us. They are not identical with our personal being, for our operations are not identical with our souls. But it is otherwise with God.[74] In him, to understand and to be are one and the same, and therefore the word uttered by God is not accidental to him. It belongs to his nature and subsists in his nature, but whatever is of the divine nature is God. Here Aquinas cites John of Damascus to the effect that the Word of God is substantial and has a hypostatic being, whereas all other words are but activities of souls.[75]

---

71 *Summa Theol.* 1, q. 34, a. 3.
72 Cp. *Summa Theol.* 1, q. 34, a. 3; and Anselm, *Monologion*, 32.
73 *Summa Theol*, 1, q. 34, a. 3.
74 Cp. again the parallel passage in the *Summa Theol.* 1, q. 34, a. 2, ad 1.
75 John of Damascus, *De fide orthodoxa*, i.1.18.

St Thomas concludes this discussion by saying that properly the Word of God must be spoken of *personaliter* in the divine, for he is not only expression and likeness of the Father from whom he proceeds but coeternal with him. Our words are always in continuous becoming (*in continuo fieri*),[76] but his Word is always in pure act (*in actu*). Our words are, as it were, artificial products; what we naturally produce is a son. But the Word of God is his Son for he proceeds from his nature and is in his likeness, coessential and consubstantial with him.[77]

In the light of the above discussion we have now to consider three things more specifically: the relation of the Word of God to the word of Holy Scripture, the interpretation of Scripture, and the use made of it in theology

1. The Relation of the Word of God to the Word of Holy Scripture

We have already seen that St Thomas could speak of the Word of God as making himself little in the incarnation for our sakes, that we may be lifted up to knowledge of God, and that therefore the way to God lies through the humanity of Christ.[78] How then does he relate that to the doctrine of the word in Holy Scripture? That is done indirectly through an analogy between the incarnate Word and our vocal word, but he draws his comparison from the side of what is human.

> To our twofold word, vocal and mental, there corresponds a twofold spirit or breath (*spiritus*). To the vocal word corresponds the breath of the body, and to the mental word the breath or spirit of inward love. Hence I say, the word according to his eternal generation is like the mental word, and so from the word there proceeds the Holy Spirit (or breath), just as love proceeds from the mental word. But the Son, according to his assumption of the flesh has a likeness to the vocal word; and as the formation of the vocable takes place through respiration, so the incarnation of the word has taken place through the operation of the Holy Spirit.[79]

---

76 *Compendium Theol.* 1.43; *De Veritate*, q. 1, a. 6.
77 *De natura verbi intellectus, Opusc.* xiv; *Compendium Theol.* 1.39, 41.
78 *Compendium Theol.* 1.1 et 2; *De Unione Verbi Incarnati*, 1.
79 *S. s. Sent.* 1, d. 11, q. 1, a. 1, ad 4.

In that passage Aquinas does not draw the analogy the other way round so as to give us an account of the vocal or written word in Scripture, but he comes nearer to doing that in another significant statement in the *quaestio de verbo* of the *De Veritate*.

> As we do not manifest ourselves to others except through a vocal word, but are manifest to ourselves through the word of the heart, which precedes the other, so the interior word is said to have priority. Similarly through the incarnate word the Father is manifested to all, but through the word begotten from eternity he makes it manifest to himself; and so the term 'word' in accordance with its incarnation is not appropriate to him. The incarnate word has some likeness with the vocal word and some unlikeness. This likeness is in each, by reason of which one is compared to the other, for as a voice manifests an interior word, so the eternal word is manifested through the flesh. But how great is the unlikeness: for the flesh assumed by the eternal word is not said to be word, but the voice assumed for the manifestation of the interior word is said to be word, and so the vocal word is different from the word of the heart. But the incarnate word is the same as the eternal word, just as the word signified by the voice is the same as the word of the heart.[80]

These are two very revealing passages, for while St Thomas compares the relation between the eternal Word and its incarnate manifestation to the relation between the interior and exterior word in human experience, he will not say that the incarnate form assumed by the Word is Word of God, for, he holds, it is only the outward instrument used by God to convey the interior or eternal Word in himself. The outward form of the Word in the incarnation, that is, the humanity of Christ, is not related to the essential and eternal nature of the Word.[81] Thus he does not say that what the Word is in the humanity of Christ he is antecedently and eternally in God, for the incarnate form does not apply eternally. Does this not mean that the incarnation of the *Word* is ultimately only an episode in the life and activity of God?

In answer to that question we may turn to a passage in the *Summa Theologica* where he discusses the relation of the eternal Word toward

---

80 *De Veritate*, q. 4, a, 1, ad 5 et 6.

81 St Thomas does hold, of course, that the divine and human natures in Christ are eternally and hypostatically united, in the way indicated by the Chalcedonian Council, but he does not seem to have thought out fully its implications either for the doctrine of the Word or the doctrine of the sacraments.

creatures, as expressive and operative of them. In that respect the term word in God imports relation to creatures but then St Thomas draws a distinction.

> Since the relations result from action, some terms import a relation of God to the creature, for they result from an action of God that passes over into an exterior effect, such as to create or to govern—such terms are applied to God in time (*dicuntur de Deo ex tempore*). But there is a certain relation which results from an action that does not pass over into an exterior effect, but remains in the agent, such as to know or to will—such terms are not applied to God in time (*non dicuntur de Deo ex tempore*). A relation of this kind toward the creature is imported in the term word.[82]

Behind this appears to lie the old idea of the utter impassibility of God and a hesitancy to think of the divine Being entering within and appropriating as his very own the creaturely relations which derive from him, which puts a question mark to the seriousness with which St Thomas understood the fact that 'the Word *became* flesh'. Apparently the human nature of Christ cannot properly be spoken of as Word, for it bears only an instrumental and episodic relation to the eternal Word.[83]

Be that as it may, Aquinas has another line of approach to the question of the relation of divine revelation to Holy Scripture, in which he makes use of the language of *light* and *vision*. Here it is the doctrine of Pseudo-Dionysius that influences him, that God reveals himself to us only in a veiled and indirect way through sensible images and parabolic forms, but Aquinas thinks it out within the framework of his Aristotelian theory of knowledge.[84]

> Concerning immaterial substances, we cannot in this life know their essences. And this is not only so as regards our natural way of cognition but we cannot even know them by way of revelation; for the illumination of the divine revelation comes to us according to our nature, enlightening our mind according to our nature. For although, by revelation we are lifted up to a knowledge of what would be otherwise hidden from us, this elevation is not of such

---

82 *Summa Theol.* 1, q. 34, a. 3, ad 2.
83 '*Non convenit aibi nomen verbi secundum hoc quod incarnatum est*', *De Veritate*, q. 4, a. 1, ad 5; cp. *S. s. Sent.* 1, d. 27, q. 2, a. 1, ad 2: '*Verbum divinum, inquantum divinum, habet quod sit permanens et subsistens*.'
84 *De Divinis Nominibus Expositio*, i.1.1 (15, 16); i.1.2 (44, 64), etc.

an order that we possess this knowledge otherwise than by means of sensible things.[85]

Because it belongs to our human nature to know in two complementary ways, through intellectual vision and through inferential reasoning from effects, it is in these two ways that we must consider the relation of the Word of God to the word of Holy Scripture.

Now the outward word of Scripture is a visible, material representation of an interior word formed in the intellect of the writer, impressed upon it by divine revelation. It is a conception formed in his mind through the action of the intelligible reality apprehended and the passion of his intellect in apprehending it.[86] The conception thus produced has a likeness both to the intelligible reality and to the intellect. Apparently, the verbal form of this conception derives from the human mind only, whereas the likeness of the conception to the reality apprehended is its truth, or adequation to what is *seen*. This is very clearly brought out by Aquinas in his interesting account of the nature and mode of prophecy which he thinks of essentially in terms of *intellectual vision*.[87] It takes place as a passion of the intellect under the action or illumination of the divine light.[88] The prophet does not, of course, see the divine Essence, but the vision is effected through intelligible images infused into his mind.[89] In his receiving of it there is both a representation of what is apprehended and a judgment on the things represented.[90] In this experience the prophet acts as God's instrument and what takes place in him is the effect of the divine light. Sometimes he is

---

85 *De Trinitate*, q. 6, a. 3, ad 1.

86 Cp. *Compendium Theol.* 1.38 et 39. Aquinas thinks of this on the analogy of natural conception through the action of the male and the passion of the female, so that the intelligible reality apprehended is as it were 'the father of the word' and the intellect its 'mother'. When this takes place in God, it is the eternal Word that is formed, God's Son, coeternal with him, but when it takes place in the human intellect it is a creaturely word or form that is conceived which is accidentally related to the intellect.

87 *Summa Theol.* 2.2, q. 171–3. The guiding text for Aquinas seems to be 1 Reg. ix.9 ('*Qui enim propheta dicitur hodie olim vocabatur videns*') which he interprets as referring to *visio intellectualis*.

88 *Summa Theol.* 2.2, q. 171, a, 2, ad 1; cp. also *Comm. in Hebraeos*, xi, leet. 7: '*Spiritus Sanctus movens mentem prophetae, sicut agens principale movet instrumentum suum . . . ad cognoscendum, sc. quandoque cum intellectueius quod videtur, sicut fuit Esaias et alii prophetae, unde dicti sunt et videntes. Qui hodie dicitur propheta, olim dicebatur videns*.'

89 *Summa Theol.* 2.2, q. 173, a. 3.

90 *Summa Theol.* 2.2, q. 173, a. 2.

moved not only to apprehend something but to speak or do something,[91] but his speech is not part of the prophecy as such so much as the means of its communication to others.[92] Thus when we read behind the exterior word of prophecy to what it signifies, we find that it signifies not a word but a *vision*. Moreover, Aquinas interprets the Old Testament expressions 'the Lord spoke', 'the word of the Lord came', to indicate merely the *transitory* way in which the prophecies were uttered. 'Word' does not belong to the essential nature of the prophecy; its nature is intellectual vision.[93]

Now the form that is conceived in the mind of the prophet signified by the exterior word is a word of the intellect formed within it in the act of intellectual vision. But this must be regarded as a creaturely form and interpreted as such.

> No similitude of whatever kind impressed by God upon the human intellect would suffice to make his Essence known, since he infinitely transcends every created form. Consequently God cannot be made accessible to the mind through created forms. Nor, in this present state can God become known to us even through the species of things that are purely intelligible, which have in a certain way a likeness to him, because our intellect is connaturally related to phantasms. Therefore it remains certain that it is only through the forms of his effects that he is known.[94]

That is the way in which Aquinas understands the word in Holy Scripture, as the creaturely effect or form of that which the prophet has seen in his vision, or, to put it the other way round, as the outward creaturely expression produced by God as 'the word of the Word'.[95] He draws a distinction between the Word of God in a proper sense and the word of God in a figurative or metaphorical sense. The term 'Word of God' signifies not only a relation to the Father but, as we have seen, a relation to the creatures he makes and knows, which may pass into some exterior effect applied to God in time.[96] Thus when it is said that the Son of God 'upholds all things by the word of

---

91 *Summa Theol.* 2.2, q. 173, a. 4; q. 176, a, 2.
92 *Summa Theol.* 2.2, q. 171, a. 1; q. 176, a. 2.
93 *Summa Theol.* 2.2, q. 171, a. 2.
94 *De Trinitate*, q. 1, a. 2.
95 *Contra Gentiles*, iv.13: '*non solum divini intellectus conceptio dicitur Verbum, quod est Filius, sed etiam explicatio divini conceptus per opera exteriora verbum Verbi nominator.*'
96 *Summa Theol.* 1.34, a. 3, ad 2.

Divine Interpretation

his power', the 'word' here has to be taken figuratively for the effect of the Word (*verbum figurate accipitur pro effectu verbi*)[97] or when creatures are said to do the word of God, what is meant is that they execute some effect to which they are ordained by the Word conceived in the divine wisdom.[98] 'The Word of God' applies properly only to God the Son, the eternal Word who proceeds personally from God, but does not apply to anything that proceeds extrinsically from God. Properly, therefore, the Word of God is what he conceives in himself and it is that Word that stands behind the figurative or metaphorical use of 'the word of God' in the Holy Scripture.[99] The word in Scripture is a creature of the Word and is not the proper Word of God, but only an instrument expressing it.[100]

Two other powerful ideas appear to be involved here: the Anselmic teaching that the Word of God is not in the likeness of the creature but the creature in the likeness of God's Word,[101] and the Boethian application of the *totum simul* to the life of God,[102] so that the Word of God is constructed as a *conceptio* characterised by 'all at onceness' and as *simplicissimum*. Thus whenever we ask Aquinas what is the word of God in Scripture, he points behind it to the divine *intellectus* and the *conceptio* he forms eternally in it. If we think of a word as having three phases, the word of the heart, its shaping into a pattern for enunciation, and its vocalization, then only the first of these is applicable to God's Word.[103] But we on our part have to use all three phases to speak of the Word of God, for we can conceive the Word of God only in an operation that terminates in a word of our intellect. We only hear the Word of God as it is formed in the likeness of our understanding as well as of itself. Thus on our side it is creaturely and finite, formed in accordance

---

97 *Summa Theol.* 1.34, a. 2, ad 5; a. 1, ad 4; *De Veritate*, q. 1, a. 1.

98 *Summa Theol.* 1.34, a. 1, ad 4.

99 *Summa Theol.* 1, q. 34, a. 1, ad 1: '*Verbum ut significat conceptum est in Deo proprie, secundum alias vero significationes eius est in Deo metaphorice tantum*.' Cp. q. 36, a. 2, ad 5.

100 Cp. *S. s. Sent.* I, d. 27, q. 2, a. 2, s. 2, ad 3: '*creatura non potest dici proprie verbum sed magis vox verbi, sicut vox manifestat verbum, ita et creatura manifestat divinam artem; ideo dicunt sancti, quod uno verbo Deus dixit omnem creaturam; unde creaturae sunt quasi voces exprimentes verbum divinum*.' See also *De Veritate*, q. 4, a. 2.

101 Cp. *De Veritate*, q. 4, a. 4, ad 2: '*Verbum divinum non est factum ad imitationem creaturae, ut verbum nostrum sed potius e converso; ideo Anselmus [Monologion, cap. XXXII] vult quod verbum non sit similitudo creaturae, sed e converso*.'

102 *Summa Theol.* 1, q. 14, a. 1, ad 2: 'God knows all things by one simple act of knowledge.' Cp. 1, q. 55. 3; *De Trinitate*, q. 6, a, 1, r. 3.

103 *De Veritate*, q. 4, a. 2; q. 4, a. 1, ad 12.

with our being, but on the other side it is divine and infinite, formed in accordance with the Being of God.[104]

In his *Commentary on the Epistle to the Hebrews*, Aquinas speaks of this question in a similar way. Whenever we human beings speak, three things are required, the *conceptio verbi* which is in our mind before it is in our mouth, a *verbi concepti expressio* through which what is conceived is made public, and *ipsius rei expressae manifestatio*, by which what is expressed becomes evident. Now God has spoken once, that is the *una conceptio ab aeterno* or the eternal generation of the Son. This is given a threefold expression: 1) in creation, which cannot be spoken of as speech (*locutio*) of God, 2) in the notions of thoughts made known to the minds of angels or men, which may be spoken of as an internal speech (*interna locutio*) which they have from God, their knowledge of the divine wisdom, and 3) in the incarnation when the Word of God was made man, in which God gave us an express manifestation of himself.[105] But when he comes to this point Aquinas does not go on to think out the relation of the speech of this incarnate Word in human form to the human form of the Scripture—rather does he fall back again upon the notion of Christ as the eternal conception of God, and insists that when Scripture speaks of the word of Christ this refers either to Christ himself (for there cannot be two words issuing from God) or it must betaken figuratively for the effect of God's Word.[106]

If, then, in the last analysis we have to think of the creaturely forms of the Scriptures as the effects produced in men through the operation of the Prime Mover, then they have to be interpreted (a) through penetration behind to the conception in the mind of God, that is, by intellectual vision, and (b) through inferential reasoning from the effects to their cause. Only metaphorically can we take the words of Scripture to be the Word of God. Now this has a decided advantage in directing attention to Christ himself as the one Word of God behind all the speech of Holy Scripture,[107] but the way in which Aquinas thinks of the relation of Scripture to that Word leads into a highly intellectualistic interpretation of it in which the meaning is inevitably schematised to the philosophical thought-forms brought to

---

104   *De Veritate*, q. 4, a. 1, ad 10: '*Dico quod verbum in divinis dicitur ad similitudinem nostri verbi, ratione impositionis nominis, non propter ordinem rei; unde non oportet quod metaphorice dicatur.*' For this idea of form see *De natura materiae et dimensionibus interminatis* 3, and also his *Expositio in librum de causis*.

105   *Comm. ad Hebraeos*, 1, *lect*. 1.

106   *Comm. ad Hebraeos*, 1, *lect*. 2.

107   *Comm. In Col*. 2, 3, *lect*. 1.

its understanding. What we find lacking in St Thomas' thought is: (1) an appreciation of the biblical teaching that the Word of God in the prophetic and apostolic witness is a living, active Word, that its coming is historical and concrete event, (2) an understanding of the Word of God in Scripture in relation to the whole Christ, including his human nature, as a real Word of God; but behind both of these, (3) it is his notion of God that is the real problem—his Aristotelian preconceptions prevented him from thinking through fully the implications of the incarnation for the Christian understanding of God.

2. The Interpretation of Scripture

When Aquinas handles the question of biblical interpretation he does not speak of *verbum hominis* and *verbum Dei* but rather of *sensus* and *intellectus* (or *verbum mentis*) and of *sensus litteralis et spiritualis*. Words are signs of intellectual meanings (*voces signa intellectuum*) and therefore we have to read the intelligible meaning lying within or behind the external word. Moreover, when we are concerned with Christian faith we have to do with something beyond the human sense (*ultra humanum sensum*).[108]

Now words are the principal signs men employ in order to signify something to others or to manifest to them their conceptions,[109] and as such they have a relation to the speaker who utters as well as to the things they signify.[110] But their primary relation is to the thing intended to what they are meant to express. They are not to be interpreted, therefore, primarily as expressions of other minds (unless, of course, they are words representing someone's understanding of himself), but are to be interpreted by looking in the direction they point, away from the speaker to what he intends to indicate. That is in line with the teaching of St Thomas that the soul does not know itself through its own essence, but only by means of its acts and through knowing external realities, for it is only then when its knowledge becomes actual that it bends back upon itself in self-knowledge.[111] It is

108 *Compendium Theol.* 1.36 f.

109 *Perihermenias,* 1.2; *Summa Theol.* 2.2, q. 55, a. 4, ad. 2; q. 72, a. 1; q. 99, a. 1; q. 110, a. 1, ad 2; 3. q. 60, a. 6, ad. 1 et 2.

110 *S. s. Sent.* 1, d. 27, q. 2, a. 2.

111 *De Veritate,* q. 10.9, 9; *Summa Theol.* 1, q. 87, a. 1–4. This is one of the important points where Aquinas came to disagree with Augustine who laid such stress upon direct inward self-knowledge. Cp. *De Trinitate,* 10.10; *De Civitate Dei,* 11.26; *Soliloquia,* 2.1, and above all the *Confessions,* passim.

otherwise with God who knows himself through his own Essence and therefore when we attend to the word which he conceives we are directed to God himself primarily, and so to the creatures he knows and creates. But when we attend to the words of men we direct our attention to them not as their self-expression, but as accidental and artificial signs that point to something other than them. The word is not the *ratio* of the intelligent subject, as we have already noted, but the *ratio* of the thing understood. It is, of course, bound up with the human processes of understanding so that the subjective element cannot be left out.[112] Therefore while it is important in interpretation to learn what the speaker or writer intends, and hence to understand him, we do not really do that unless we look with him at what his words are intended to indicate, or receive from him what he means his words to convey to us.

Now when we examine the sense of the Scriptures, according to St Thomas we have to reckon with a literal or historical sense, and a spiritual sense; the former is primary and essential, the latter is derived and based on the former.[113] But the literal sense includes the metaphorical or parabolic sense, and therefore may itself be twofold.[114] That is to say, while some words of Scripture are to be taken directly in a univocal sense, others cannot be so restricted.[115] By including the parabolic sense in the literal or historical sense Aquinas seems anxious to allow for a dimension of depth other than the transferred senses developed by tradition in allegorical interpretation. There is much more in one word of Scripture than many expositors discern or expound, he says, for it goes back to divine authorship—the Word of God contains no less than the knowledge of God himself—but even when we consider the human authorship there may be a twofold sense intended as when a prophet like Isaiah speaks of present affairs and yet intends at the same time that they should have a future reference,[116] or when Scripture has a proper sense and a metaphorical or figurative sense.[117]

---

112 Cp. *De Veritate*, q. 4, a. 2: '*Verbum intellectus in nobis duo habet de sua ratione; scilicet quod est intellectum, et quod est ab alio expressum.*'

113 *Summa Theol.* 1, q. 10; *Q. Quodlibet*. q. 6, ad 1, et ad 3.

114 Cp. R. Garrigou-Lagrange, *The One God, A Commentary on the First Part of St Thomas' Theological Summa*, pp. 88ff.

115 *Summa Theol.* 1. q. 1a, where Augustine, *Conf.* 12.18 et 19 is cited. Cp. also *S. s. Sent.* II, d. 12, q. 1, a. 2, ad 7; *De Potentia*, q. 4, a. 1.

116 *Q. Quodlibet*. 7, q. 6, a. 2, ad 5; *De Potentia*, q. 4, a, 1.

117 *Comm. in Gal.* iv, lectio 7 fin.

Recalling Augustine's fourfold distinction in determining the sense of the Old Testament, the historical, aetiological, analogical, and allegorical, Aquinas declares that all but the allegorical are to be included in the literal sense. History is the straightforward account, aetiology is the causative account, and analogy is the comparative account in which the truth of one passage is shown not to contradict the truth of another. To that Aquinas adds, as we have noted, the parabolical sense, in which something is figuratively but properly signified by the words, remarking that the literal sense is not the figure of speech itself but the reality it signifies.[118] In these several ways the literal sense is that which refers to things or objects directly or indirectly. In the first place that may be a reference to sensible or material objects, but in and through them it may be to divine and eternal realities—in that event, however, the reference is always grounded in the plain text. The rule to be followed is that all the senses are built upon the literal sense, and that argument and doctrine are to be taken from the literal sense alone, never from the allegorical or spiritual sense.[119] Aquinas is very emphatic about this. Thus in reference to the interpretation of the Old Testament he says that the literal truth must be observed,[120] and in reference to narrative passages, that historical truth must be kept as the foundation while spiritual expositions are to be built on top of it.[121] To wrest the Scripture to an alien end is a form of spiritual adultery,[122] and to prevent or hide its true meaning is a form of spiritual theft.[123]

By the spiritual sense Aquinas refers in traditional terms to the allegorical, tropological or moral, and the analogical senses.[124] All of these can be included under the heading of allegory.[125] But he insists that Scripture does not teach under the spiritual or mystical sense anything necessary for faith which it does not clearly teach under the literal sense.[126]

---

118 *Summa Theol.* 1, q. 1, a. 10, ad 2 et 3; 1.2, q. 102, a. 2, ad 1; *De Veritate*, q. 12, a. 10. 14; *Comm. in Gal.* iv, *lectio 7*.

119 *Summa Theol.* 1, q. 1, a. 10, ad 1; *De Potentia*, q. 4, a. 1; *Q. Quodlibet*, 7, q. 6, a. 3.

120 *Q. Quodlibet*. 3, q. 14, a. 1: '*observanda est veritas litteralis*'.

121 *Summa Theol.* 1, q. 102, a. 1; *De Potentia*, 6.7.

122 *Comm. in 2 Cor 2, lectio 3, fin.*, in *2 Cor 4, lectio.* 1.

123 *Comm. in Psalm 49, fin.* Cp. *De Potentia*, 4.1.

124 *Summa Theol.* 1, q. 1, a. 10; 1.2, q. 102, a. 2; *S. s. Sent.* I, prol. A. 4; IV, d. 21, q. 1, a. 2, q. 1. 3; q. 1, a. 3, q. 23. *Q. Quodlibet*. 7, q. 6, a. 1; *Comm. in Gal.* iv, *lectio 7*.

125 *Summa Theol.* 1, q. 1, a. 10, ad 2.

126 *Summa Theol.* 1, q. 1. 9, ad 2; q. 1, a. 10, ad 1; *Q. Quodlibet*. 7, q. 6, a. 1, ad 3.

Aquinas on Scientific Hermeneutics

In any case no conclusive arguments can be drawn from these senses, for symbolic theology of this kind has no weight of proof.[127]

Aquinas distinguishes between the literal sense and the spiritual sense by positing two kinds of signification.[128] On the one hand there is the signification whereby words signify things; that is the kind of signification involved in the literal sense, which is interpreted by looking at the facts the author intends to signify by his words.[129] This kind of signification we have in every other field of knowledge, but in Holy Scripture we have another kind of signification as well, whereby God not only accommodates words to mean certain things, but so arranges the things themselves as to make them in their turn figures of other things. The second signification does not allow us to go beyond the literal sense, but in looking at the things literally signified, we have to examine the order in which they are disposed by the divine author of Scripture, for he has truth to convey to us in that way.[130] What Aquinas has in mind here is the whole relation of the Old Testament to the New Testament, and the pattern of sign and fulfilment in the Covenant. And therefore the second signification, founded on the first, proceeding from it, and guided by the analogical relation of Old Testament passages to New Testament passages, directs us to Christ.[131] This is the spiritual sense which is certainly not to be found everywhere, but which may have a typological and a mystical reference. The Old is a figure of the New and the New of the Heavenly Realities. In seeing the relation between the Old and New Testaments we discern how God has adapted events in the Old to be types of fulfilment in the New, and in interpreting this we discern spiritual truth in the mystical relations between Christ and his Church, the head and the members, the union between God and the soul in the life of the Church and the celestial or future union between God and the Church triumphant—in all these three ways, the allegorical, the tropological and

---

127 S. s. Sent. I. prol. 5; De Trinitate, a. 3. ad 5; Q. Quodlibet. 7, q. 6, a. 1, ad 4.

128 Summa Theol. 1, q. 1, a. 10; Q. Quodlibet. 7, q. 6, a. 1.

129 Summa Theol. 1, q. 1, a. 10.

130 Q. Quodlibet. 7, q. 6, a. 1: 'Manifestatio vel expressio alicuius veritatis potest fieri de aliquo rebus et verbis; inquantum scilicet verba significant res, et una res potest esse figura alterius. Auctor autem rerum non solum potest verba accommodare ad aliquid significandum, sed etiam res potest disponere in figuram alterius. Et secundum hoc in sacra Scriptura manifestatur veritas dupliciter. Uno modo secundum quod res significantur per verba: et in hoc consistit sensus litteralis. Alio modo secundum quod res sunt figurae aliarum rerum: et in hoc consistit sensus spiritualis.'

131 Q. Quodlibet. 7, q. 6, a. 2: Summa Theol. 1, q. 1, a. 10.

the analogical, we see how God makes visible things to reveal invisible things.[132] The whole purpose of the spiritual sense is twofold, to give moral teaching to guide our conduct and spiritual teaching to aid our faith.[133]

The primary necessity, therefore, is to study the text. We have to see the parts in relation to the whole and the whole in relation to the parts that make it up. That applies to the words in relation to their sequence and to the composition of the sentences in their relation to the whole. Significance lies in the form which the whole and the parts have together. No part separated from the rest has the form of the whole any more than a hand separated from a person has human form.[134]

But we must also examine the actual words in order to see how they are used so that we may take everything that the words signify in their proper way. That includes the application to persons of imaginary forms drawn from nature, e.g. when Christ is spoken of as the stone cut out of the mountain without hands. If we take that properly it does not refer to historical facts but it does belong to the literal or historical sense of the text and we must take it as such and not confuse it with a spiritual sense that there may be discerned in addition to the literal. Passages in the Bible have to be interpreted in their setting in the relation between the Old and New Testaments, so that the later derive significance from the earlier. Thus something which in an earlier passage can be expounded spiritually may be spoken of literally in a later passage, but the reverse does not apply, and so what is said literally of the relation of Christ and his Church, for example, cannot be given an allegorical interpretation, although some of it may have an eschatological reference.[135] Thus a spiritual interpretation depends upon the actual course of events in the providential direction of God, and it can only be derived from it by superimposition upon the literal sense.[136]

The Use of Scripture in Theology

From start to finish St Thomas is a rational, scientific thinker. It is not surprising therefore that he should act in the same way with regard to

---

132   Q. *Quodlibet.* 7, q. 6, a. 2, ad 1.5; cp. Pseudo-Dionysius, *De Coel. Hier*, 2 et 4–5. See also *S. s. Sent.* I. *prol.* 5.

133   Q. *Quodlibet.* 7, q. 6, a. 2 et ad 2 et 3.

134   *Perihermenias*, i.4, 6.

135   Q. *Quodlibet.* 7, q. 6, a. 2, ad 1 et d. 5; *S. s. Sent.* III, d. 24, q. 3. 51, ad 3.

136   Q. *Quodlibet.* 7, q. 6, a. 3.

Sacred Scripture. Now a science, according to St Thomas, is the way of knowledge in which from things already known we derive a knowledge of things previously unknown. This involves a reasoning process from first principles to conclusions (*discurrere de principiis ad conclusiones*) through which knowledge is sifted out and arranged in an order which the intellect seeks to see as a whole. No science can prove its first principles, for it is in the light of them that it knows what is less knowable, but in ordering its matter in the light of the first principles it does succeed in connecting the contents rationally together and so directs attention back again to the first principles. They on their part can now be discerned more clearly and the intellect is the more convinced of their truth because through the light they cast other things become knowable and evident.[137]

Now when we apply this scientific method to theology, Aquinas claims, Sacred Scripture occupies the place of first principles, and it is in the light of the truths they reveal that the whole ratiocinative process of theological activity is undertaken, in order that these same truths may be more perfectly apprehended by the intellect.[138] We must not presume to demonstration, but this does not mean that the truths of faith are closed to scientific investigation and argument; rather must we seek to show their comprehensibility by using scientific concepts drawn from other areas where our knowledge is derived from naturally known principles.[139] In this way theology employs a parabolic mode of argumentation which is in accordance with its material content, beginning with God and going from God to his creatures.[140]

But Aquinas also reminds us that there are two kinds of science. Some sciences are grounded on their first principles that are *per se nota* or immediately evident to the natural intelligence, such as arithmetic and geometry, but there are others that operate under the light of God's own knowledge, that is, in the light of truths that are *per se nota* in the knowledge which God has of himself, and which he manifests to us through the words of Scripture acting as his messengers.[141] This means that while on the one

---

137 *Summa Theol.* 1, q. 7, a. 8; 1.2, q. 54, a. 2; 1.2, q. 57, a. 2; 1, q. 79, a. 3 et 4; 7, q. 85, a. 1; 2.2, q. 1, a. 5; *De Trinitate*, q. 1, a. 3; q. 2, a. 1-a. 3; *De Veritate*, q. 1, a. 9; q. 10, a. 5, q. 11, a. 1.

138 *Summa Theol.* 1, q. 1, a. 2; a. 3; a. 5, ad 2; a. 7; a. 8, ad 2; q. 79, a. 8; 2.2, q. 2, ad 7, etc.

139 *De Trinitate*, q. 2, a. 1 et a. 2; *Contra Gentiles*, 1.8.9; *Summa Theol.* 1, q. 1, a. 8.

140 *S. s. Sent. prol.* 5; *Contra Gentiles*, ii.4; iv.1.

141 *De Trinitate*, q. 2, a. 2; *Summa Theol.* 1, q. 1, a. 2; *S. s. Sent. prol.* q. 1, a. 3.

hand we have to defend the truths of the Scriptures as the first principle of sacred science, within the Scriptures we have to operate with the basic principles of faith and seek to interpret the whole in the light of them. The principles of faith with which we operate here are what we understand of the divine revelation, but actually it is the divine intellect itself that is really the first principle.[142] Thus we begin by assenting to the truths of a superior science (*the scientia Dei*) but faith goes on through discursive examination of what it has believed to reach understanding for itself. Every science begins like that, relying on the authority of its first principles, before clarifying its understanding of their truth, but in theological science we begin with the highest authority of all, that of God himself, and yet even here we do not proceed without discursive reasoning in going from principles to conclusions before returning to the principles again.[143]

There are three main things here that concern us.

(a) St Thomas unequivocally bases the doctrines of theology upon Sacred Scripture. Theological science receives its *principia* immediately from God through the divine revelation given to the prophets and apostles. The authoritative pronouncements of the canonical books have supreme place—sacred doctrine can only make use of other authorities or teachers as extrinsic and probable arguments.[144] And so again and again in St Thomas' systematic works *sacra scriptura* and *sacra doctrina* are taken as equivalents.

(b) This appeal to Scripture as the source of theology means in effect appeal to 'principles of faith' or 'articles of faith' or 'the truth of faith' found in the Holy Scriptures, for it is in the light of them that the Scriptures are scientifically interpreted.

> Now the *veritas fidei* is contained in the sacred scriptures in a scattered form and in various modes, in some of them obscurely. Therefore in order to elicit the truth of faith from sacred scripture long study and practice are required, which is not within the reach of all who must know the truth of faith, many of whom have no time for study, being occupied with other affairs. And so it was necessary for some clear summary to be gathered from the utterances of the sacred scripture which might be set before all for

---

142 *De Trinitate*, q. 2, a. 2, ad 7; *Summa Theol.* 1, q. 1, a. 7.
143 *De Trinitate*, q. 6, a. 1, r. 1; *Summa Theol.* 1, q. 1, a. 8
144 *Summa Theol.* 1, q. 1, a. 5, ad 2; a. 8, ad 2; 2.2, q. 1, a. 5, ad 2; *Contra Gentiles*, 1.9; 4.1.

belief. This was not an addition to the sacred scripture but rather something derived from it.[145]

The earliest and most authoritative summary was the Apostles' Creed. It is then in the light of the articles of faith which the Church derives from Scripture that the various writings of Scripture are interpreted but what we are concerned with behind all this interpretation and in all the articles of faith is the *prima veritas* of God. Faith adheres to all the articles of faith through the medium of its relation to the *prima veritas* as rightly understood in accordance with the teaching of the Church.[146] Now it is undoubtedly admitted that the articles of faith and the understanding of them by the Church are derived from and are subordinate to the Scripture, but practically St Thomas' method meant, not only assent to the authoritative interpretation of the Church to begin with, but the guidance of all understanding of the Scriptures by the Church.

In this method St Thomas was consciously applying a scientific principle to hermeneutics, i.e. to the understanding (*intelligere*) of the Scripture by reading within (*intus legere*) it the *veritas* lying behind its many outward expressions. This scientific principle he describes thus:

> The discourse of reason always begins from an understanding and terminates at an understanding (*discursus rationis semper incipit ab intellectu, et terminatur ad intellectum*); for we reason by proceeding discursively from certain understood things and then the discourse of reason is completed when we reach the point where we may understand what was previously not known. Therefore when we engage in reasoning, we proceed from something previously understood.[147]

Applied to interpretation that results in the so-called hermeneutical circle, but in Aquinas's application of it there are two deficiencies.

(i) He does not recognise sufficiently that the completion of the circle involves a critical reassessment of the prior understanding with which interpretation began, that is, not a criticism of what Aquinas calls the formal object of faith, the *prima veritas*, but of the material object of faith or the medium through which faith assents to certain beliefs in the *prima*

---

145 *Summa Theol.* 2.2, q. 1, a. 9, a. 1.

146 *Summa Theol.* 2.2, q. 5, a. 3, ad 2; cp. q. 1, a. 8 et a. 9. Cp. further passages adduced by Wicksteed, *The Reactions between Dogma and Philosophy Illustrated from the Works of St. Thomas Aquinas*, 197ff.

147 *Summa Theol.* 2.2, q. 8, a. 1, ad 2.

DIVINE INTERPRETATION

veritas,[148] namely, the understanding and teaching of the Church. Aquinas lays it down that in science we do not form propositions except in order to have knowledge about things through their means, and so it is in faith, for the act of the believer does not terminate in a proposition but in a thing.[149] But in refusing to allow the propositions of the Church to come under the criticism of the thing, the *prima veritas*, he has virtually identified them, and practically made the authority of the Church dominant over the *veritas*.

(ii) St Thomas recognised that if the Church is to occupy an authoritative place in interpretation of the Sacred Scripture, that authority must be derived from the Scripture itself, and he sought to prove that out of the Scripture, even to the extent of adducing scriptural evidence for an unwritten tradition in the Church deriving from the Apostles.[150] But even if we suppose that this could be proved, it does not follow that the Church is the inerrant interpreter of the Scripture, or that her opinions are to be treated like first principles, that is, truths through which we know but which do not themselves fall within the region of confused knowledge needing analytical and critical clarification. Thus not only is St Thomas' method lacking in scientific rigour in its application to hermeneutics, but his argument seems to be deficient in logic at a very crucial point.

(c) The application of the scientific method to the interpretation of Sacred Scripture meant not only the investigation of it in an argumentative form but also 'the use of Philosophy in Sacred Scripture', as he himself expressed it. This derived from St Thomas' conviction that in divine things we speak according to our own mode which our minds develop in their scientific investigation of inferior things.[151] In other words, this involved the application of thought-forms, developed outside the biblical revelation both to the interpretation of the Scriptures and the ordering and assimilating of its results. The ground for this lies in the constitution of human nature as occupying a place between the world of sensible and the world of intelligible realities. But St Thomas sensed acutely the problems and dangers this involved.

Thus he claimed that

---

148 *Summa Theol.* 2.2, q. 1, a. 1; q. 2, a. 3; q. 5, a. 4.

149 *Summa Theol.* 2.2, q. 1, a. 2, ad 2.

150 *Summa Theol.* 2.2, q. 1, a. 9 et 10; q. 2, a. 7; q. 5, a. 3. Cp. Wicksteed, *Reactions between Dogma and Philosophy*, 169f., 204f.

151 *De Potentia*, q. 2, a. 1.

in the use of philosophy in sacred scripture, there can be twofold error: in one way, by using doctrines contrary to the faith, which are not truths of philosophy, but rather error, or in abusing philosophy, as Origen did. In another way, by using them in such a manner as to include under the measure of philosophy truths of faith, as if one should be willing to believe nothing except what could be held by philosophic reasoning; when on the contrary, philosophy should be subject to the measure of faith, according to the saying of the Apostle (2 Cor. 10:5), 'Bringing into captivity every understanding unto the obedience of Christ.'[152]

On the other hand, St Thomas claimed that 'those who use philosophical doctrines in sacred scripture in such a way as to subject them to the service of faith, do not mix water into wine, but change water into wine.'[153]

There can be little doubt, however, that in spite of his sincere intention to give the Scriptures and sacred doctrine their supreme place, as Hans Meyer has said, 'in his *Theological Summa*, as well as in his other writings, philosophy is more conspicuous and receives more extended consideration than theology.'[154] St Thomas had a giant mind, to which there have been few equals, but his own immense intellectual powers laid him open to great temptations. His prior understanding of human experience, of the intellect and the soul, his masterful interpretation of Aristotelian physics, metaphysics and psychology, proved too strong and rigid a mould into which to pour the Christian faith. It is philosophy that tends to be the master, while theology tends to lose its unique nature as a science in its own right in spite of the claims advanced for it. Insofar as the contents of theology surpass the powers of scientific investigation they are to be accepted as revealed truth but in the end the authority of ecclesiastical tradition outweighs in practice the authority of Sacred Scripture so that interpretation of revealed truth is schematised to the mind of the Church. And yet in spite of the criticism that we may offer, we must acknowledge unhesitatingly the immense contribution of St Thomas, not least in the judicious and rational handling of his material, and his application of careful scientific method to biblical and theological interpretation.

---

152 *De Trinitate*, q. 2, a. 3.

153 *De Trinitate*, q. 2, a. 3, ad 5.

154 Hans Meyer, *The Philosophy of St. Thomas Aquinas*, pp. 45f. Meyer seeks, however, to defend St Thomas from the charge that he permitted his philosophy to absorb his theology.

CHAPTER 6

The Hermeneutics of John Reuchlin, 1455–1522[1]

John Reuchlin is generally acknowledged to be the father of Hebrew studies in the Western Church, for it was through his early work on Hebrew grammar and vocabulary, *De Rudimentis Hebraicis*,[2] that the learning of Hebrew really became possible for Christians, and through his zeal and persistence that interest in the Hebrew Scriptures increased rapidly in spite of opposition. Apart from his contributions to humanism, in Latin, Greek and Hebrew letters, Reuchlin's great importance for the history of Christian thought lies in the new understanding of the Word for which he had struggled so hard in attempting to set it free from the sophisticated and syllogistic thinking of the Schoolmen. What helped him perhaps most of all was what he called the *veritas hebraica*,[3] the new way of looking at things that he had acquired from his knowledge of Hebrew and of the Hebrew Scriptures. His characteristic humanist fascination for language led him to reflect upon the nature of Hebrew and its distinctive idioms and peculiarities, but this coincided with something he had learned from Plato's *Cratylus*[4]—the relation of language to the realities it is employed to denote. Hence he drew a close connection between true knowledge (*vera*

---

1 This essay originally appeared in James E. Bradley and Richard A. Muller (eds.), *Church, Word and Spirit: Historical and Theological Essays in Honor of Geoffrey W. Bromiley* (Grand Rapids: Eerdmans, 1987), 107–21. Reprinted with permission.

2 Reuchlin, *De Rudimentis Hebraicis* (1506) and *Primi Graecae et sacrae Hebraicae linguae* (1537). For a complete bibliography of Reuchlin's works see Josef Benzing, *Bibliotheca Bibliographica* 18 (Bad Bocklet, Bavaria: 1955).

3 Reuchlin, *De verbo mirifico* (1552) 2.11 (p. 144) and *De accentibus et orthographia linguae Hebraicae*, fol. aii, etc.

4 *De verbo mirifico* 2.7 (p. 129); 2.8 (pp. 136f.); 2.9 (p. 196); 3.5 (p. 249); 3.12 (p. 283).

apprehensio rei) with the study of language (*ponderanda verborum vis est*).[5] In this way he made a discovery which gave him the leitmotif for all his future work: the contrast between the scholastic understanding of *Word* as essentially an intellectual occurrence, and the biblical understanding of *Word* as a wonderful and creative happening. That is the subject of his early and (for our concern) most important work, *De verbo mirifico*, which was first published in 1494 at Basel. This discovery lent greater fascination to his study of Hebrew and Hebrew writings, all of which was directed to elucidate the *miraculum* of God's Word communicated through the Scriptures.

By orientation and temperament Reuchlin belonged to the Augustinian tradition in the Western Church, with a more mystical slant.[6] Moreover, as an interpreter of the Scriptures Origen held a special place in his affection. The Platonic influence mediated to him through these sources was reinforced by Pythagorean and Neoplatonist elements acquired through his contact with the Italian leaders of Renaissance thought, Marsilio Ficino and Pico della Mirandola. But through the latter Reuchlin's interest in the *Jewish Cabbala*, with its strange mystical and linguistic lore,[7] was also reinforced; and that, together with the *veritas hebraica* which he imbibed more and more from his study of the Hebrew Scriptures, modified considerably his Platonic tendencies. That is apparent, for example, in the way in which he holds the distinction between the *mundus intelligibilis* (or the *mundus superior sive archetypus*, as he often prefers to call it), and the *mundus sensibilis*,[8] and in his rejection of the Orphic notion of humanity's participation through likeness or proportion in divine being.[9]

For Reuchlin God is essentially the creator who made the world out of nothing and is infinitely transcendent over it. As the Light of all light he created also the invisible and intelligible world, for there is no understanding and no light apart from his. He is *supersupremus* over both the *mundus sensibilis* and the *mundus intelligibilis*.[10] It is his creative Word alone that

---

5 *De verbo mirifico* 1.8 (pp. 54, 60); *Der Augenspiegel* 13, 14.

6 See *De arte cabalistica* (1612) 1 (p. 617), where Reuchlin speaks of the human soul as born from the mouth of God and breathed into his face by the divine Spirit as the illumination of his mind.

7 See Reuchlin's *De arte cabalistica* as well as the *De verbo mirifico* for these tendencies; also *Der Augenspiegel* 12f.

8 *De arte cabalistica* 1 (pp. 641f., 665ff., 719f.); *De verbo mirifico* 2.18 (p. 174); 2.21 (pp. 214, 220).

9 *De verbo mirifico* 1.2; see also 3.10–12.

10 *De arte cabalistica* I (pp. 642f.); 2 (pp. 665f., 689ff., 707); 3 (pp. 715ff.).

Divine Interpretation

bridges the chasm between God and the creature and makes communication between them possible, giving rise to true human knowledge of God.[11] It is this *verbum mirificum* that is the secret of all human life and knowledge, and indeed of all creation. It is the understanding of this *Verbum Dei* that Reuchlin seeks as he weighs the force of the Hebrew through which this knowledge has been mediated.

One might well describe this as a 'mysticism of the Word', for what Reuchlin rejoices in is a mystical experience through hearing the ineffable rather than through vision.[12] He does not contrast these sharply, for vision, the seeing of the invisible, has its proper place.[13] But because it is only through the Word that emanates from the innermost Being of God that he is known, it is in the experience of hearing the Word—*receptio ab auditu*[14]—that there takes place the transition or ascension of man into the divine mystery.[15] Like God's name, his Word is inexpressible by man; yet it is expressed through the speech of God and must therefore be heard in a wonderful way appropriate to its ineffable nature.

That is what Reuchlin is struggling with in his curious reflections upon the Tetragrammaton (YHWH):[16] the communication to man in his 'imbecility' of the transcendent self-revelation of God. To justify this ultimate experience in hearing God's miraculous Word Reuchlin tends to appeal to Aristotle's notion that first principles are by their very nature beyond demonstration,[17] and to have recourse to Cabbalistic and Pythagorean mystical speculations, which he often mixes up in weird ways with his reflections upon the biblical narratives. There is much here that is inevitably quite strange to us and rather undisciplined; yet it does represent something extremely important: Reuchlin's rejection of any attempt to penetrate into knowledge of the divine being by processes of reasoning, and also of any attempt to reduce what we know of God to syllogistic

---

11 *De verbo mirifico* 3.2; *De arte cabalistica* 1 (p. 642). Reuchlin likens the Word to Jacob's ladder. *De arte cabalistica* 2 (p. 670); *De verbo mirifico* 2.9.

12 *De verbo mirifico* 3.10 (pp. 271ff.); 3.3 (p. 236).

13 *De verbo mirifico* 1.9 (p. 61).

14 *De arte cabalistica* 1 (p. 623); 2 (pp. 657f.); see also *Der Augenspiegel* 17 and following.

15 *De verbo mirifico* 2.6 (pp. 122f.).

16 *De verbo mirifico* 2.18 (pp. 191ff.); 3.13 (pp. 288ff.).

17 *De verbo mirifico* 2.9 (pp. 183f.); *De arte cabalistica* 2 (p. 659).

argumentation or to corrupt it by 'the sophisms of Aristotle'.[18] He will have nothing to do with the mixing up of divine knowledge with natural things, nor with appeals to Gregory Nazianzus and Athanasius in support.[19] Knowledge of God is by faith alone (*sola fide*)—the proper faith (*recta fides*) that comes from hearing—and is rooted in revealed truth, in God's own pronunciation of his divine name. In *De arte cabalistica* this tends to be seriously obscured with naive and almost superstitious ideas, but in *De verba mirifico*, written before Reuchlin became so steeped in Cabbalistic lore, there is a clear line of thought of great importance for our inquiry.

The latter book is constructed on the basis of a dialogue which Reuchlin (under the name Capnion) conducts with a representative of Greek philosophy (Sidon, a Pythagorean) and a representative of the wisdom of Judaism (Baruch). Over against the views of the Greeks, in which he has obviously steeped himself, Reuchlin maintains that the Word or *Logos* of God is *Verbum* as well as *Ratio*. And over against the view of the Jews he maintains that the Word or *Dabhar* of God is his *Hand* (that is, his Deed) as well as his Word. To both he insists that it is only through this creative and wonderful Word and the communication or conversation it sets up between God and humanity that humanity can acquire knowledge of God or read the sublime things that utterly transcend his feeble capacities.[20] This is the Word that became flesh in Jesus Christ. Therefore it is in and through him, and in accordance with the human form which the Word has taken in him, that human beings may attain to the knowledge they desire. Hence Reuchlin seeks to bring his Greek and Jewish interlocutors to faith in Jesus Christ as the Way, the Truth, and the Life leading to the Father.

After the opening discussion with Sidon and Baruch, the book moves on to the main theme in which Reuchlin, through the exposition of Capnion, sets out his doctrine of 'the one Word'. At the outset a distinction is drawn between the knowledge of inferior and mutable realities which is really *opinio* and the knowledge of superior and immutable realities which is *sapientia* or *scientia* in the proper sense. These sublime realities are beyond the capacity of humanity, for we are unable to penetrate into them through the power of our own reasoning (*cogitatio*), but they may be

---

18 This is all the more significant in view of the fact that Reuchlin had a thorough knowledge of the works of Aristotle, to the study of which, he says, Greek recalled him. Yet the complaint was that these studies alienated him from Roman piety. See his *De accentibus et orthographia linguae hebraicae*, fol. aiif.

19 *De arte cabalistica* 2 (pp. 659ff.).

20 Cf. *De arte cabalistica* 2 (pp. 659ff.).

Divine Interpretation

discerned by us, by the eye of the mind (*acis mentis*), although not apart from the shining of divine light and truth.²¹ The mode of this perception or knowledge is *faith*. Just as through our senses we apprehend sensible things, and through the intelligence apprehend intelligible things, so through faith we know God in a way appropriate to him.²² This takes place through a covenant relation (*pactum, unio, confoederatio*) which God sets up between humanity and himself, as he places humanity in the midst of the universe in which he shares alike in things below and things above, directing faith to what is above and reason to what is below.²³ While there is no proportion between God and humanity (*nulla hominis erga deum proportio*), because God is infinite and humanity is finite, God nevertheless freely enters into relations with humanity (*libenter versari cum hominibus*), establishing fellowship (*societas*) and communication (*communicatio*) between himself and humanity. It is faith that is the bond (*vinculum*) between the love of God for humanity and the hope of humanity for God—but faith answers to the miraculous act of God through his Word in which he gives us to participate through an indescribable union.²⁴ Here Reuchlin admits that we are up against something ultimate, like the presuppositions or first principles or axioms with which we work in mathematics and physics, something which we can only acknowledge in joyful obedience.²⁵ To this Capnion's companions readily assent, but they press him to fulfill his promise to speak about the Word by which we are placed in nature, but through which we may rise above nature, and by which miracles are wrought.²⁶

Before resuming the argument Reuchlin pauses to note that here, where we are concerned with God who precedes all and who effects everything, the proper approach is one of wonder and reverence. It is through humility that we are made fit hearers of something so great, while faith, hope and love all play their part in our understanding.²⁷ 'Blessed be the God of Israel who only does wondrous things', he cites—God alone works miracles,

---

21 '*Nisi revelation divina*', *De verbo mirifico* 1.9 (p. 62); '*nisi lucent Deo*' 1.11 (p. 71). Cf. also 1.17 (p. 90): '*nulla ratione prompta coactus, nisi sola divinae revelationis auctoritate*'; and *De arte cabalistica* 2 (pp. 662f.).

22 *De verbo mirifico* 1.9 (pp. 60f.).

23 *De verbo mirifico* 1.10.

24 *De verbo mirifico* 1.11; 1.19 (p. 96).

25 *De verbo mirifico* 1.15; cf. *De arte cabalistica* 2 (p. 658).

26 *De verbo mirifico* 1.17 (p. 92); 2.1 (p. 99).

27 *De verbo mirifico* 2.2.

and not humanity. Therefore when we know him it can only be through an 'indescribable union' with him created by the miraculous power of his Word.[28] We acknowledge that our understanding of this wondrous operation can never be adequate to it, so that in our act of knowing we have to rely upon revelation from above and attribute everything to his glory.[29]

When Reuchlin attempts to offer an account of this relationship between humanity and God set up by the divine Word he is at a loss, for he has no adequate tools with which to set forth his understanding of it. He is determined, however, not to reduce it through syllogistic reasoning to the knowledge of clear-cut apprehensibility loved by the Schoolmen, for that would not be to respect its divine majesty. He keeps on saying that it is 'indescribable' (*innarrabilis*) and that it can be apprehended only in a way appropriate to its mysterious character (*proprietate occulta*).[30] He does try to feel his way forward through analogies taken from nature and from language which are not very helpful and often obscure his exposition, but the main line of his thought is fairly clear, even if at times it is somewhat fanciful.

Reuchlin points out that the relationship through the Word with which he is concerned is not something irrational but on the contrary arises in the divine employment of the human mind as his instrument through admitting it into a fellowship with the divine Mind. The conversation that results from this is grounded on a divine decree before the creation of the world and is rooted in the eternal *Logos*, for even from eternity God rejoiced to have fellowship with us.

> Accordingly the Lord of eternity rejoicing in our society and counting among his delights the sanctified human mind as, so to speak, bordering on his own nature and deriving from him, when he sees it submitting to him in sedulous worship and constant devotion, continually strives as an exceedingly abundant nutritive power to transform it, as far as human weakness allows, not only by the warmth of his love but by a secret propriety to direct it toward himself; so that we may migrate into God and God may dwell in us.[31]

---

28 *De verbo mirifico* 1.2 (p. 71); 2.5 (p. 116).
29 *De verbo mirifico* 2.3; *De arte cabalistica* 2 (pp. 662f.).
30 *De verbo mirifico* 2.3, 6(2).
31 *De verbo mirifico* 2.6; cf. *De arte cabalistica* 2 (p. 670).

Divine Interpretation

This migration into communion with God is established and fortified by covenant acts (*pacta*) on a confederation (*confoederatio*)[32] such as that into which God placed Israel when he drew it out of the workhouse of the Egyptians (*de ergastulo Aegyptorum*), delivering it from servitude and redeeming it by his mighty arm and great judgments, taking it to be his people and giving himself to them as their God.[33] But at its heart this is an operation of God which is secret and hidden from us, like the vegetative and digestive activities in nature of which we stand in ignorance.

> Thus in this utterly divine movement unto God [*in hoc divinissimo in Deum transitu*] there are some words [*verba quaedem*] which we know and some which we do not know. But this *vinculum verborum* unites both parties, *Deus enim spiritus, verbum spiratio, homo spirans*. God is called *Logos*, named Word by the same term by which the human reason is expressed in a similar way of speaking. God is discerned by mind, and conceived by the Word, so that as he makes the mind his invisible abode, he takes up his audible dwelling in words—not all words, not any words that happen to be used, but those which God has first provided for us, and which human ingenuity has not thought up. For God knows the thoughts of men, that they are vain. But God's thoughts are redemptive and saving, permanent, invincible, and sure. As he thinks, so it will be; as he determines, so it will come to pass. The Lord commands the universe and who can hinder him? Therefore not all words carry the divine presence [*igitur non omnia verba numen possident*].[34]

God himself, the great God of the world and of humanity, or his sharp-sighted angels, have composed, at his command and by his providence, the words that echo the music of eternity and, in accordance with his saving economy, convey to us divine things. Hence we have the literary form of God's revelation which has been handed down to us from ancient times.[35]

This raises a discussion about the nature of the Hebrew language which, according to Reuchlin, is the medium in which God converses with the angels—not that God speaks Hebrew with himself, for the Word in

---

32 *De verbo mirifico* 2.18 (p. 193).

33 *De verbo mirifico* 2.6; 2.18 (p. 192).

34 *De verbo mirifico* 2.6 (pp. 122f.).

35 *De verbo mirifico* 2.6 (p. 123); *De arte cabalistica* 3 (pp. 725ff.). It is the inner aural receiving and handing on of the divine word that is the theme of Reuchlin's cabbalistic musings.

God is something utterly transcendent and ineffable, and which cannot be grasped by the human mind. That is the significance of the unpronounceable divine name, YHWH, which as he pronounces it to humanity is his divine self-revelation.[36] But Hebrew does have a peculiar and unique place in the divine economy; it was not only the original language of revelation but remains the language in relation to which even the New Testament is to be understood.[37] Most of the rest of the second book of *De verba mirifico* is taken up with the question of inspired writings, and especially of the idioms and distinctive characteristics of the Hebrew Scriptures—the *veritas hebraica*.

The significance of this may be judged from a comparison with the view of Aquinas that God and the angels converse wordlessly.[38] However fanciful Reuchlin's notion may appear to us,[39] he is insisting that Word has an eternal place in the Being of God. Because God is Word in himself, he converses with his creatures in words. It is from a source in God's creative speech that all our ability to employ words is derived. But words as such have no divinity about them and tell us nothing about God. Just as no one knows what is in a person's heart but their own spirit, so no one knows God or his Mind except his own Spirit and those to whom he grants revelation of himself through his Spirit and Word.[40] The Scriptures, however, are the written form of God's Word because they are the providentially formed and appointed medium through which he comes to converse with us by the power of his Spirit.[41] Reuchlin's view of the relation of this divine speech to angels is governed in part by Aristotle's idea that word is the *messenger* that announces to another what is in a person's mind—that is, a sort of *angel*.[42] It involves a creative act on the part of God's Word, but what he communicates is through creaturely media. Hence in the union

---

36   *De verbo mirifico* 2.8, 15ff.

37   *De verbo mirifico* 2.8 (p. 136); 2.11 (pp. 144ff.); 2.12 (pp. 154f.).

38   Thomas Aquinas, *Summa Theologiae* 1a, q. 107, a. 1.

39   Reuchlin reminds us that we have to speak of these sublime things *humano more, propter imbecillitatem nostram*. See *De verbo mirifico* 2.18 (p. 176).

40   *De verbo mirifico* 2.13 (pp. 155ff.).

41   *De verbo mirifico* 2.6 (p. 123); cf. *Der Augenspiegel* 15: *Die schrift ist ain zaichen der wort*.

42   *De verbo mirifico* 2.13 (pp. 155ff.); 3.3 (pp. 236f.). See also *De arte cabalistica* 2 (pp. 722f.), where Reuchlin relates it to Exodus 23:20f. The influence of Philo is also apparent here in his assimilation of *logoi* with *angelos*. See *Opera Philonis*, ed. L. Cohn, 1.152, 463.

Divine Interpretation

set up between humanity and God by his words, there is a nonobjectifiable element and an objectifiable element—or, as Reuchlin expresses it, some of these words we know and some we do not know. That is as it ought to be for at the heart of our conversation with God we are concerned with an intractable miraculous event.[43]

This helps us to understand another aspect of Reuchlin's teaching in which he directs close attention to the *idiomata* of the Hebrew text, pointing out that they are so distinctive that they cannot be adequately translated into another language, and that unless we read the Scriptures in their original Hebrew we shall not understand them properly.[44] This does not mean that somehow the divine revelation is to be discerned in the peculiar structure of the Hebrew language as such, but that through study of the *idiomata* and *proprietates* of the Hebrew Scriptures we are paying attention to the sign-language (*signa, symbola, signacula*) which they employ to direct us beyond to the unique and ineffable speech of God.[45] That is why Reuchlin never tires of insisting that we encounter *miracle* in the Bible. We can get the Word of God no more through etymological or philological examination of the Hebrew than through the logical argumentations of the Schoolmen. But we must allow ourselves to be guided by the nature of what is actually and literally written to *hear* God speaking—it is in that act of hearing, which is essentially a miracle, that we really hear the Word of God. In other words, it is *by faith* that we hear, and *through hearing* that we understand God's Word, that is, in a way appropriate to the wonderful nature of God's speaking.[46]

Another aspect of the Word of God that Reuchlin is concerned to emphasise is the dynamic force. God's Word exercises the widest *imperium* and the fullest power resides in it.[47] God's Word includes his act, so that when he utters it, it fulfills what he intends.[48] He remains faithful to it and supports it with his divine being. Thus in the Old Testament the self-revelation of God through his Word and the making bare of his mighty arm

---

43 *De verbo mirifico* 2.6 (pp. 122f.).

44 *De verbo mirifico* 2.11; 2.12; 2.18.

45 This is what Reuchlin called *symbolica theologia* at *De arte cabalistica* 3 (p. 713). It is partly for this reason that Reuchlin is so fascinated with the *Cabbala*.

46 Compared to that divine speaking, Reuchlin says, citing from Origen, humanity must be considered not only ineloquent but even mute. *De verbo mirifico* 2.15 (p. 163).

47 *De verbo mirifico* 3.2 (p. 229); *Der Augenspiegel* 17f.

48 *De verbo mirifico* 1.15 (p. 81); 2.6 (p. 123); 2.11 (p. 150); 2.18 (pp. 192f.).

mean the same thing.[49] God's Word is his Hand as well as his Word.[50] That is why it is not amenable to treatment in mere ideas or logical connections, and why understanding of it can only begin after the action of God upon us, in a reflection upon what he has both spoken and performed, and through participation in his Spirit. The Word of God is a mighty, active, creative thing, a life-giving emanation, as it were, of his own divine energy.[51]

That is the point at which Reuchlin begins his account of the Word in the third book of *De verbo mirifico*, in which he seeks to carry his readers through to a profounder understanding of the Word incarnate in Jesus Christ.[52] This is the *verbum rationale* or the *ratio verbalis*, the creator of the universe and the disposer of everything. Using the familiar analogy of the *verbum internum hominis* which proceeds from the mind, Reuchlin proceeds at once to speak of Christ as the Word who proceeds from the Father's Mind, the only begotten Son of God, whose name, according to Isaiah, is called Wonderful (*Mirificum*),[53] but to whom David and others also give the name of God's *Hand*.[54] Just as it is the office of the word to announce what goes on within the mind, to fetch out from the depths the secrets of thought, and to lay open the will of the speaker, so he is most aptly deemed to be the Son and Word of the Father, since no one has ever seen God, but the only begotten Son who is in the bosom of the Father has announced him to us. He is therefore the Angel or Messenger of the great Counsel who reveals to mortals the sublime purposes of God.[55] He is in fact the substantial and substantive Word of the Father, the wholly adequate Word and perfect Image of God, through whom we know him who previously was not known by us. He that hath seen me, said Jesus, has seen the Father. Thus the whole substance of God is revealed in one brief Word (*tota substantia brevi sermone aperta*). No one knows the Father

---

49 *De verbo mirifico* 2.18 (p. 192).

50 *De verbo mirifico* 3.3 (pp. 235f.); 3.11 (pp. 276ff.). See *De arte cabalistica* 3 (pp. 765f.).

51 Cf. *De arte cabalistica* 2 (pp. 660ff.); and *Johan Reuchlins Briefweschsel* (L. Geiger ed.; Tübingen, 1875) 125, letter 17.

52 His biblical starting point is Hebrews 11:3; John 1:1ff.; Revelation 19:16; 1 Corinthians 1:28. *De verbo mirifico* 3 (pp. 228f.).

53 Isaiah 9:6; *De verbo mirifico* 3.3 (p. 234). This is of course what gives Reuchlin the title for his work.

54 Psalm 74:11, etc.; *De verbo mirifico* 3.3 (p. 235).

55 *De verbo mirifico* 3.3 (p. 236).

except the Son and those to whom the Son reveals him. He is the *imago vivens et volens* of God.⁵⁶

We need not follow Reuchlin's account in detail, but we must note the point of supreme importance he is intent on getting across: *the consubstantiality of the incarnate Word* with the eternal Father, for in Jesus the eternal hypostatic expression of the Father has been given human form. That is the astounding novelty (*novum*) that God has created in the earth; he now converses with us humanly as Immanuel, God with us. In Jesus the deity of the Word has assumed human nature and is united to it, so that he who was from the beginning, as John says, the Word of life, has been heard with human ears and seen with human eyes, and handled with hands. That is the Word that is announced in the gospel. That is, the ineffable Word, the unpronounceable name of God, can now be spoken by a human mouth.⁵⁷

Reuchlin goes on to expound the Chalcedonian Christology and the doctrine of the Holy Trinity and the traditional terminology, but he applies it with immense emphasis to the epistemological question that concerns us in this inquiry. In Jesus, God the Word is present hypostatically, in his own proper person, speaking to us face-to-face, humanly. What is in the stream is in its source, what is in Jesus is in the God of eternity. It is as such that Jesus is the Way, the Truth and the Life, and he is that so exclusively that there is no way to God the Father but by him.⁵⁸ 'Hence the Word, although he is the eternal Son of God, born of the substance of the Father before the ages, nevertheless was born of the substance of the virgin in time, perfect God and perfect human of a rational soul and subsisting in human flesh.'⁵⁹ It is in and through him that the indescribable communion between humanity and God through the miraculous operation of God's Word is consummated, that the sublime self-revelation of God to which nothing on earth is commensurate is made apprehensible to us, that the ineffable name of God can be taken on human lips. Thus in the divine *economy*, 'the Word clothed himself with human flesh that we through his saving contact with us may more easily follow up our accommodation to him, when with these eyes and our several senses we embrace that very Word, no longer

---

56 *De verbo mirifico* 3.3 (p. 237). Reuchlin speaks of Christ as *mentis nostrae objectum supremum . . . per quem plane tandem in Deum transeanus in comprehensibilem*. See *De arte cabalistica* 1 (p. 649).

57 1 John 1:1, *De verbo mirifico* 3.4 (pp. 240ff.).

58 *De verbo mirifico* 3.8; see esp. p. 263.

59 *De verbo mirifico* 3.8 (p. 254); cf. 3.11 (pp. 276f.).

ineffable as before, within the compass of letters, but can even denote it with an utterable word and an understandable sound'.[60]

There follows a discussion of the names *Christ* and *Jesus*, Messiah and Savior,[61] in the course of which Reuchlin sets out to show in his abstruse linguistic reflections how the miraculous and wonderful name of the Word comes to be uttered by a human voice. The Word himself descended into human flesh and spoke human words with a human voice in such a way that divine speech passed into human speech and letters; yet this happened in such a way that the human speech and letters retained the imprint and seal or character of the divine Word. What Reuchlin tries to do, admittedly not very clearly, is to apply the classical doctrine of the two natures of Christ in one person to the relation between divine utterance and human utterance in the incarnate Word. It is a miraculous relation that we have there, and therefore is only explicable from the side of the divine creative act. That is denoted by the saying that the Word is Arm or Hand of God as well as his Speech. As he became incarnate through the Spirit, as it is the Spirit who utters the Word of God in the Incarnation, so it is only through the power and unction of the same Spirit that we may hear and understand the Word.[62] Reuchlin notes the importance of rejecting the heresy of Nestorianism and affirming the teaching of the Council of Ephesus that in the person of the incarnate Word who came out from the eternal Father, divine and human natures cannot be separated.[63]

In the concluding sections of his book Reuchlin shows that it is in the name of Jesus and through his Word that God is still at work miraculously among humans to reveal himself to them and save them. God manifested his name to Christ; and he has manifested it to the disciples, and through them to the world, so that it is in and through Christ and his cross that we are adopted into communion with God. There is no Christ without the cross—that in fact is the *ratio* of the incarnate Word and of our participation in the mystery of God.[64]

---

60   *De verbo mirifico* 3.10 (p. 273). See also 3.11 (pp. 279f.); and 3.16 (pp. 302ff.).

61   According to Reuchlin *Jesus* (*yhshwh*) is the revelation of *Yahweh* (*yhwh*), the addition of the *shin* to the Tetragrammaton standing for the Name (*shem*) of the Messiah. *De verbo mirifico* 3.12 (pp. 280f.); *De arte cabalistica* 3 (p. 770).

62   *De verbo mirifico* 3.11–13.

63   *De verbo mirifico* 3.14 (p. 296). See also *Der Augenspiegel* 12.

64   *De verbo mirifico* 3.16–20.

Divine Interpretation

How are we to describe the application of this, then, to the actual interpretation of the Holy Scriptures? In seeking to answer that we must not forget that after writing *De verbo mirifico* Reuchlin went on to write his epoch-making work on Hebrew grammar and vocabulary, *De rudimentis Hebraicis* (1506), followed by a short textbook for reading Hebrew, *In septem psalmos poenitentiales hebraicos interpretatio de verbo ad verbum* (1512), and then his second book on the Hebrew language, *De accentibus et orthographia linguae Hebraicae* (1518). The mysticism of the Word had its counterpart in a severely linguistic and grammatical treatment of the Scriptures. And then on top of that again we have to take into account *De arte cabalistica*, published in 1517, in which he developed his symbolic philosophy of Hebrew mysteries.

(1) First of all we must emphasise that Reuchlin was a humanist of a special kind: he was a lawyer with a religious passion for truth, the truth of letters, the truth of equivalence in statement, the truth at the bottom of things, in the original sources. His first insistence therefore was upon reading exactly what stood in the text, every jot and tittle of it. Hence of his book on Hebrew rudiments he once wrote: '*In hoc enim rudimentorum libro saltem hoc unum te docebo, ut scripta legas, non ut legenda scribas.*'[65] At this stage he keeps theology out of things, and so he wrote in the same work that he was not concerned to write as a theologian about statements but as a grammarian about words.[66] Grammatical knowledge when carefully undertaken, he maintained, did not yield superficial results, but served to reveal the true and genuine sense of Scripture through bringing to our attention the distinctive properties of the words used.[67] Hence when he produced his edition of the penitential Psalms he offered a word-for-word (*de verbo ad verbum*) interpretation in order to help the student discern the inherent characteristics and distinctive properties of the language.[68] This involves the conviction that the Scriptures cannot be properly understood or interpreted except on the basis of the original languages in which they were written, for in interpreting one language into another it is not possible

---

65 Cited from Ludwig Geiger, *Johann Reuchlin. Sein Leben and seine Werke* (Leipzig, 1871) 127.
66 *De rudimentis hebraicis* 123.
67 *De accentibus et orthographia linguae hebraicae*, a.iii.
68 See *Johann Reuchlins Briefwechsel*, 189, letter 163.

to carry through into it these distinctive characteristics or all its original power.[69]

It is interesting to note how Reuchlin's training and profession as a lawyer and judge influenced his method here: it must be specified and defined *(descripta definitaque methodus)*.[70] Two examples of that may be given. In his Hebrew dictionary, which he assembled with great labor and sweat and persistence,[71] he determines the meaning of each word by noting definite cases. He then builds up their meaning, not primarily on etymological grounds (there is very little of that in Reuchlin), but on the grounds of specific instances of employment. The importance of this emerges as he keeps on pointing out how much the old Latin translation has mistaken the meaning of the Hebrew.

A different example of his method is to be seen in the little work *De arte praedicandi* which he wrote for the preachers of Denkendorf Abbey in thanks for their kindness to him. While the little handbook does have something to say about how to compose and deliver the sermon, it is mostly concerned with arid grammatical distinctions and connections, precisely the sort of thing that a juristic hermeneutics would require in order to determine in the most matter-of-fact way the plain sense of the statements and no more than that. On the other hand, when it comes to the application of the exposition to the lives of people, Reuchlin falls back upon the familiar threefold sense of Scripture (i.e. in addition to the literal sense determined by grammar alone): the tropological which is its 'moral' application to the individual, the allegorical which is the 'civil' application to our relations with fellow Christians and the anagogical* which concerns men's relations with divine things.[72] Along with the literal sense, and the grammatical exegesis appropriate to it, it is the anagogical sense that is most important, for here the Sacred Scriptures must be handled in such a way that they fulfill their purpose in *raising humanity up* to communion

---

69 *De verbo mirifico* 2.12 (p. 155).

70 *De accentibus et orthographia*, xix.a.iv.

71 *Johann Reuchlins Briefwechsel*, 175, letter 151.

72 *De arte praedicandi*, fol. aii. See also *De arte cabalistica* 3 (p. 716), where Reuchlin mentions, in addition to the literal and allegorical senses, a great variety of other ways in which to interpret the Scriptures. Here he has in mind the 'fifty gates' through which Cabbalistic art reaches the mysteries of the sacred writings. [Ed. Torrance has the last of these, indicated by the *, as *analogical*, but it is clear from its use here that he meant *anagogical*, especially since that is the word he uses in the following sentence. I have therefore rendered it *anagogical* here.]

Divine Interpretation

with God and so to a spiritual understanding that exceeds nature *(naturam excedit)*. This carries us to the second thing that has to be emphasised.

(2) The Scriptures must be read and interpreted in a new way in which we let God himself speak to us through them directly. This was the significance that Reuchlin attached to his study of Hebrew and his interpretation of the Hebrew Scriptures. After trying various versions, he says, nothing he learned out of all the languages joined him to God more *(plus me deo conjungit)* than his occupation with the Scriptures in Hebrew.[73] They have the divine seal or character inwardly imprinted upon them, a majesty that points back to God the divine speaker.[74] This was greatly reinforced by his conviction (which we have already noted) that in the Hebrew Scriptures we have the language of the original revelation. 'In reading Hebrew,' he says, 'I seem to see God himself speaking, when I consider that it is by means of this language that God and the angels have passed through their communications to men in a divine manner. Thus I am shaken with dread and fear, yet not without a certain unspeakable joy following wonder or rather amazement, which I will call wisdom, about which the divine Word says, "The fear of the Lord is the beginning of wisdom."'[75]

This represents a very basic shift in the conception of the Word, which was bound to affect exegesis and interpretation. It came about through the turning away from the Latin text to the Hebrew and through the fresh understanding of the biblical teaching that that opened up. We learn in it that 'the great God wills to be signified not by any likeness or representation or image, but by the voice alone' *(maximum Deum nulla similitudine, nulla effigie, nulla imagine, nisi sola voce significari velle)*.[76] It is the voice that mediates between God and man,[77] the voice which we hear in the Scriptures, but God's voice is his Spirit *(Vox Spiritus est)*. Reuchlin cites from John 3:8: 'His Spirit blows where he wills, and you hear his voice but do not know where he comes from and where he goes.'[78] This means that

---

73 *Johann Reuchlins Briefwechsel*, 123, letter 115.

74 *Johann Reuchlins Briefwechsel*, 16.

75 *Johann Reuchlins Briefwechsel*, 123, letter 115.

76 *De verbo mirifico* 3.12 (p. 283). Cf. *De arte cabalistica* 1 (p. 651): *id est Spiritus, Verbum, Vox*.

77 *Johann Reuchlins Briefwechsel*, 105, letter 102: '*Vox enirn fuit mediatrix Dei at hominum, at in Pentateucho legimus, at non quaelibet vox, sed tantum Hebraica, per quota Deus voluit arcana sua mortalibus innotescere.*'

78 *De verbo mirifico* 3.12 (pp. 283f.).

while we know God through reception of his Word by hearing (*ab auditu*), it is not everyone who hears, for the hearing is a wonderful and miraculous happening corresponding to the miraculous activity of the Spirit.[79] That is the kind of hearing to which we have to learn to lay ourselves open in the reading and interpreting of the Sacred Scripture, giving attention to 'the new and original kind of speaking in the divine scripture, which is called the mouth of God' (*novum et nativum in divina Scriptura dicendi genus, quale os Dei locutum est*).[80]

As Reuchlin makes clear in *De verbo mirifico*, this leads straight to Jesus Christ, for he is the wonderful Word of God who has penetrated into human existence and into human speech. It is his Word that is articulated in the letters of the Scripture, for in him the ineffable is spoken, and the unutterable is pronounced and may be pronounced. Moreover, what happened in Christ Reuchlin considered to have a backward reference to the Old Testament writings. What is written in the Old Testament as well as in the New Testament all relates to him and his work, for all else that happened before the time of Christ was ordained to point forward to him.[81] In the human nature and form of Christ we have the Word that proceeds from the Father and has come down from the heavens. In him the Lord has thrust out his hand from above, and God is seen on earth in conversation with humanity.[82] That is the Word we encounter and hear in the Holy Scriptures, the potent, living, energetic Word of God which heals and saves, and which is identical with the name of Jesus Christ.[83]

When Reuchlin writes in this vein it is difficult not to think of him as a forerunner of the Reformation, and certainly he had not a little influence upon Melanchthon, his nephew, and upon Luther himself. But we must note another side to Reuchlin that affected his approach to interpretation:

---

79 *De arte cabalistica* 1 (p. 623).

80 *Priori Graecae at Sacrae Hebraicae Linguae* a2. While Reuchlin speaks realistically like this of *audire sermonem ab ore Dei*, he insists that that must not be understood anthropomorphically as if the Spirit breathed the Word through lips, etc., but understood *divinitus*, in a divine manner. See *De arte cabalistica* 1 (pp. 623ff.).

81 The Sacred Scripture, whether written by the instrument of Hebrew or Greek letters, is all of Christ *(ista Christi)*. *In septem psalmos poenitentiales hebraicos interpretatio*, fol. a3.

82 *De verbo mirifico* 3.11 (p. 279).

83 It is significant that when Reuchlin spoke of 'the three states of the Word' as 'God, the Son, and the Incarnate', he does not mention the written word of the Scripture. *De verbo mirifico* 3.4 (p. 242).

DIVINE INTERPRETATION

his application of the anagogical method to the disclosure of abstruse mysteries.

(3) Two of Reuchlin's great insights were that the relation between the one Word of God and the words of the Sacred Scripture was miraculous and that Hebrew, like any other language, had highly distinctive traits and characteristics that must be taken into account if the Old Testament writings are to be adequately and properly interpreted. But since Hebrew was the original language of revelation, Reuchlin concluded that the distinct characteristics of Hebrew were not unconnected with the miraculous relation between the wonderful Word of God and the speech of the Bible.[84] Reuchlin was so deeply convinced of the peculiar nature of each language that he insisted on learning Greek from Greek teachers and Hebrew from Jewish teachers. It is not surprising, therefore, that in order to understand these *idiomata et proprietates* of the Old Testament language he should turn to other Hebrew literature and to the judgments of Jewish scholars, such as the rabbis whose teaching is recorded in the Talmud, or to commentators like Rashi and Kimhi, or to thinkers like Maimonides.[85] But in this extracanonical Jewish literature he found in the Masoretic tradition a slavish reverence for the peculiarities of Hebrew, down to the very points and apexes of the letters. And he found in the Cabbalistic tradition mystical and speculative tendencies that claimed a higher wisdom not given to the multitude in virtue of which the deepest secrets of the sacred writings could be unraveled. Fascinated by this sapiential literature and speculation, Reuchlin could not refrain from probing into the wonderful relation between the Word and the words, so he developed an esoteric philosophy of Scripture that seriously distorted his Christological insight into the doctrine of the Word and damaged his influence both within and without the Roman Church.

Reuchlin's peculiar view may be described by saying that he transposed the basic *eikonic* relation between words and what they signified from the *eidetic* to the *acoustic* realm, for it is only in word that God's Word can be imaged or signified. Hence it is through meditating upon the distinctive features of the sacred letters that we discern the *signacula* or *symbola* that aid our hearing the secret speech of God. That is what he called the

---

84 Sacred letters, he held, had a 'majesty' about them in which the 'divine character' originally imposed upon them could be discerned. *Johann Reuchlins Briefwechsel*, 16; cf. also p. 189.

85 *Der Augenspiegel* 8, and passim.

anagogical method of interpretation, for through it our minds are elevated to the heights where we are in touch with divine reality.[86] This is what he called wisdom, *sapientia, sophia*, a mode of 'philosophy' in which he claimed to transcend ordinary knowledge by breaking through the visible world into the invisible and archetypal world of divine patterns in the light of which all else becomes lit up with supernal truth.[87]

Reuchlin's veneration for the *idiomata et proprietates* of Hebrew Scriptures is rather like the veneration for icons that one finds in the Eastern Church—except that this involves a meditation through contemplation. Behind both there are latent or Neoplatonic tendencies that can become particularly powerful and damaging to the interpretation of the Scriptures or the formulation of doctrine when it is worked out into some kind of philosophy of eidetic or acoustic representation.

Reuchlin's great contribution to biblical interpretation lies in his insistence that the text must be understood in accordance with the nature of the divine Word mediated to us through it, for behind the speech of the biblical writings there is the Word that eternally inheres in the Being of God and is made audible in and through the divine revelation that reached its fulfillment and finality in the Incarnation. It also lies in his recovery of the insight that this Word of God heard in and through the Scriptures is God's mighty arm, for God's Word has not only being in God but comes forth from him as his creative act and is at work in the Church in healing and saving activity—that is, in the healing and saving activity of Jesus Christ. Thus whereas for the Greeks and for the Schoolmen word was primarily an expression of intellectual activity, for Reuchlin word is primarily a dynamic force. God's Word is thus Word which includes his act within it so that in our hearing it he acts upon it miraculously and unites us to himself in a communion that transcends nature. Hence the significance of biblical statements is not independent of the divine utterance that lies behind them and may be reached only through a consideration of the force with which they are laden.

But Reuchlin fell down badly at the very point where he rejected the methods of the Schoolmen. In rejecting their sophistical *quaestiones* and

---

86 See *De arte cabalistica* 1 (pp. 641f.).

87 Reuchlin's 'theosophical' attempt to penetrate more deeply into the relation between the Word and the words has a parallel in modem 'sophiology', in which attempts have been made (e.g. by S. Bulgakov) to penetrate behind negatives of the Chalcedonian Christology into a deeper and more positive understanding of the relation between the divine and human natures in the person of Christ.

distinctiones which they imposed upon the Scriptures, he also rejected the all-important argumentative mode of interpretation in which the reader of the Scriptures does not simply interpret language with grammatical and syntactical rigor, nor simply meditate upon what is written in order to be lifted up to communion with God, but thinks the realities that are denoted by them and allows his mind to be shaped and directed by the inner logic of those realities. Reuchlin came near to doing that in the last book of *De verbo mirifico*, but when he veered off into his abstruse sapiential speculations he deprived himself of the one discipline that would surely have corrected his thinking and prevented him from straying into the fatal morass of hermetic and Cabbalistic fancy. And yet for all that he did insist that he was not expounding the Holy Scriptures in any way contrary to what the Church taught, for what the Church believed he believed, and by what the Roman Church taught he allowed himself to be guided. He remained therefore an opponent of the Reformation, which was to benefit so much from his opening up of the study of the Scriptures in Hebrew.

Reuchlin's influence upon his contemporaries may be judged from the collect composed by Erasmus and published in his *Soliloquies* in the essay entitled 'The Apotheosis of Capnio'. I give it in the seventeenth-century translation of Sir Roger L'Estrange.

> O God that art the lover of mankind, and by Thy chosen servant John Reuchlin, hast renewed to mankind the gift of tongues, by which Thy Holy Spirit from above did formerly enable the Apostles for the preaching of the Gospel; grant that all people may in all tongues, preach the glory of Thy Son, to the confounding of the tongues of the false apostles, who being in confederacy, to uphold the wicked tower of Babel, endeavor to obscure Thy glory, by advancing their own, when to Thee is due all glory, etc.

CHAPTER 7

The Hermeneutics of Erasmus[1]

While it cannot be claimed that Erasmus was the father of Greek as Reuchlin was of Hebrew studies in the Western church, he was without doubt the ablest and the most influential humanist scholar of his age, who made immense contributions to biblical interpretation. In fact, it was he more than any other who laid the foundations of modern scholarship in the investigation and handling of the text of the New Testament. He was not such a great Greek scholar as Budaeus or such a careful and profound commentator as Calvin, but it was largely owing to him that the dialectical and (as he called it) 'barbarous' treatment of the Scriptures by the later Schoolmen was brought into disrepute, and a new approach was initiated in which all the available knowledge of the original languages and the cultures to which they belonged was utilised in the aid of sober and patient exegesis.[2]

He owed a great deal to others, most of all—apart from the ancient scholars to whom he constantly appealed—to Lorenzo Valla and John Colet. From Valla he learned much in the appreciation and use of 'good letters' and in a critical approach to the Latin text of the New Testament,[3] and from Colet he learned not a little how to bring humanist studies to serve the elucidation of the Holy Scriptures, and their liberation from the sterile legalisms and syllogisms of the Schoolmen, through a pure devotion to Jesus and his teaching.[4] 'This learned discipline, this philosophy, this

---

1 This essay originally appeared in Elsie Anne McKee and Brian G. Armstrong (eds.), *Probing the Reformed Tradition: Historical Studies in Honor of Edward A. Dowey, Jr.* (Louisville: Westminster/John Knox Press,1989), 48–76. Reprinted with permission.

2 See especially Erasmus, *Antibarbari* (*Opera Omnia* 10:1691–1744).

3 L. Valla, *Elegantiae Linguae Latinae*, 1471 (edited by Erasmus, *Opera Omnia* 1:1069ff.). Cf. Erasmus, *Opus Epistolarum* (eds. P. S. and H. M. Allen, and H. W. Garrod), 1.23, and *De ratione studii ac legendi interpretandique auctores* 4; and L. Valla, *In Latinam Novi Testamenti interpretationem ex collatione Graecorum exemplarium adnotationes* (published by Erasmus in 1505).

4 See the discussion of W. Schwarz, *Principles and Problems of Biblical Translation:*

speech for understanding Christ, for celebrating the glory of Christ: this is the aim of all learning and speech.'[5]

Two basic factors appear to determine all of Erasmus' work of biblical interpretation.

1. From an early age in his career, apparently during his studies in Paris, Erasmus revolted sharply against the subtleties and cavilings of the 'neoteric theologians.' He detested the way in which they *played* with biblical statements and convictions, distorting them to quite alien meanings through notions derived from the peripatetic philosophy or simply out of their own proud ingenuity. He derided their habit of elaborating subtle distinctions and frivolous questions and then projecting their conclusions into God, thus thinking of him in a quite worldly way instead of respecting his majesty and deity. One of Erasmus' outstanding contributions in this period was his successful attack on the nominalist notions of grammar and syntax, which he stigmatised as barbarous, for these involved a radical separation of language from culture and so abstracted the interpretation of biblical statements from the living context of meaning in the civilization in which they were expressed that they gave rise to an arid and frigid theology which could have no real relevance to the spiritual and human life of people.[6]

Although he never rejected a proper use of dialectic, especially if it were kept subordinate to the proper aim *(scopus)* of theology, Erasmus thoroughly distrusted all speculation and could never bring himself to agree that the kind of logical connections Scholastic theologians employed in their disputations were apposite to 'Christian philosophy', which was essentially spiritual rather than intellectual.[7] The *Logos* with which we are concerned in Christian studies is not reason but the divine speech *(sermo)*, i.e., not a word of our own devising which we project into God in order

---

Some Reformation Controversies and Their Background (Cambridge, 1955), 108ff., and J. H. Lupston, *A Life of Dean Colet* (London, 1887), ch. 5, 59ff.

5 Opera Omnia 1:1026. [Ed. This translation is mine. Torrance quotes the Latin as follows: 'Huc discuntur disciplinae, huc philosophia, huc eloquentia ut Christum intelligamus, ut Christi gloriam celebremus. Hic est totius eruditionis et eloquentiae scopus.']

6 This is a theme that runs throughout the *Liber Antibarbarorum (Opera Omnia* 10).

7 See *Enchiridion militis Christiani*, prefatory epistle (CCCXXIX); and *Ratio seu methodus compendio perveniendi ad veram theologian (Opera Omnia*, 1703, vol. 5), 126f., 136.

to make him speak our language and think our thoughts, but a word that derives through the prophets and apostles and which is the expression of the Spirit or mind of Christ.[8] On the other hand, Erasmus was never able to develop a proper answer to the false dialectical theology of the 'Scotists', for he never managed to penetrate far behind organised language to the inner connection of the realities denoted—that had to wait for the Reformers and their development of a positive theology on the ground of biblical exegesis. Erasmus was content merely to develop narrations of the biblical teaching, and to imbibe 'the Spirit of Christ' and work it out in the moral connections of human life. Thus for Erasmus interpretation was essentially a descriptive and paraphrastic science, and its results were ethical and social rather than evangelical and theological.

2. Erasmus took over the theory of Valla that language and culture belong inseparably together—decay in letters reflects the general decline in civilization. He was convinced that the converse was equally true, that progress in culture must come about through an advance together of good letters and liberal arts. Indeed, Erasmus was so forcibly seized with that conviction that the whole of his life was devoted to its embodiment and achievement.[9] Applied to the question of biblical studies, this resulted in the realisation that, for the Bible to be made perspicuous, it required a new context in which to reflect its meaning, a new civilization which could be employed to serve its interpretation and implement its teaching. Erasmus felt that the interpretation of the Bible in the Middle Ages corresponded to the barbarity of people's attitude to good letters, for how could the Bible reflect its meaning properly in the arid dialecticism of the Schools or in the crudity and illiteracy of the monks? He longed for a recovery of the old culture of Greece and Rome, and a new appreciation of the old theologians and interpreters who used Classical culture to reflect the meaning of the Bible and who at the same time Christianised the ancient culture by the philosophy of Christ.[10] Hence he made it the task of his life to work for the recovery of purity and eloquence in language, and in and through that medium to let 'evangelical truth' subdue the barbarity and crudity of humanity, which it would recreate in a new civilization.

---

8 *De ratione concionandi I* (*Opera Omnia* 5:771f.; and *Paraclesis, id est, Adhortatio ad Christianae philosophiae studium* (*Opera Omnia* 5:137–44).

9 See again the fine account of Schwarz, *Principles*, 94f.

10 This is vividly clear throughout the *Enchiridion militis Christiani*.

It was Erasmus' stand for a Christian humanism that gave direction to his many activities and even lent a real consistency to many of his most contradictory statements. He aimed at a reconciliation of the culture of Classical antiquity with the Christian spirit and was convinced that it would result in the elevation of humanity in an era of tolerance, wisdom, peace and progress.[11] Judged from the perspective of the late eighteenth and the nineteenth centuries, he was essentially 'modern'.[12]

Like Reuchlin and his friend Sir Thomas More,[13] Erasmus reacted against Aristotelian philosophy even in its classical form, preferring, as he said, with the great majority of philosophers and poets, to follow the teaching of Plato.[14] It was Plato, moreover, who had influenced some of the old theologians and expositors that Erasmus most admired, such as Origen, Ambrose, and Augustine, so that it is not surprising that he too should revive the old Hellenic distinction between the *mundus sensibilis* and the *mundus intelligibilis*.

> The intelligible world, which we may also call the angelical world, is that in which God dwells with blessed minds; the visible world comprises the celestial spheres and all that they involve. Then let us imagine man as a sort of third-world participant in both, in the visible in respect of his body, in the invisible in respect of his soul. In the visible world we are strangers *(peregrini)* and ought never to be at rest, but whatever we experience through our senses we must refer by some apt analogy *(apta quadam collations)* to the angelical world, or (which is more profitable) to the morals of man and that part of him that corresponds to it. What this sun is in the visible world, the divine mind is in the intelligible and in that part of you which is most akin to it, I mean, the spirit.[15]

Erasmus also took over the teaching of the Platonic Socrates that humanity's highest wisdom is to know ourselves,[16] and so he held that, when our eyes are directed inward to self-understanding, they are directed upward to the intelligible world to which we are akin in our spiritual

---

11 See W. H. Woodward (ed.), *Desiderius Erasmus, Concerning the Aim and Method of Education* (New York, 1964), 35ff., 39ff.

12 In some respects Erasmus is the forerunner of Herder and Dilthey, especially in his view of the relation of language to the expression of the culture to which it belongs.

13 See the *Moriae Encomium Declamatio*, 1511 (cf. *Bibliotheca Erasmiana*, 122f.).

14 *Enchiridion* 13 (*Opera Omnia* 5:29).

15 *Enchiridion* 13, p. 27.

16 *Enchiridion* 3, p. 12, and 5, p. 16.

natures. Under the influence of Origen, however, Erasmus thought of humanity's constitution as threefold: flesh, soul and spirit. The flesh is the vile part of us, the spirit that part in which we are in the similitude of God and are united to him, while the soul occupies a place midway between the flesh and the spirit, and which may be carnal or spiritual according as it yields to the influence of the flesh or the spirit.[17]

This combination of Platonic philosophy and Origenistic anthropology had an important influence on Erasmus' hermeneutics, for it directed him to look for the meaning in an inward and purely spiritual experience. He shows some evidence of having studied Plato's *Cratylus* and having adopted from it the notion that words are naturally and mimetically related to the things they signify. But he developed that in his own way. Thus he insisted that even if no likeness between some word and the thing it signified could be discerned, there must be some invisible reason for it other than mere convention, and he tended regularly in his interpretation of letters, whether profane or Christian, to interiorise the meaning—that is, to look not so much to the language as significant of things or events but as expressive of mental states and moral attitudes.[18]

Typical of this whole approach is Erasmus' work *On the Use and Abuse of the Tongue*,[19] for throughout he emphasises the fact that it is the moral personality of the speaker that is determinative in the use of language. God alone perceives what is hidden in our hearts, but the tongue has been given to us for this purpose, that we may get to know the mind and spirit of another through its internuncial function. It is fitting, therefore, that the image should correspond to the archetype. Mirrors reflect *bona fide* the image of the objective reality, but what are called 'lying mirrors' are held up for ridicule. Hence the Son of God who came to earth in order that we might get to know the mind of God through him, wished to be called the *speech* of the Father (*Sermo Patris*), and likewise the *truth* (*Veritas*), because it is extremely base that the tongue should differ from the spirit. God in heaven, how rare among Christians is fidelity of speech (*linguae fides*).[20] Two points may be noted here.

---

17   *Enchiridion* 4, pp. 11f., and 7, pp. 19f.

18   *De pronunciatione* (*Opera Omnia* 1:930); *De ratione concionandi* III (*Opera Omnia* 5:852, 958).

19   *Lingua, sive de linguae usu atque abusu* (*Opera Omnia* 4:657ff.).

20   *Lingua*, p. 691.

1. Erasmus prefers the Augustinian translation *sermo* to *verbum* for the Greek *Logos* applied by the fourth Gospel to the Son of God, for it does not lend itself easily to a misinterpretation in a rational direction. But by *sermo* Erasmus means something rather different from the divine speech which interested Anselm so deeply, the objectivity of God's eternal Word behind the revealed Word. That is not altogether lacking in Erasmus, but with him *sermo* bears a connotation that quickly passes over into *letters*. That is the slant he gives to the classical doctrine of the incarnation of the Word.

> God speaks very rarely and sparingly, but his speaking is supremely true and efficacious. The Father spoke once, and begot his eternal Word. He spoke again, and by his omnipotent Word he founded the whole fabric of this universe. Again he spoke through his prophets through whom he handed on to us sacred books, concealing under a few simple words the immense treasure of divine wisdom. Finally in sending his Son, that is the Word clothed with flesh, he brought forth his speech in a succinct form upon the earth, drawing everything together as if in one epilogue.[21]

The peculiar slant that Erasmus gave to this doctrine comes out particularly clearly in one of the most significant of all his works, his little biography of Jerome,[22] the patristic authority who more than any other was for him the epitome of Christian humanism and sober scholarship. In Jerome, Erasmus found a theological account of the Christian faith that was essentially undogmatic and was mediated through pure and eloquent speech, *bonae litterae*, rather than through the elaboration of sophisticated arguments and definitions such as one finds among the Scholastics, be they Thomist, Scotist, or Occamist. If *dialectica* is needed for the exposition of the Christian faith, what could be better than that of Augustine? But Erasmus himself preferred the *eloquentia* of Jerome, for it is nearer to the kind of speech handed down to us from the apostles.[23]

2. True and healthy speech is that which faithfully reflects the mind of the speaker—hence, both in speaking and in interpreting, it is the relation of the tongue to the heart that is all-important.

---

21 *Lingua*, p. 696. See also *De ratione concionandi* (*Opera Omnia* 5:771f.).

22 *Hieronymi Stridonensis Vita*, ed. W. K. Ferguson, *Erasmi Opuscula, A Supplement to the Opera Omnia* (The Hague, 1933), 134–190.

23 *Hieronymi Stridonensis Vita*, 178ff.

> What the Father is in divine things, who produces his Son out from himself, the mind is in us, for it is the source of our thoughts and speech. As the Son is born of the Father, so in us speech proceeds from our spirit. The Son is said to be the image of the Father, so that he who knows one or the other knows both. In us speech is the mirror of the spirit—hence the famous saying of Socrates, 'Speak that I may see you.' A handsome youth was brought before him, whose appearance bespoke natural ability. But Socrates did not see the youth as long as he was silent, for the spirit does not shine out in the face so much as in the speech. It is not so much from the face as from the tongue that physicians detect the signs of disease. But the surest signs of a healthy spirit, or of a sick spirit, are in the tongue, which is the face of the mind.[24]

Erasmus was convinced that speech, whether in its written or spoken form, derives from the inner depths of the personal being, so that its power for good or evil depends on the veracity or mendacity of the relation between the word and the inward state which it expresses. Thus speech can be corrupted in two ways, either through a false or insincere relation between outward expression and inward conviction, or through inner impurity defiling speech at its source. The Scholastics corrupted biblical speech in the first way, forcing it by their depraved interpretations to lie, and the monks corrupted it in the second way through the impurity of their living.[25] It is the recovery of divine speech through faithful attention to good letters that will allow the healing virtue of God's Word to operate effectively among people. The human tongue may be a source of poison, but (Erasmus cites from Prov. 12:18) 'the tongue of the wise is sanity'. What is needed is a *lingua medica* to cure those infected with a pestilent tongue. That can come only from God: *Emisit sermonem scum et sanavit eos*, as the psalmist declares.[26] It is the function of the biblical expositor to mediate that divine speech to his generation so that through it they may become assimilated in their inward thoughts and spirits to the divine mind and the divine Spirit as imaged in Jesus Christ. It is in him that God has tempered the sublimity of his celestial speech to us and spoken to us more within our capacities so that through hearing and imitating him we may obtain eternal salvation.[27]

24 *Lingua*, p. 698.
25 *Lingua*, pp. 700ff.
26 Ps. 107:20; *De ratione concionandi* I (*Opera Omnia* 5:836).
27 *Lingua*, p. 748.

We are fortunate in having from Erasmus several works on method (in this too, he was decidedly modern) that help us not a little in understanding the principles of his hermeneutics. In addition to the *Enchiridion militis Christiani* of 1503, in which he set forth his program for the recovery of the philosophy of Christ, there are the *De ratione studii ac legendi interpretandique auctores* of 1511, the *Ratio seu compendium verae theologiae* of 1519, and the *Ecclesiastes sive de ratione concionandi* of 1535. We can hardly do better than look at them in that order, drawing from the *Enchiridion* at relevant points.

I. *De Ratione Studii*

The *De ratione studii* is particularly instructive for it sets forth for the ordinary student what Erasmus considered to be the proper method of reading and interpreting authors without having Christian authors particularly in mind, although not all that he has to say here is relevant for us.[28]

The work opens with an important distinction between the knowledge of things (*cognitio rerum*) and the knowledge of words (*cognitio verborum*). If the former is thought to be preferable, it must be remembered that the latter comes first in time and must not be neglected. Since things are known only through verbal signs (*per vocum notas*), he who does not have an expert knowledge of the power of language will be blind in his judgment of things and cannot but suffer delusions. None are more likely to fall into captious arguments anywhere than those who boast that they are concerned with things themselves and not with words.[29] However, when we ask Erasmus what the *cognitio rerum* is, he appears to point only to factual information such as can be acquired from ancient writers on geography or natural science or medicine, and all that is useful for the understanding of classical literature, he says, but he seems to have little understanding of what 'real studies' are. This is characteristic of Erasmus, for all through his works, and not least in his exegetical writings, he stops short of penetrating through language to an objective knowledge of the realities denoted. That in turn radically affects his interpretation.

---

28 *Opera Omnia* 1:522–30. See Woodward, ed., *Desiderius Erasmus ... Education*, 162ff.

29 *De ratione studii*, p. 522.

The Hermeneutics of Erasmus

Erasmus makes it clear, then, that grammar must have the first place in the order of our studies (in this he includes Greek and Latin). He insists, in contrast to the mediaeval grammarians, that the proper method of mastering grammar is not through rules and definitions but through reading the classical authors themselves. Only grammar acquired in that way will be appropriate for their interpretation. The rules of grammatical structure, of prosody and rhetoric, are important because they help us to appreciate the styles of the authors and to develop a precision in the study of their characteristic use of expressions, archaisms, and figures of speech. Logic, of course, has its place, but dialectic is no guide to the understanding of style. What is important is that the interpreter must steep himself in the literature he is studying, and there is no better way to become acquainted with it than to teach it, for then we discover how much we really do and do not know.[30]

In turning to the content of the ancient literature, Erasmus lays stress on the study of history[31] and of proverbs or *adagia*.[32] What Erasmus has to say about these sheds not a little light on his fundamental approach to literature and its interpretation. Erasmus' attitude to history is highly ambiguous. He is deeply committed to the movement of return to the sources of Western civilization in the Classical culture of Greece and Rome, and he applies that throughout to his understanding of Christianity, probing into its historical origins as one can see very clearly by the way in which he treats the problems of the text of the New Testament.[33] He was capable of writing a historical biography of Jerome in which he insisted on using only original sources and allowing them to call into question the tradition about Jerome that had become overlaid with legend and fictitious story.[34] But when Erasmus comes to speak of *historia* itself he reveals what W. H. Woodward has called 'an entire absence of historical perspective'.[35]

---

30 *De ratione studii*, p. 522.

31 *De ratione studii*, p. 523.

32 *De ratione studii*, p. 525. The immense importance of this for Erasmus' conception of literature is apparent from his own laborious collections of proverbs published in the different editions of his *Adagia*, of 1500 and after, to which the entire vol. III of the *Opera Omnia* is devoted.

33 Cf., for example, the discussion of the opening verses of the Acts of the Apostles, *Opera Omnia* 6:433.

34 *Erasmi Opuscula*, 134ff. Cf. the remarks of Ferguson, op. cit., 129f.

35 Woodward, ed., *Desiderius Erasmus. Education*, 130. Cf. *De rerum copia* II (*Opera Omnia* 1:106), where Erasmus points out that historical writers are allowed to

Historical writing is looked on only as a form of literature, to be included, in fact, under the general umbrella of *grammatica*[36] and to be valued mainly for the fact that historical narratives illustrate moral and spiritual truth.[37] That is to say, the importance of historical narrative lies not in its direct but in its oblique sense.

That is why Erasmus laid such great stress on proverbs, parables, allegories, and myths, for it is in the tropical turns of speech that not only natural phenomena but profane and even crude narratives may be made to yield 'something divine', i.e. timeless truth or a moral or spiritual nature.[38] He applied this method of interpretation not only to the Classical authors such as Homer and Vergil but also to the historians and philosophers. To cite Woodward again:

> Unfortunately Erasmus did not confine himself to considering the particular 'allegorical' interpretations which may have been intended by Plato or Vergil, he opened the door to floods of arbitrary glosses and moral lessons such as the mediaevalists had applied to all departments of thought. On the other hand this should be said. The allegorical method is the intermediate stage between a conscious antinomy and its historical solution. ... The historical attitude being impossible, the allegory was the only instrument of reconciliation. But such allegories rested upon no critical basis, they were at the disposal of the ingenious mind, and could take any form which the exigencies of the argument required. Hence to the neutral inquirer, with no specific cause to advance, such a method served to bring to light, rather than to solve, the problem to which it was applied.[39]

We shall have to return later to Erasmus' use of allegory in the interpretation of the biblical documents, but our interest at the moment lies in his idea that attention must be directed to the style and form of the author's diction, to his use of language, his elegance of phrase, rhetorical devices, and above all to his use of metaphorical or tropical turns of speech in order to let

---

invent speeches, for nothing is more admirable for their purpose, but he doubts whether Christians may do this.

36 *De ratione concionandi* II, p. 853.

37 *De ratione studii*, p. 523. Hence he can even say: '*Sunt qui Novi Testamenti historiam ad allegoriam trahunt: quad ego sane vehementer approbo*' (*Ratio verae theologiae* V, p. 125).

38 *De ratione concionandi*, pp. 865, 1028f.

39 Woodward, *Desiderius Erasmus ... Education*, 49f.

them serve as clues to guide our intuitive penetration into the mind and individuality of the author. '*Postremo ad philosophiam veniat et poetarum fabulas apte trahat ad mores, vel tanquam exempla, ut Pyladis et Orestis, ad amicitiae commendationem, Tantali fabulam ad avaritiae detestationem.*'[40]

A more succinct account of how Erasmus advises study of some classical piece of writing is given in the *De conscribendis epistolic*, where he suggests a fourfold reading.[41] An initial reading is necessary in order to inform oneself of the general point of view. A second reading should follow in which care is taken to examine grammatical structure and individual words and sentence forms. Then the third reading ought to be directed to an investigation of the rhetorical devices and characteristic features of the composition. The interpreter must inquire into the author's mind and his reasons for the language used; but if he finds himself deeply moved, he must keep his feet on the ground and calmly assess his emotional reaction to find out what is the occasion for it and why he has not reacted in the same way to others. If he comes across some adage or proverb or anything similar, let him appropriate it and make use of it for himself. In a final reading, however, consideration must be given to anything that admits of practical or philosophical use, and especially to any instance that can serve a moral end. But, further, discussion of the text with others will help the interpreter to revise his judgment and correct his understanding.

Quite clearly this method of interpretation is fraught with serious danger, for in spite of the fact that it requires such a serious and thorough examination of what is actually said, the concentration on the style and the aesthetic form, and the employment of the interpreter's prior intent as the ultimate guide to understanding, can lead only too easily to a reading out of the author what the interpreter wants to find in him. That is particularly apparent when Erasmus seizes on the adages or myths as the instrument through which to open up the inner meaning of what is written. He takes the myth of Narcissus as an example, for it is a striking parable of the truth that supreme love goes together with the greatest similarity or affinity. Narcissus caught sight of himself in a fountain of limpid water and was immediately inflamed with love for what he saw. 'What is more like ourselves than our image?' Erasmus asks. 'Therefore when one man of learning loves another man of learning, he loves nothing else but his own image in the other, yet in

---

40 *De ratione studii*, p. 527.
41 *Opera Omnia*, xxx I, pp. 447f.

another sort of way. So it is also with the sober, the modest, or the upright man, each is attracted to his own kind.'[42]

Although Erasmus had profane authors in mind here, it is his own extremely sympathetic study of Jerome that provides about the best example of this method of interpretation. Quite clearly he was attracted to Jerome by the reflection of himself in him. What he had to say of him and of his method was important for Erasmus, therefore, as a sort of *apologia pro vita sua*. One can certainly appreciate that in the interpretation of Jerome, but what about the application of this method to Paul or John or Peter? Erasmus' views of the right way in which to apply this approach to the Scriptures were set forth initially in the *Enchiridion*, to which we must now turn to supplement what he had to say in the *De ratione studii*.

Three things guide his handling of biblical texts.

1. Erasmus has a profound reverence for the sacred Scriptures; they come from God and must be handled with humility. It is like the manna that came down from heaven and was given in small quantities—that is to say, the Scriptures have come by inspiration from God, but divine truth is communicated to us through them in a humble and lowly way, for under the homeliness, under rude words, are included great mysteries. This is not the doctrine of mortals, which is vitiated by error, but the teaching of Christ, which is altogether pure and bright and clean.[43]

> Therefore you must always remember that the divine letters are not to be handled except by cleansed hands, that is, with the greatest purity of spirit, lest that which is given to you as an antidote may be turned into poison, and the manna start to putrify if you do not take it into your innermost affections. First of all, then, you must have a high regard for the scriptures, thinking of them as the very oracles that have come out from the sanctuary of the divine Mind. You will then feel yourself moved by divine power, formed and carried away, and changed in an indescribable way, if you approach the scriptures religiously, with veneration and humility.[44]

2. Because the teaching of Christ which we hear in the Scriptures is essentially simple and unsophisticated, we must bring to the reading of the text the simple and bright eye, the purity of heart and faith of which the Gospel speaks; that is to say, we must govern our life by the rule and pattern of the

---

42 *De ratione studii*, pp. 527f.
43 *Enchiridion militis Christiani* (*Opera Omnia* 5:6f).
44 *Enchiridion*, prefatory epistle (CCCXXIX) (*Opera Omnia* 3:340f.).

love of Christ if we are to hear what he has to teach us, letting him always occupy the central point in all our relations with him and with others.[45] This means that we have to renounce the sophistications which we are tempted to bring to the text, for they can only corrupt our understanding of it—they derive either from false dialectics or from false affections, in which we seek to wrest the Scripture to serve our own ambition and to bolster up our own aims. Erasmus admits that the teaching of the Scriptures in this way is a perilous undertaking, for it cuts across so many interests and concerns to which others have given themselves, and rouses their hostility.[46]

3. Essentially simple though the divine teaching or the philosophy of Christ is, it is hidden in the Gospels and Epistles of the apostles behind strange and extremely difficult forms of expression, figures and oblique turns of speech (*figurae tropique obliqui*), so that we often have the utmost difficulty with what is actually written before we can perceive the real meaning. This sends us to study the most approved interpreters of the Scriptures, to aid us in acquiring a brief and simple summary of Christ's philosophy to serve as a regular guide in interpretation. Study and read again and again, Erasmus says, chiefly the old doctors and expositors, and choose especially those who go farthest from the letter of the Scripture, such as Origen, Ambrose, Jerome and Augustine.[47]

The chief conviction that appears to determine Erasmus' handling of the Scriptures is this:

> the Spirit of God has His own tongue and His own figures of speech which you must get to know above all through diligent observation. The divine Wisdom prattles to us like some obliging mother, accommodating His words to our infancy. He gives milk to infants in Christ, soft food to the weak. Do you therefore hurry on with your growth, and advance to solid food. God's Wisdom has stooped down to your lowliness, but you must rise up to His sublimity.[48]

The way to do that, Erasmus goes on to say, is to break the shell and dig into the marrow—that is to say, to break through the 'letter' or the 'flesh' into

---

45 *Enchiridion*, prefatory epistle, pp. 339f.
46 *Enchiridion*, prefatory epistle, p. 339.
47 *Enchiridion* II, p. 8.
48 *Enchiridion* II, p. 8. Cf. *Responsio ad notationes Eduardi Lei in Mattaeum* (*Opera Omnia* 4:140).

Divine Interpretation

spiritual knowledge, for the 'letter' kills but the 'spirit' quickens and gives life. Spiritual things must be compared with spiritual things.

> Do you therefore who are endowed with a productive mind (*ingenio tam felici praeditus*) resolutely refuse to linger in the sterile letter, but hasten on to more hidden mysteries, and as a help to your constant endeavour add frequent prayers until He who has the key of David opens for you the book sealed with seven seals— He who shuts up the secrets of the Father which no man opens, for no one knows the Father but the Son and he to whom the Son has willed to reveal Him.[49]

It is worth noting that Erasmus considers this to be only an adaptation of the method which is to be adopted in the interpretation of profane literature. What is basic to both is the distinction between the body and the soul, the letter and the spirit, so that interpretation must advance beyond the literal sense to the inward or oblique meaning. This applies, he says, to all poets and philosophers, and principally to the followers of Plato, but most of all to Holy Scripture, which like the Silenus of Alcibiades under a rude and foolish exterior presents divine and holy things—but they are to be interpreted therefore as allegorical statements.[50] The Scripture and even the Gospel have their flesh and their spirit, and it would be folly to stick in the flesh and not penetrate beyond to the spirit.

> What is the difference then between your reading the book of Kings or of Judges in the Old Testament and your reading of Titus Livy, if you pay no attention to the allegory in either? In the latter there is much that amends common behaviour, and in the former there are some things which appear quite absurd, but which if understood superficially, will hurt behaviour, such as David's theft, adultery with homicide, etc. Therefore, despising the flesh of the Scripture, especially of the Old Testament, make it your point to search out the mystery of the spirit.[51]

Erasmus is aware, however, that this kind of investigation must be controlled, else it will become quite arbitrary, and so he insists that 'in digging for mysteries, you must not follow the conjectures of your own mind, but you must learn the method and the art which Dionysius has handed down in his book *De divinis nominibus* and St Augustine in his

---

49 *Enchiridion*, p. 9.
50 *Enchiridion* 13, p. 29.
51 *Enchiridion* 13, p. 29.

De doctrina Christiana. After Christ it was St Paul who opened up certain sources of allegory, and it was He whom Origen followed, and in that part of theology is easily supreme.'[52] The mediaeval theologians certainly concerned themselves with allegorical interpretation, but they treated it quite unfruitfully, because they lost the art of eloquence and were content to follow only Aristotle, throwing out the followers of Plato and Pythagoras although they were preferred by Augustine.[53]

When Erasmus applies the same procedure to the New Testament, he insists that even there a distinction must be drawn between the flesh of the Gospel and the spirit—the body without the spirit, he says, can have no being, but the spirit of the body is in need of nothing. It is Paul who teaches us to have no confidence in the flesh.[54] This cannot be taken to mean that Erasmus despised the historical acts of the incarnate Son, in the life, death, and resurrection of Jesus, but rather that we must seek to be assimilated to the inward revelation of God mediated to us in that way—learning to hear inwardly God's Word (*intus audire verbum Dei*), for the Lord speaks His Word inwardly (*Dominus intus dicit verbum*).[55]

Another way he has of expressing this is to speak of it as the image of the divine Mind, or the image of Christ's mind to which we must be assimilated if we are to interpret the Gospels properly. 'You honour the image of Christ's face formed in stone or wood, or portrayed with colours. Much more religiously ought you to honour the image of His Mind which by the operation of the Holy Spirit is expressed in the language of the Gospels.'[56] That is the essential thing for Erasmus, the interiorizing of the Gospel, the contemplation of the beauty and serenity of the Spirit of Christ as it is represented in the simplicity of the evangelical truth, and through that contemplation the assimilation of the mind of the interpreter to 'the spirit and pattern of His divine mind.'[57] He thinks of that movement as parallel to that which Plato had in mind when he spoke of the wings which spring up in our spirits through love of the truth.

> Move upward, then, from the body to the spirit, from the visible world to the invisible, from the letter to the mystery, from

---

52 *Enchiridion* 13, p. 29.
53 *Enchiridion* 13, p. 29.
54 *Enchiridion*, p. 30.
55 *Enchiridion* 13, pp. 37f.
56 *Enchiridion* 13, pp. 31f.
57 *Enchiridion*, p. 32.

sensible things to intelligible realities, from complicated things to simplicities, raise yourself upward as with the certain steps of Jacob's ladder. If you draw near in that way, the Lord in His turn will draw near to you. If you try with all your strength to rise up out of your darkness and the confusion of your senses, He will accommodate Himself to you and come to meet you out of His inaccessible light and unthinkable silence in which not only all the tumults of the senses but the images of all the intelligible realities cease and become silent.[58]

In view of statements like this, which are by no means isolated, it is impossible to agree with many writers who declare that Erasmus had little or no mystical side to his nature or his faith. The influence of Dionysius and Augustine on him was immense, although he kept it in control—or, to use his own expression, he kept his feet on the ground. The problem is rather how far he allowed this Origenist and Augustinian notion, that we must transcend even the flesh or 'carnal history' of Jesus in order to attain to the heights of divine Revelation, to affect his exegesis of the evangelical records and his interpretation of the Gospel itself. Certainly, in the debate over his use of *sermo* to interpret the Johannine *logos* he made it clear that the divine speech which was made flesh and which we hear in the Gospels is not something passing or transient—'*sermo non est temporarius quemadmodum noster, sed aeternus*'.[59] For a fuller answer to the problem we have to turn to the other two main works of Erasmus which we have selected for discussion.

II. *Ratio seu Methodus Compendio Perveniendi ad Veram Theologiam*

This was originally written as a short statement on method (*Ratio seu compendium verae theologiae*) to act as a preface for Erasmus' edition of the New Testament in 1516. But it was greatly enlarged for the second edition of 1519 *et seq.* (with the extended title given above) and really became one of his most important works, if only because it initiated a series of works on theological method from Reformed and Lutheran theologians later on in the century. Although it can stand alone, and has been published separately,

---

58 *Enchiridion*, pp. 38f.
59 *Apologia pro in Principio erat Serino* (*Opera Omnia*, 9:117).

The Hermeneutics of Erasmus

much of its significance lies in its immediate relation to the text of the New Testament and its explication.[60]

Erasmus recalls right away the works of Augustine, *De doctrina Christiana*, and of Dionysius, not only the *De divinis nominibus* but the *De mystica theologia* and the *De significativa theologia*, but without wishing to contradict them; he has other things to put forward. The first thing he demands is a tranquil and quiet spirit in order that the image of the eternal truth may shine more distinctly in the interpreter as in a placid stream or in a smooth and clean mirror. No admission to divine colloquy may be gained without cleansing and purification. The eye of faith must be single and characterised by simplicity if it is to discern celestial things. The only entrance into the royal secrets of heaven is through a lowly door; all that is inimical to the truth, such as the love of fame, arrogance, or impious curiosity, must be left behind. Far from trusting his own judgment, the interpreter must allow himself to be formed and shaped by what he learns.[61] Every human discipline has its own aim which it must disentangle from those of others if it is to be carried out properly. Likewise with theological studies: 'This is your first and only aim, this is your commitment, this is the one thing you are to do, to be changed, to be carried away, to be fashioned, to be transformed into what you learn.'[62]

This requires discipline as well as prayer and great diligence. First of all, it is necessary to learn the three languages—Hebrew, Greek and Latin—for without languages we cannot read and understand what we read; but it also requires incessant study of the ancient expositors and doctors and a copious supply of information drawn from the classical cultures, without the distortion of foolish questions and problems elaborated in disjunction from the actual subject matter we are investigating. There can, of course, be no Christian theology without grammar and dialectic; but once we have mastered all these tools, we have to put them to proper use within the perspective and objective of theological study, and then to that we must bend all our powers like some athlete in the games.[63]

It is certainly the question of aim or objective, the *scopus*, that Erasmus makes primary in this treatise, for everything depends on getting

---

60 *Opera Omnia* 1:75–138

61 *Ratio seu methodus*, p. 76.

62 *Ratio seu methodus*, p. 77: 'Hic primus et unicus tibi est scopus, hoc votum, hoc unum age, ut muteris, ut rapiaris, ut affleris, ut transformeris in ea quae discis.'

63 *Ratio seu methodus*, pp. 77–84.

Divine Interpretation

the perspective right and developing the kind of method appropriate to the nature of the subject matter. The one and only objective is Jesus Christ, and that must be considered objectively and subjectively. He is himself our frame of reference, so that everything in theological studies and in Christian things must be referred to him as the one center of all (*omnium unicum centrum*). We ourselves have to be directed to him so that it belongs to our objective to be assimilated to him, to grow up in him into the measure of his fullness.[64] It is characteristic of Erasmus that these two aspects should be held together. The devotion of the exegete to Christ in the center carries with it the renunciation of all alien philosophies, the shedding of our own unreality and hypocrisy, the readiness to live in accordance with what is learned from Christ, and throughout all a passionate devotion to the subject, sacred letters and in and through them Christ himself.

As Erasmus sees it, the determination and clarification of the *scopus* are essential to proper interpretation, but interpretation is needed to clarify and determine the *scopus*. These two activities have to proceed side by side. After the initial clearing of the ground, and the preparation of a brief summary (*summa*, or *compendium*) of the general trend of the teaching of the New Testament, that can be used as a working guide for the longer task of drawing out in fuller detail the main elements that form the contents of the Christian message.[65]

In the initial activity of clarifying and determining the *scopus*, particular attention must be paid to what is actually said, by whom it is said, to whom it is said, by what words and at what time, and on what occasion, to what precedes and to what follows each passage elucidated.[66] Note must be taken of 'the distinction of times' if we are not to run into confusion, especially in the relation of the teaching of the Old Testament to that of the New.[67] But it is as we are able to develop our narration of the contents in series of expositions that we will find that the more obscure passages and doctrines have light thrown on them from others which are clearer. It often happens that, when we try to explicate the meaning of the words, we clarify the meaning of the sentences, but the reverse is also true.[68] But it is

---

64 *Ratio seu methodus*, pp. 84, 88.
65 *Ratio seu methodus*, p. 84.
66 *Ratio seu methodus*, pp. 85, 128.
67 *Ratio seu methodus*, pp. 86–88; *De ratione concionandi* IV, pp. 1075f.
68 *Novum Testamentum* i (*Opera Omnia* 6).

The Hermeneutics of Erasmus

as the *scopus* becomes clearer to us that we will find obscurity vanishing.[69] Thus a certain order of authority or importance in the unity and variety of the books of the Bible will become apparent if they are looked at from a center in Christ, their *scopus*. Erasmus considers, for example, that Isaiah should be set before Esther, and that Matthew should have precedence over the Apocalypse, and Paul's epistle to the Romans over the epistle to the Hebrews, and so forth. In this way the variety does not lead to confusion but ministers rather to fullness of understanding.[70]

The major bulk of the *Ratio seu methodus* is given over to the task of drawing out the main teaching of the New Testament insofar as it affects the procedure to be adopted in exposition and interpretation; that is to say, Erasmus is keenly aware of the fact that the actual subject matter must be allowed to influence the method to be used in its elucidation. But far from taking the form of a *summa* of dogmatic principles, this summary takes the form of an unfolding through narration of the essential teaching of the New Testament. This is for Erasmus primarily a descriptive rather than an explicatory task. Divine things, as he has said elsewhere, are more to be indicated than explained (*'magis indicanda sunt quam explicanda'*).[71]

Along with this, however, goes the problem of bringing out the inner spiritual meaning of the New Testament, and since 'almost the whole speech of Christ is oblique with figures and tropes' (*'totus sermo Christi sarmo figuris ac tropis obliquus est'*), care must be given to allegorical interpretation as the instrument through which the oblique sense is drawn out.[72] This does not mean that Erasmus despises the historical sense, for he regards it rather as the foundation for allegory.[73] No allegorical interpretations can be allowed which are only a pretext for the accommodation of Scripture to some philosophy, but only those which are in accordance with the demands of the subject matter.[74] On the other hand, Erasmus insists once again that the truth is to be found in allegories which make up almost the whole of Scripture through which the divine wisdom prattles with us, as it were (*'per*

---

69 *Ratio seu methodus*, pp. 85, 89, 131.

70 *Ratio seu methodus*, pp. 91f.

71 *Apologia ad Jacobum Fabrum* (*Opera Omnia* 9:51).

72 *Ratio seu methodus*, pp. 85f.

73 See *De anthill ecclesias concordia* (*Opera omnia* 5:470: *'Nec oportet historicism sensum reiicere, quo locus fiat allegoriae, quum ille sit huius basis et fundamentum, qui cognitus facit, ut aptius tractetur intelligentia retrustior ac mystica'.*

74 *Ratio seu methodus*, p. 126.

quam aeterna sapientia nobiscum veluti balbutit'). Quite often the open meaning is quite false—indeed ridiculous and absurd—if the sense of the words is accepted in a straightforward way.[75] Allegorical interpretation, however, is not to be used to develop fantastic doctrines but rather to help us penetrate beneath the common sense to a deeper meaning ('*a communi sensu ad sensum penitiorem*') which is the truest and the most salubrious.[76]

A disciplined treatment of allegory will follow the rules laid down by the classical interpreters, such as the seven rules of Tychonius as expounded by Augustine.[77] Every passage must be examined carefully for itself, no biblical testimony is to be torn out of its context and distorted in order to justify some extraneous notion, and the meaning which is taken out of obscure words must answer to the whole orb of Christian doctrine, to the Christian life and to natural equity. If we use the sacred writings in this way, they will minister salvation. Nothing is worse than playing with divine Scripture or abusing the mystical words in scurrilous jokes.[78] Erasmus is convinced that a great deal of misinterpretation and distortion can be avoided if the interpreter is himself a man of moral integrity and sincerity who puts his investigation of the Holy Writings to a spiritual and ethical end, and keeps in front of him the true *scopus* to which the whole of the Scripture is directed.[79]

III. *Ecclesiastes Sive de Ratione Concionandi*

This work was written not so much for the scholar as for the preacher of the gospel (*concionator evangelicus*) and must be taken to represent Erasmus' mature views, for it appeared in 1535 not long before his death.[80] There is much here that we have already discussed and need not repeat, and much more that does not concern us, which we must leave aside. We single out three principal elements that have a contribution to make to our study.

1. The whole work is prefaced with a discussion of the relation between the incarnate Word and the incomprehensible Speech (*Sermo*) of God, for Erasmus is aware that it is the mighty power that lies behind faithful

---

75 *Ratio seu methodus*, p. 124.
76 *Ratio seu methodus*, p. 119.
77 See also *De ratione concionandi* III, pp. 1058ff.
78 *Ratio seu methodus*, pp. 131ff.
79 *Ratio seu methodus*, pp. 134f.
80 *Opera Omnia* 5:770–1100.

preaching of the Gospel. Christ is the sole Word of God who expounds him and reveals him. He is the omnipotent Speech of God who is without beginning and without end, and who eternally proceeds from the heart of the Father. Through him the Father has made all things, governs all things; through him the fallen race of man is restored and the Church is united to himself. Through him in a wonderful and indescribable way he wished to make known to the world, that through him he would quicken the dead, pour out the gifts of the Holy Spirit, add his secret energy to the sacraments of the Church; through him he will judge the world, separating the goats from the sheep, and make a new heaven and a new earth, and inspire the citizens of the Heavenly Jerusalem, and fill them with his riches. He is the incomprehensible Speech of God, the surest Expositor of the divine Mind; at no point is there any discrepancy between him and the Archetype of the *Summa Veritas*. It is through him that the eternal divine Mind has miraculously spoken to the created world, and in manifold ways to us by the prophets. Through him he has spoken to us most distinctly, in his mission on earth, as man born of man, so that now he may not only be heard but perceived with our senses and handled with our hands.

Just as the speech of man is the truthful image of his mind and does not proceed from man apart from his spirit—for as his speech is so is his spirit—so Christ the incarnate Word proceeds from the Father as his omnipotent Speech, revealing the divine Mind that transcends all that we can think or imagine. He is the *Sermo* of God, his image and his voice. He it is who dwells with us by his Spirit and speaks himself to us. Hence the tongue of the preacher has no other efficacy than that which derives from the Spirit of Christ dwelling in his heart, governing his speech and adding to his uttered words hidden power. The voice of the preacher reaches the ears of the hearers, but it is God alone who by his secret force transforms men's minds. Jesus Christ is the Way, the Truth, and the Life, God speaking through his Son, Christ himself speaking to liberate the world from error.[81]

That would appear to be as exalted a view of the proclaimed Word as one can find anywhere in the Reformation. In spite of his opposition to what he regarded as the more tumultuous aspects of the movement for reform, and his failure to think out the profound implications of what he himself narrated of the Gospel, Erasmus was gripped by the power of the living, active Word of God and realised that that was the power and reality with which we have to do in the interpreting and proclaiming of the evangelical

---

81 *De ratione concionandi* I, pp. 772f.

message. It is not surprising that Erasmus as well as Luther should leave his mark on John Calvin, who published the first edition of his *Institutio* in the year following the *De ratione concionandi*.

2. In this work Erasmus shows more evidence of taking seriously the relation of speech to the realities it is employed to denote. Thus he insists that the meaning of words, even in their transferred sense, is not to be taken from the words themselves considered as names (in the Platonic sense) but rather from their relation to the realities which they denote.[82] He is apparently aware, too, that words may denote more than they can express, as we can see in the use of emphasis.[83] But more important is the suggestion that, in expounding the Scriptures, the preacher should expound the Scriptures in accordance with the order (*ordo, consequentia, tenor consequentium*) which the Scripture itself supplies, which reminds us of the insistence of Athanasius that in interpretation it is the sequence or connection of the actual content of a passage, rather than that manifested by the words, that must be followed.[84] Elsewhere Erasmus insists that while words and meanings are related to one another like body and soul, it is the sequence of meaning (*sententia*) that must be brought out in a translation rather than the word-for-word sequence of the original text.[85] That is well illustrated by his *Paraphrases* on the New Testament, where he insists, as he says, in bringing his own thoughts to the rule of what is revealed in the text rather than the other way around.[86] The paraphrase is thus a method of bringing out the meaning of the text through constructing an amplified sequence of thought that brings out as fully as possible the sequence lying behind the grammatical sense of the Scriptures.

Yet this remains the great weakness of Erasmus' hermeneutics, for he cannot get beyond a descriptive, paraphrastic interpretation. As soon as he comes up against the realities denoted by the language of the New Testament, he tends to draw back and take refuge in a purely literary exposition. Thus his spiritual and theological judgments are never very profound. He was content as an interpreter to present the evangelical narrative as far as he could, freed from the glosses which had obscured it in the Dark and Middle Ages, with the confidence that the inherent power and truth of God's Word

---

82 *De ratione concionandi* I, pp. 796f.; II, p. 852; III,, p. 958.

83 *De ratione concionandi* III, p. 1005.

84 *De ratione concionandi* III, pp. 953, 1019, 1026f., etc.; of the *Apologia*, xx2, to the *Novum Testamentum* (*Opera Omnia* 6).

85 *Contra morosos quosdam ac indoctos* (*Opera Omnia* 6, xx6).

86 *Tomus primus paraphraseum in Novum 'Testamentum*, 1523, p. a5.

would leave their impact on the reader. To the end he rejects dialectic as useless in biblical exposition.[87]

3. Erasmus offers here a more careful and critical account of the relation between the historical sense and the spiritual sense of Holy Scripture. As in the *Ratio verae theologiae*,[88] he accepts the fourfold sense that was held by the Fathers and the Schoolmen, the grammatical or historical, the tropological, the allegorical, and the anagogical, although he related the allegorical or parabolic more to doctrine. But he clearly prefers the simpler twofold distinction by the ancient Fathers, between the grammatical, or literal, or historical, and the spiritual.[89]

It is the natural or direct sense (*germanus sive rectus sensus*) of Scripture that is the primary one, and therefore it is to it first of all that attention must be directed. It is the foundation for everything else and must not be subverted in the slightest. If the basis is crooked, everything else will be distorted. But the Scriptures do not just have a human sense, and they are seriously distorted if their meaning is reduced to that. They have a spiritual sense, which, so far as the language used is concerned, is tropical or allegorical; but if this spiritual sense is to be grasped and expounded aright, it cannot be torn away from the natural sense, for it serves the natural sense. If it does not serve it, it is to be rejected; but if it does serve it, it cannot be rejected. The direct sense taken by itself may well be quite absurd, and therefore needs the spiritual sense even to be an acceptable direct sense. It is adherence to the direct or natural sense that prevents us from being 'lords of the Scripture' and checks our use of allegorical interpretation, so that it does not become a violent instrument in our hands with which we make the Scriptures say what we want them to say. When we do that, we convert divine authority into human authority.[90]

Erasmus points out that frequently the Scriptures use words which have a natural meaning in the profane world or in ordinary life, but when they are applied to divine things their meaning necessarily undergoes a modification. It is that change from the ordinary natural sense (*germanus sensus*) that he has in mind when he speaks of the spiritual sense. To use these terms as if there were not that change or modification in their meaning would be quite abhorrent. It is the true sense of the Scripture (*verus*

---

87 *De ratione concionandi* II, p. 906.
88 *Ratio seu methodus*, pp. 127f.
89 *De ratione concionandi* III, pp. 1034f.
90 *De ratione concionandi* II, p. 906.

Scripturae sensus) that we must seek to elucidate.[91] But biblical statements have a depth of meaning into which we must probe, and that is the purpose of the fourfold sense. Rightly taken, that does not bring confusion but reveals the fertility of the Scripture, i.e. that it is always pointing out to us far more than can be expressed directly in human speech.[92] Holy Scripture has an inexhaustible depth of meaning.[93]

Erasmus is clearly more anxious than ever to point out the dangers of tropical exegesis, for it lends itself so easily to violent treatment. Even Jerome, he points out, was sometimes violent in his interpretation of the Scriptures, forcing passages to bear a meaning that were not germane to them and were not properly indicated by them.[94] What we must try to disentangle is the metaphorical element in scriptural statements, for metaphor, he says, is the source of all allegorical and tropical meanings, and if we can discern how the allegorical moment arises necessarily out of the actual sense, we have a method in which to check and control allegorical interpretation.[95] It is for this reason that Erasmus likes the simplicity of the twofold sense (*geminus sensus*) which we treat in such a way that we allow the underlying reality (*alētheia*) to break through into manifestation (*dēlōsis*).[96] Although he does not say so, that stands much nearer to the analogical understanding of biblical language advocated by Thomas.[97] He insists, however, on drawing a firm line at the anagogical sense, for at the point where our human speech in the Bible points up to what utterly transcends us, it breaks off, and it is impossible—indeed, irrational—to attempt to go farther.[98] We must keep to a *sobria mediocritas* in all determination of allegorical or typical

---

91 *De ratione concionandi* III, pp. 1019f.; 1028f., cf. *Lingua* IV, pp. 700f.

92 *De ratione concionandi* III, pp. 1020, 1026.

93 *De ratione concionandi* III, pp. 1026f.

94 *De ratione concionandi* III, pp. 1029, 1031. He points to Origen as a good example of an interpreter. 'He did not derive his allegories from the philosophers, or from the Talmud or the Cabala, or out of the dreams of his own head, but out of the scriptures themselves, comparing passage with passage.' 1. *Origenes Libros censuriae* (Opera Omnia 8:440).

95 *De ratione concionandi* III, pp. 1033ff.

96 *De ratione concionandi* I, p. 796.

97 *De ratione concionandi* III, p. 1061, where Erasmus refers to Augustine's distinction between the *aetiological* and *analogical* treatment of Scripture in the *De utilitate credendi*, 5–8.

98 *De ratione concionandi* III, pp. 1037f.

meanings.[99] The art of allegorical interpretation is a gift of the Spirit called *prophecy*, but it must be kept in control.[100]

But there are the other tests and checks which we must apply. Everything must be made to point to Christ as the center and scope of the biblical revelation, and nothing can be derived from this or that passage by allegorical interpretation that in any way conflicts with the doctrines established from the whole body of the biblical teaching.[101] Every statement which we deduce by this means which conflicts with the dogmas of the faith must be rejected.[102]

Toward the end of the work Erasmus makes a distinction which once again recalls the teaching of Athanasius. In Christ there are three natures, he says, body and soul according to his human nature, and his divine nature.[103] When we understand the meaning of the Holy Scripture on that basis, we have to distinguish between a bodily sense and a spiritual sense and, over against them, the divine sense to which both the bodily and the spiritual senses of the Scripture point. Although this is not the way in which Erasmus used to think, his point of view might be expounded by saying that what he was concerned to reject here was an Apollinarian exegesis of the Scriptures, i.e. the elimination of the human mind in it which is assimilated to the divine Mind without vanishing into it. That may well be the element of truth for which Erasmus was constantly fighting in his championing of a Christian humanism in the interpretation of sacred letters. But if so, he should have gone further in his doctrine that God prattles to us in our human speech,[104] by saying that the human speech with which God's Word is clothed is so united to the divine Speech that it is, so to speak, the most powerful sacramental reality and force in the life of the Church. That is to say, he might have gone on to relate the doctrine of the consubstantiality of the human nature of Christ in an applied form to the Word of God heard in the Holy Scripture, but that was precisely the explosive thing about Luther's doctrine of the Word which shook Erasmus and made him hesitate and draw back. He was not prepared for the full consequences that the Reformation doctrine of the Word contained.

99   *De ratione concionandi* III, p. 1043.
100 *De ratione concionandi* I, p. 825.
101 *De ratione concionandi* III, pp. 1043ff., 1047f., 1056.
102 *De ratione concionandi* III, p. 1054.
103 *De ratione concionandi* III, p. 1057.
104 *De ratione concionandi* IV, pp. 1072f.

But it must be said that Erasmus did not appreciate the problems in their real depth, for he failed entirely to see that the tropical exegesis which he advocated in deflecting the direct sense of the New Testament message could not but lead to a tropical theology of the acts of God in Christ—that is, to the menacing error which appeared in so many different forms in the early church and which Athanasius, whom Erasmus appreciated so much, had to contend with throughout his whole life, against Arians and semi-Arians, against Macedonians and Tropici. Now a form of this same error was raised again by Erasmus through a tropical exegesis that was detached from the dialectical control imposed on it by the Thomists. The ancient battles had to be fought all over again. That is why, when Calvin came upon the theological scene, he rigorously opposed all forms of allegorical and tropical exegesis and championed the *homoousion* in its application to the communication of divine Revelation and Grace.

How, then, are we to assess Erasmus' contribution to the development of biblical hermeneutics?

There can be no doubt that he did immense service in clearing the ground of the rank growth of gloss, invention and sophism which derived from the mixture of mystical sense and irrelevant dialectics. He turned the eyes of Christendom back to the ancient scholars of the Church and through them forced the Church to look again at its historical origins. He uncovered the text of the New Testament and at the same time supplied the tools of exegesis, and he took at least the first major steps toward its elucidation. The importance of his annotations on the text of the Gospels, Acts and the epistles can hardly be exaggerated; for centuries they continued to force scholars to face up to what the text actually said, and by comparing the views of the classical interpreters brought some real measure of objectivity into the judgment of the serious reader. In this work he opened up the avenues of historical criticism and reconstruction, at least so far as the establishing of the original text was concerned, and so called in question the habit of interpreting through adding layer on layer of ecclesiastical opinion to the biblical documents. His rigid adherence to the descriptive or narrative and paraphrastic method of elucidation helped considerably to enable the Church to interpret the Scriptures out of themselves, without forcing them into alien moulds in order to make their meaning relevant to the ongoing life of the Church and the world around it.

At the same time Erasmus realised the problems involved in translation, for all translation is inevitably involved in interpretation, if only because it is the meaning that has to be transferred and not the word connections or sentence connections from one language to another. Language thus constitutes an interpretative medium through which the material contents of documents are translated out of one historical or cultural context into another. This was brought home to Erasmus when his annotations on the New Testament were attacked by Edward Lee for being more than translations, and for involving *inventions*. Erasmus replied that, far from being inventions, they were extended forms of translation which brought out the real meaning and did not simply give a word-for-word or sentence-for-sentence translation as if there were no difference in the essential nature of the languages concerned. But there was a deeper problem here. How can translation be truly effected unless at the same time something of the essential culture in which the original language is embedded and has its basic meaning is also translated into the new context? It was one of Erasmus' greatest contributions to the modern world that he discerned this and set about his task of Classical and biblical studies in such a way that he took account of it, i.e. in a resolute refusal to separate language from culture or to interpret written documents in abstraction from the civilizations out of which they were produced and in which their language had the original orientation which gave it meaning. It was false abstraction between language and culture, Erasmus held, together with the nominalist notions of grammar and syntax and 'Scotist' terminism to which it gave rise that had led to the degeneration of culture and created a generation of 'barbarians'. Hence he bent all his energies to achieve a new synthesis between *bonae litterae* and Christian tradition in which he hoped that the great inheritance of the Classical cultures could be recovered and combined in a purified form with evangelical truth to form the basis of a new civilization.

The rejection and refutation of linguistic barbarianism became all the more important to Erasmus when, under the influence of Colet, he turned to devote himself especially to biblical studies. He realised that since the Scriptures are records of the Speech of God to man, are therefore the communication of the Word of God in human form (*humano more*), they cannot be investigated and understood in abstraction from the human life and human understanding to which they are addressed. To become perspicuous in each generation, the divine Scriptures must be allowed to create for themselves a human way of life which in turn will be the continuing medium through which their meaning is reflected in the understanding and life of men. Thus Erasmus combined human studies with spiritual understanding of the Gospel and used every tool he could find in the Classical cultures to enable him to carry that out. Precisely because he sought in the Scriptures more than human documents, he insisted that a way of interpreting them must be found which would allow that other and twin sense to be brought to light. The tool universally used for that purpose in profane and Christian literature alike was some form of allegorical hermeneutic, and he set himself to shape that into an instrument that would suit his purpose; but he failed to see that it could only lead back into the same or at least similar entanglements from out of which he had done so much to extricate the Scriptures.

Hence over against his great positive achievements we must set some fundamental failures. He failed to discern adequately the relation of biblical language to the acts of God in history, and therefore failed to penetrate very far beyond a merely literary activity in the interpretation of the Scriptures. When it came to essential meaning, to doctrine, his understanding of history was superficial. Although he did discern, as few of his immediate contemporaries, the need for historical research and historical understanding, when it came to the actual point he turned aside from it through his assessment of history as having merely illustrative value. At the same time this oblique approach to history helped him to face the challenge of breaking through language to the realities it is intended to denote, and therefore of understanding language from its objective relation to the independently real as well as its subjective relation to the realities of the speaker and his spiritual and mental experiences.

But behind this there was a deeper failure. He had very little sense of the conflict between the truth and the mind of the natural man. In some respects this is surprising, for he was constantly in conflict with others who objected to his devotion to 'Hebrew and Greek truth' and who saw their way of life and thought menaced by his exposure of the errors in the received and authorised Latin text of the Bible. But he tended too easily to put that down to barbarity and ecclesiastical dogmatism or false dialectics, and he had too easy a view of the power of the truth once revealed to eliminate error. That is why Luther felt that Erasmus was so superficial—at heart Erasmus was a humanist not only in the literary sense but in the theological sense. He never had the struggles that Luther had in suffering the attack of the truth on his preconceptions, and the exposure by the truth of man's own profound enmity to it. This failure to see the epistemological relevance of the Cross which was one of Luther's greatest insights into the Gospel, to understand the profound meaning of repentance as the radical change of mind and heart that comes from reconciliation with Christ, meant that interpretation involved no struggle, no battle with the self, no facing up to the objection of the divine Truth to the interpreter as one whose innermost being distorts what he hears and understands. Hence it was comparatively easy for Erasmus to fuse together evangelical truth and profane Classical culture into a new Christian philosophy. But this meant, and could not but mean, that he failed finally to interpret the Scriptures objectively, out of the depth of their saving message, but interpreted them as he was able to build out of them a new way of life, or, as we might say today, a new ideology.

The fact is that Erasmus stopped short of serious interpretation of the Scriptures out of their own objective depth. He only went halfway in letting them reshape his mind and fashion habits of thought with which to appreciate them and so brought to them habits of thought and attitudes of mind that were alien to them. There can be no question about the fact that it was his passion for the oblique sense of the Scripture and for allegorical exegesis that contributed to this immensely. Instead of letting the message of the Scriptures call the traditional forms of thought and the habits of mind he brought with him into question, he interiorised them, stripped them of their crudities and intellectual rigidities, and spiritualised them so that they would serve a placid way of life. Thus he substituted for the casuistical ethic of the Middle Ages a new psychological ethic concerned with the development and adornment of the human personality. But it was ultimately Pelagian and served to deflect the full force of the biblical message, and so inhibited serious exegesis and theological penetration. The whole problem of preconception and presupposition had to be raised more openly and faced more courageously before the great contributions of Erasmus to biblical interpretation could be fully utilised. But as he stood, Erasmus was the great forerunner of liberal and romantic hermeneutics.

CHAPTER 8

Hermeneutics according to F. D. E. Schleiermacher[1]

Friedrich Daniel Ernst Schleiermacher was born on the 21st day of November 1768, and died on the 12th day of February 1834. It is altogether fitting that as we honour the birth of this great man by dedicating to his memory this number of the *Scottish Journal of Theology*, we should consider that aspect of his thought which has continued to influence us in the twentieth century so powerfully.[2]

Basic to Schleiermacher's thinking was the old Hellenic distinction between the *sensuous* and the *spiritual*, that is, between the realm of physical events and the realm of consciousness, and the idealist resolve to transcend the distinction through a co-ordinating principle drawn from the realm of the spirit and of consciousness. It was this realm that was regarded as ultimately real. In comparison with it the realm of sense appeared to be lacking in reality so that it required to be re-interpreted and given meaning through being taken up into the realm of the spirit and of consciousness. While this determination to transmute the sensuous into the spiritual affected every aspect of Schleiermacher's thought, it was for him the particular concern of the Christian religion, which he regarded as

---

1 This essay originally appeared in *Scottish Journal of Theology* 21.3 (1968) 257–67, © Scottish Journal of Theology Ltd., reproduced with the permission of Cambridge University Press.

2 See especially F. D. E. Schleiermacher, *Hermeneutik, Nach den Handschriften neu herausgegeben und eingeleitet von Heinz Kimmerle* (Heidelberg, 1959), and the discussion of H. G. Gadamer, *Wahrheit und Methode* (Tübingen, 1960), 172ff. Also, 'Ueber den Begriff der Hermeneutik mit Bezug auf F. A. Wolfs Andeutungen und Asts Lehrbuch', *Werke* (Berlin, 1835), III.3, 344ff; *Hermeneutik und Kritik, mit besonderer Beziehung auf das Neue Testament*, ed. F. Lücke, *Werke* (Berlin, 1838), 1.7. For a brief account of Schleiermacher's Hermeneutics in English, see H. A. Hodges, *Wilhelm Dilthey* (London, 1944), 234ff. Hodges sees Schleiermacher through the eyes of W. Dilthey, *Die Hermeneutik Schleiermachers* (Berlin, 1860).

Hermeneutics according to F. D. E. Schleiermacher

the culminating development of the human spirit in its ascendency over nature.[3] In the Christian tradition, however, the spiritual is presented in forms that are bound up with the physical and the sensuous, which applies not only to cultic and sacramental acts but to the historic tenets and dogmas of the faith. To the purified self-consciousness these are mythological forms thrown up by sensuous thinking, but since they are expressions of man's inner life and spirit they must be retranslated and made understandable as determinations of the religious self-consciousness. A double activity is involved here: an act of penetration through the external forms and expressions into the inner life and spirit in order to achieve understanding of them, and an act of re-formulation and communication which makes them understandable today.

It was in the application of this movement of understanding to the interpretation of literary texts that Schleiermacher made his great contribution to hermeneutics. He insisted that along with the traditional philological discipline, and passing beyond it, there must be another in which we probe into the author's mind and reach a fundamental understanding with him through reproducing in ourselves the basic determinations of his spirit and give them appropriate expression in our own forms of speech. Since for Schleiermacher thinking was a form of inward speech, and speech was an external form of thinking, it is not surprising that he should have developed a theory of hermeneutics that was entirely consistent with his theory of knowledge. What was common to them both was *Verstehen* or *understanding*.[4]

The great presupposition with which the interpreter must go to work, according to Schleiermacher, is that he is concerned with speech or language, with what is spoken and heard in acts of communication between subject and subject.[5] That must not be forgotten even when it is a written text that is to be understood. As a part of speech or a component of a language every word belongs to a whole sphere of meaning, and therefore it must be interpreted not as a particular on its own but through its relation to the whole, although it makes its own contribution to the whole. This is a

---

3 Schleiermacher, *The Christian Faith*, 4; *Kurze Darstellung des Theologischen Studiums zum Behuf Einleitender Vorlesungen*, ed. H. Scholz (Darmstadt, 1961). See also F. Flückiger, *Philosophie und Theologie bei Schleiermacher* (Zürich, 1947); and P. Löftier, 'Selbstbewustsein und Selbstverständnis als theologische Prinzipien bei Schleiermacher und Bultmann,' *Kerygma und Dogma* II.4 (1956) 304ff.

4 See Gadamer, op. cit., 166f, 172ff.

5 *Hermeneutik*, 38. Cf. Kimmerle's *Introduction*, 17.

fuller application of the so-called 'hermeneutical circle', which all scientific hermeneutics has made use of since Aristotle: the understanding of the whole from its parts and of the parts from the whole.[6] In order to achieve this understanding, recourse must be made to comparative methods in which words or notions are studied in the fullness of their manifold applications. It is when we have grasped the unity of the general and the particular that we penetrate into the sphere of meaning or the essential unity of words.[7]

Now every text has an 'external form' and an 'inner form' requiring respectively objective and subjective interpretation. These two approaches are what Schleiermacher calls the 'grammatical' and the 'technical' or 'psychological'. It is the task of grammatical interpretation[8] to examine and clarify the linguistic phenomena, subjecting them to formal analysis in order to learn their principles and inherent possibilities, clarify obscurities and ambiguities and so to remove every hindrance to understanding. To this end interpretation must employ all the philological and historical scholarship it can muster. All this is concerned with the outward appearance or form. It is the task of technical interpretation[9] to probe behind that to the inner form which is given expression in external utterance or written text, that is to say, into the author's style or distinctive and characteristic use of language.[10] But it is more than that, for it involves a penetration into the ideal form or inner connection of thought in the author's mind and an appreciation of his individuality. Schleiermacher also spoke of this as psychological interpretation,[11] for it involves as much as anything else an understanding of the human life and personal being. It is much more an art than a discipline, a distinctively personal act rather than a procedure according to certain rules.

Both the grammatical interpretation and the psychological interpretation require to be carried out in two ways: through the comparative method, i.e. the operation of the hermeneutical circle, and through intuitive penetration which Schleiermacher called 'divination'.[12] In grammatical interpretation the sense of each word and sentence must be

6 *Hermeneutik*, 45f, 48f, 75f, 90f.
7 Ibid., 61f.
8 Ibid., 57ff, 90ff, 161f.
9 Ibid., 107ff, 113ff.
10 Ibid., 116f.
11 Ibid., 165ff.
12 Cf. Gadamer, op. cit., 178, and Hodges, op. cit., 12f.

understood in the light of the whole context, and the context in the light of the whole work and indeed in the light of all the literature of that kind. But the grammatical interpretation has its limits, which become apparent when we are up against 'the tone and accent' of the whole text behind which lies the productive spirit, the originality and individuality of the author. It is here, however, that Schleiermacher brings in what he calls the divinatory approach through which the interpreter in an act of imaginative and sympathetic understanding appreciates the individuality of the author that comes to expression in his style.[13]

Schleiermacher also insists that both these approaches apply to psychological interpretation. The psychological understanding of a text makes use in its own way of the hermeneutical circle, for as it penetrates into the nexus of thoughts in the author's mind it must treat each thought in the whole context of the author's life and as an act in which his life is given particular expression. The comparative method here has its limits too, and therefore if understanding is to be achieved we need to advance further through the divinatory approach in which we penetrate into the basic orientation of the author's mind, or into the fundamental determination of his soul, for it is only then that we get at the germ from which the whole work has emerged, and are able to reconstruct it in such a way that we can make it understandable to ourselves.

This is undoubtedly where the distinctive character in Schleiermacher's hermeneutical theory lies, for it involves a hermeneutical circle through a comparison which the interpreter makes between himself and his subject; it is a dialogical encounter, as it were, in which the interpreter, as well as the author, takes part, which is possible for both belong to a common consciousness, the realm of human spirit.[14] There are three important points. First, interpretation presupposes not only the treatment of language as a movement of human life and its expression, but an understanding of the interpersonal structure of human life and existence as the 'whole' within which communication takes place.[15] The relation of the individual to the community and the community to the individual is all-important.[16] Secondly, interpretation is directed not to the understanding of the things

---

13 *Hermeneutik*, 87f, 109. Cf. Gadamer, op. cit., 177f.

14 *Hermeneutik*, 109; cf. *Werke*, I.7, 147, and *Hermeneutik*, 136ff.

15 *Kurze Darstellung*, 55f.

16 Cf. R. R. Niebuhr, 'Schleiermacher on Language and Feeling', *Theology Today* 17.2 (1960) 150ff.

spoken about or of speech in its relation to those things—that is only of subsidiary importance.[17] Nor is it an attempt to step into the place of the first readers or of the original hearers in order to recover their understanding—again, that is only a historical problem of subsidiary importance. It is directed toward the understanding of the original author himself whose life expression is mediated in written form, by the text. That is to say, as Gadamer has expressed it, Schleiermacher's problem is not that of a dark history but that of a dark *Thou*.[18] Hermeneutics is the art of penetrating into the innermost determinations of the other's mind and understanding him better than he himself.[19] That can be carried out, however, and this is the third important point we note, only through a movement in which the interpreter traces the creative process lying behind a work to its germinal source in the author, and then reconstructs it by a movement of participation, and of reproduction in the mind of the interpreter himself. Thus his understanding depends upon his own ability or art to recreate in himself the basic determination of consciousness he finds in the author.[20]

This is the principal element in Schleiermacher's hermeneutics which was taken over and developed by Dilthey in his notion of hermeneutics as the re-discovery of the I in the Thou through a transposition by the interpreter of his own self into the other and a reliving of his experience in himself.[21] From these views of Schleiermacher and Dilthey no extension is needed to the theory that the key to the interpretation of a text, whether of Plato or of St Paul, is self-understanding.

In order to see how Schleiermacher's hermeneutic was oriented to the New Testament we have to turn back to the distinction between external form and internal form. For Schleiermacher, that constitutes more than a distinction, for there is a real discrepancy between them, corresponding to the discrepancy between appearance and idea.[22] That discrepancy may be widened for us if the text we are seeking to interpret is in a foreign language or if it has come down to us from another period of history and so is severed from its native context in the life and society where it has its fullness of meaning. It is because of such discrepancies that Schleiermacher

17 Cf. Gadamer, op. cit., 173f and 180.
18 Ibid., 179.
19 *Werke*, I.7, 32.
20 Cf. Kimmerle, op. cit., 23.
21 Hodges, op. cit., 119.
22 Kimmerle, op. cit., 201.

held that hermeneutics is more than a science; it is an art.[23] It does have a scientific aspect which is necessary for the investigation of the objective side of the text, but because much more lies behind language than can be conveyed in words, something more than philological, grammatical and literary disciplines is necessary. In order to penetrate into that other inner aspect on the other side of the discrepancy an act of divination is necessary which depends more on talent than on method.

The interpreter of the New Testament, however, is faced with a double problem.[24] On the one hand, he must cope with the fact that there is a serious discrepancy between the speech-world and the thought-world in the text. While the thought-world is mainly Hebraic the speech is Greek which is bound up with a different sphere of meaning. To a certain extent this discrepancy is overcome by the impact of Christianity upon the speech of the New Testament, for Christianity has what Schleiermacher called 'language moulding power.' But the discrepancy remains. It was through reflecting upon this, and particularly upon the Epistles of St Paul, that Schleiermacher developed his hermeneutical theory, and came to hold that psychological penetration and divination were of supreme importance in enabling us to bridge the gap and achieve understanding.

On the other hand, the interpreter must cope with the fact that the discrepancy in the biblical text between the external appearance and the internal idea is as wide as that between the sensuous and the spiritual. Hence it is all the more necessary that the interpreter should divine the seminal determination in the consciousness of the biblical author in order to reconstruct and reproduce it as a determination in his own consciousness and so to remodel it in his own understanding. This is of course consistent with Schleiermacher's fundamental approach to Christian doctrine in his effort to transpose it into another conceptual form and so to make it understandable in the culture of modern Europe. Yet what in point of fact Schleiermacher did, especially through his concentration upon the psychological and divinatory aspects of hermeneutics, was to lift it out of specialised disciplines and to generalise it as the fundamental act of human understanding concerned with the unity of the universal and the particular especially as they are embodied and expressed in human individuality.[25]

---

23 *Hermeneutik*, 3ff, 79ff; cf.. Gadamer, op. cit., 175f. See also Schleiermacher's *Kurze Darstellung*, ed. H. Scholz, 53f.

24 *Hermeneutik*, 93ff.

25 Cf. K. Barth, *Theologische Fragen u. Antworten*, 77f.

But the application of Schleiermacher's hermeneutics to biblical statements and texts does have the effect of subjecting Christianity to the self-reflection and self-interpretation of the human spirit in culture, for this interpretation of the Christian message is carried out in a comprehensive pursuit which provides general principles and notions that determine its procedure and so are the test of its acceptability and truth.[26]

This brings us to consider the other idealist presupposition that lies behind Schleiermacher's hermeneutics: the radical dichotomy between the given and the not-given, or between the objectifiable and the non-objectifiable. We recall that idealism is the moment of thought that probes behind the correlation between subject and object and questions the limits of the knowledge that takes place within it, but on its positive side it seeks to penetrate behind the given, the objectifiable, and the finite to the ultimate presupposition of what is given, objectifiable and finite, in what is not-given, non-objectifiable and infinite. This does not mean that idealism rejects objectivity or objective thinking, for it does not just bypass experience but looks for its ultimate legitimation and substantiation beyond. Hence idealism describes a sort of hyperbola in which it rises above the objectifiable to what is non-objectifiable and then moves back to the objectifiable to reinterpret it in the light of what is not-given beyond it.[27]

Now there can be no doubt that serious thinking about God must draw a distinction between the givenness of God and the givenness of all other being, a distinction so fundamental that the Being of God is treated in relation to all other being as not-given or non-objectifiable. Hence theology also engages in a similar movement of thought in which its reflection upon the actuality of God involves a transcending of the actuality of our knowledge of God to its ultimate truth in God Himself, and then a downward movement in the understanding of 'the given' in the light of 'the not-given'. This does not mean that theology wishes in any way to deny the actuality or givenness of God in His revelation, but that it seeks to understand the Truth through it in order that the Truth may illumine it, apart from which it would not be God's actual revelation. To heed this transcendence of God over what is given to us, means that we take seriously the inadequacy of all our human statements about God and are on our guard against the substitution of objective statements for God Himself in His revelation. Thus the 'idealist' element in theological thinking can only

---

26 *The Christian Faith*, 12ff.
27 Cf. K. Barth, *Theologische Fragen u. Antworten*, 77f.

mean a retracing of the actual ways in which God has revealed Himself to us in order that we may lift up our minds to Him above ourselves, and above all efforts at self-interpretation and self-understanding on our part.

But this is precisely the difficulty with Schleiermacher. There can be no doubt that on the one hand his critical idealism was the negative or obverse side of a very serious realism, for his doctrine of the feeling of absolute dependence on God was intended by him to be a decisive expression of the ultimate objectivity of God, that is, the un-objectifiable transcendence and otherness of God, which we must not confound with our own objectivities.[28] But in point of fact it led his thought into the opposite direction for it posited such a dichotomy between the given and the not-given in God that Christian doctrines were conceived to have their ground not in an activity of God within our actuality nor in any direct communication of truth, but in the emotions of the religious self-consciousness. Hence to understand God man is thrown back upon the interpretation of his own feelings of dependence and his own self-understanding, while Jesus plays the part of a creative co-determinant in man's religious self-consciousness.

The problem we are concerned with here is: how are we to relate the ultimate objectivity of God Himself to the objectivities of this world within which He gives us knowledge of Himself, for the polarity between 'the given' and 'the not-given' in God is other than the polarity between 'the given' and 'the not-given' in our intramundane experience? It is because the polarity of 'the given' and 'the not-given' of God intersects the polarity of 'the given' and 'the not-given' in our intramundane experience that it is so easy to confuse the one with the other and to identify the invisibility of our own spiritual life with that of God and so to substitute human spirit in the place of God's Spirit. This is what inevitably happens when Schleiermacher's hermeneutics is applied to the interpretation of the Christian Gospel. God Himself is not objectifiable, and He does not give Himself as such (in word or act) to our experience, but what is given to us is an awareness of Him in the experience of the individual and of the community in the form of determinations of the religious consciousness. That is what Schleiermacher found in St Paul's Epistles, and therefore he insisted that interpretation of them must penetrate down to the fundamental orientation of his mind, to the profound determinations of his soul in his awareness of God, for it is only in that way that we can reach understanding of the Epistles themselves.

---

28 *The Christian Faith*, 12ff.

Divine Interpretation

Then it is the task of theology to reflect upon them and to reinterpret them as living co-determinants of the human spirit in the present.

Three comments may now be offered.

(1) Interpretation of a biblical text involves the setting up of a polar relation to a subject-matter which by its very nature entails a polar relation between the witness and God Himself. No hermeneutical method or art can be justified which neglects the objective pole in the text and absorbs the subjective pole into its own polar movement. This is particularly evident when it involves such a penetration of the interpreter himself into the soul of the author that through his own self-understanding he claims to understand the author better than himself; for this is to make it impossible for the interpreter to distinguish what is being objectively communicated to him from his own subjective conditions and states.

(2) It is indeed true that biblical interpretation and theological thinking cannot be separated from one another, but for that very reason it ought to be clear that biblical interpretation, like theological thinking, arises and moves not from a centre in ourselves but from a centre in God; that is to say, it arises from a centre in the ultimate Word of God and moves from God to man, and therefore it must reject any form of thinking that proceeds first through the self-reflection and self-interpretation of the human spirit and seeks in that way to rise to some ultimate word worthy of the name of the Word of God. Thus by its very nature theological thinking calls in question every form of human thinking that seeks to establish from the side of man some congruence between man's thinking and God's reality, and so theology performs, as it were in reverse, the function of the idealist critique by questioning the adequacy of idealist correlations.

(3) The third point that must be made is that the radical dichotomy posited by idealism turns the hermeneutical circle into a vicious circle, for by making the relations between man and God reciprocal it thinks away all free ground for such a correlation in God. By taking its starting-point in man's self-consciousness, and making its ultimate criterion man's self-certainty it can only move ultimately from self-understanding through self-interpretation to a self-understanding. Thus it has no objective ground independent of its own movement, and no point where its circular movement comes to an end, since the 'God' at the opposite pole is only the correlate of man's self-consciousness and so points back to man for its testing and truth.

Hermeneutics according to F. D. E. Schleiermacher

We may now specify by way of summary the chief elements in Schleiermacher's positive contribution to hermeneutical theory and method as follows.

(i) Schleiermacher both widened and deepened the scope of hermeneutics, by making it the essential core of understanding. As such it is both general, applicable to every field, and yet particular for it must be appropriate to the individuality of the special text being interpreted. General hermeneutics is more concerned with the grammatical and philological aspects of interpretation, and its special application is more concerned with peculiarities of language, style, and the inner form that comes to expression in external speech.

(ii) The Aristotelian principle, that the particular must be seen in the light of the whole and the whole in the light of the particulars that make it up, is to be applied in the most thorough-going way both to the objective and to the subjective approach to the text. Hence the place that 'the hermeneutical circle' has occupied in hermeneutics ever since.

(iii) Hermeneutics requires not only exhaustive work in comparative philology, especially where foreign and ancient languages are concerned, and the comprehension of a text in the historical, cultural and political context of its origin, but it requires an understanding of the structure of the living personal and social relations in which human speech is the means of self-disclosure and the medium of communication.

(iv) Because genuine understanding must rest upon the fundamental affinities in life and personal being, hermeneutics is as much an art as a science or discipline operating within the limits of determinable laws or rules. In addition to a clarification of the sense through the formal analysis of the linguistic phenomena and a removal of ambiguities and obscurities, interpretation involves a movement of sympathetic and intuitive penetration into the mind of the author, divining the basic disposition in his soul out of which the work emerged, and a movement in which the interpreter retraces the creative activity of the author in order to reproduce it in himself and so to understand it from within. This requires empathy, and talent, and an affinity for the genius of the author.

(v) It follows that interpretation of biblical texts cannot be carried through without theological thinking. This does not mean that dogmatic presuppositions are to be brought uncritically to the text, but that interpretation must proceed along with a development of the thoughts of the author and a re-translation through which they will be made understandable in the present. Thus when the philological and historico-critical work has been done on the text, properly speaking the work of understanding the author and making him understandable has only begun, yet it is a clear implication of Schleiermacher's hermeneutics that we cannot even handle the philological and historico-critical work without some real theological understanding.

How far the philosophical and cultural presuppositions of Schleiermacher, or his psychological slant, allowed him to carry out these principles is another matter, but they have had as much influence upon others who did not share those presuppositions as upon those who did.

CHAPTER 9

Karl Barth, Theologian of the Word[1]

When I was introduced to the teaching of Karl Barth through John McConnachie and Hugh Ross Mackintosh, I first read *The Word of God and the Word of Man*, *The Doctrine of the Word of God* and then *God in Action*, which initiated me into a much deeper understanding of the Word of God. Like Karl Barth, I had been brought up by my parents in the Evangelical and Reformed Faith and learned from them how to dwell in the Holy Scriptures by reading several chapters of the Bible every day and letting them soak into the depths of my being, a habit which I have continued all my life. The godliness of my father and mother begot in me a biblical and theological instinct similar to their own upon which I have implicitly relied in all my basic judgments and decisions as a minister of the Gospel and a theologian. I cherished the Bible as the Word of God spoken to mankind.

However, when I opened the pages of Karl Barth's books and read the Holy Scriptures in the light of the startling questions he asked about the strange new world within the Bible and the dynamic nature of the Word of God; my study of the Bible changed into a higher gear. I found myself sharing with him his awareness in reading the Bible of 'something like the tremors of an earthquake or like the ceaseless thundering of ocean waves against thin dykes'. 'What really is it that beats at the barrier and seeks entrance here?'[2] It is the direct Word of God, not the Word of God as man utters it, but *the Word of God as God himself utters it*, in fact *the Word of God which God himself is*, for *he is identical with his Word*.[3] That is the new

---

[1] This essay originally appeared in *Karl Barth: Biblical and Evangelical Theologian* (Edinburgh: T. & T. Clark, 1990), 83–120. Reprinted with permission from Bloomsbury Plc, London.

[2] *The Word of God and the Word of Man*, tran. D. Horton (London, 1935), 29.

[3] See Torrance, *Karl Barth. An Introduction to His Early Theology, 1910–1931* (London, 1962), 96.

world to which the Bible opens the door, the World of God sovereignly and actively present *revealing himself as God*. This is what makes the Bible such an altogether extraordinary book: the contents of the Bible are 'God', and God himself, the one, ever present, eternal and living God, is the content of those contents. God himself, and nothing less than God, is the content of his revelation.[4]

1. Revelation Is God Himself

With that insight acceptance of the Bible as the Word of God, which I shared with Barth, takes on a new dimension of depth. The revelation which it has been inspired by God to mediate is not just something divine coming from God to man, but '*God speaking in Person*', as both Athanasius and Calvin used to express it, for in his Word and through his Word and as the Word in the words, God communicates to us his very self, the eternal *I Am* who in the beginning made heaven and earth and who in the fullness of time has come among us as man in the Lord Jesus Christ. Because God himself is this Word, the *Holy* Bible is to be approached and read and heard with the utmost awe and reverence for it is the appointed place where God addresses us directly and personally. We draw near to him like Moses at the burning bush bidden to take the shoes off his feet for the ground on which he trod was holy, like Elijah on Mount Horeb when he wrapped himself in his mantle at the sound of the 'still small voice', and like Isaiah when he saw the Lord upon his throne, high and lifted up, before whose presence the seraphim covered themselves with their wings and cried, 'Holy, holy, holy is the Lord of hosts: the whole earth is full of his glory'.

The Revealed Word of God

Karl Barth's discovery, or rediscovery, of the Bible as the revealed Word of God in this profound dynamic and ontological sense broke in upon him in his struggle to take seriously his calling as a parish minister to preach to his people week by week, when he was 'surprised by the truth as by an armed man'. That is what explains the arduous work he devoted to the Epistle to the Romans. In the first instance it was an attempt to help him understand his own questions as a minister of the Word: What is preaching?—not How

---

4 Cf. the opening chapter on 'Revelatio'" in *God in Action*, Eng. tran., E. G. Homrighausen and K. J. Ernst (New York, 1936), 12–19.

does one do it? but How *can* one do it?[5] Hence, as he explained to a meeting of ministers in 1922, it arose simply out of what was felt to be 'the need and promise of Christian preaching'. 'For twelve years', he told them,

> I was a minister, as all of you are. I had *my theology*. It was not really mine, to be sure, but that of my unforgettable teacher Wilhelm Herrmann, grafted upon the principles which I had learned, less consciously than unconsciously, in my native home—the principles of those Reformed Churches which today I represent and am honoured to represent in an official capacity. Once in the ministry, I found myself growing away from those theological habits of thought and being forced back at every point more and more upon the specific *minister's* problem, the *sermon*.[6]

The discovery of the strange new world within the Bible governed by the identity of God with his Word increased his perplexity as a minister of the Word, for how could he, a mere man, preach the Word of God if that Word is God himself? 'As ministers we ought to speak of God. We are human, however, and cannot speak of God. We ought therefore to recognise both our obligation and our inability and by that recognition give God the glory. That is our perplexity. The rest of our task fades into insignificance in comparison.'[7] 'The Word of God is at once the necessary and the impossible task of the minister.'[8] The very perplexity of the minister in his obligation to speak of God and in his inability to do so is also his promise: for God who only can speak of God calls us to speak of him and is pleased himself to speak the Word that he is in our speech of him. Thus it may be, as Barth says,

> that the Word, the Word of God, which we ourselves shall never speak, has put on our weakness and unprofitableness so that *our* word *in* its very weakness and unprofitableness has become capable at least of becoming the mortal frame, the earthen vessel, of the Word of God. It may be so, I say; and if it were, we should have reason not so much to speak of our need as to declare and publish the hope and hidden glory of our calling.[9]

---

5 *The Word of God and the Word of Man*, 103.
6 Ibid., 100.
7 Ibid., 186.
8 Ibid., 213.
9 Ibid., 216.

Divine Interpretation

Thus preaching of the Word of God is God's Word spoken by himself through the service of those specially called to expound the Bible and proclaim its message to others as if they heard it directly from God themselves. Just as the very hearing of the Word of God always implies an acknowledgment of the miracle by reason of which that hearing has actually taken place, so the preaching of the Word of God rests upon the promise of a miracle by reason of which the preaching may indeed be the preaching of the Word of God. 'When God's Word is heard and proclaimed, something takes place that for all our hermeneutical skill cannot be brought about by hermeneutical skill.'[10] Such is the wonder of the proclaimed Word of God.

It is highly significant that when Karl Barth moved from being a parish minister in Switzerland to being a professor of theology in Germany he regarded the theological task assigned to him in the University in much the same way.

> We cannot speak of God. For to speak of God seriously would mean to speak in the realm of revelation and faith. To speak of God would be to speak God's Word, the Word which can only come from him, the word that *God becomes man*. We may say these three words, but this is not to speak the Word of God, the *truth* for which these words are an expression. Our ministerial task is to say that God becomes *man*, but to say it as *God's* Word, as God *himself* says it.[11]

That is the perplexity and the miracle of preaching and teaching the Word of God in the name of the Father, the Son and the Holy Spirit.

In many respects this conception of the Word reached by Barth was a return to the doctrine of the Word of God put forward by the Reformers, by Martin Luther and John Calvin. In their epoch-making recovery of the Pauline doctrine of justification by grace, the Reformers recognised that the free gift of grace is not just something imparted by God but is identical with God the giver. Likewise in their rediscovery and reappropriation of the Word of God in the Bible they recognised that the Word of God is not just some communication of truth about God but is identical with God himself speaking in Person. As the grace of God is the grace of God who is of and through himself alone such that its giving is backed up by God's own ultimate being and incomprehensible love, so the Word of God is the

---

10   *CD*, I.1, 148.

11   Ibid., 198f; see also *Die christliche Dogmatik im Entwurf, Die Lehre vom Worte Gottes* (München, 1927), 411f.

Karl Barth, Theologian of the Word

Word of God who is of and through himself alone such that its speaking is backed up by the living force of God's own ultimate being and ineffable self-utterance. For Barth this identity of the gift of grace with God the giver, and the identity of the Word of revelation with God the revealer, constituted the cardinal truth for which the Church contended in the fourth century when it confessed belief in Jesus Christ as of one being with God the Father.[12] But whereas the immediate focus of attention in the great Nicene theology, when the doctrine of the Trinity was at stake, was on the consubstantiality of the incarnate Son, the immediate focus of attention in Reformation theology, where the doctrine of free grace was at stake, was on the consubstantiality of the incarnate Word. Everything hinged in both on the identity of God with the content of his saving revelation. There is one Mediator between God and man, the man Christ Jesus who as God and man in one Person is the very grace and the Word of the mighty, living God of the Bible. When such a recognition of the personal nature of the Word of God strikes home, then reading and understanding of the Bible undergo a vast paradigmatic shift of an intensely realist kind. We are swept along by the mighty driving wind of the Spirit into direct encounter with the wholly other reality of God who may be heard only through his own self-witness and be understood only through the eternal Word that he himself is and has caused to become incarnate in the world, made flesh in the midst of Israel in Jesus Christ.

The Written Word of God

What, then, does Karl Barth think of the Holy Scriptures themselves? They are the inspired writings of prophets and apostles brought into being by the patient self-revealing of God through his Spirit to mankind in the historical existence of Israel and finally in acutely personal and concrete form in Jesus Christ his incarnate Word. The Bible itself is not to be thought of as an incarnate transcription of the ineffable speech inherent in the eternal Being of God, for that would presuppose a latent identity between the word of man and the Word of God. 'The Bible is not the Word of God on earth in the same way as Jesus Christ, very God and very man, is that Word in heaven.'[13] Nevertheless in God's saving and revealing purpose he has uniquely and sovereignly coordinated the biblical word with his eternal Word, and adapted the written form and contents of the Bible to his Word,

---

12 Refer again to *God in Action*, 13ff.
13 *CD*, I.2, 513.

Divine Interpretation

in such a way that the living Voice of God is made to resound through the Bible to all who have ears to hear. The Bible is thus constituted by God to be the written Word of God, the holy medium of the very revelation that God himself is. It is the understandable and communicable form which God's Word has freely taken and decided to use in the actualisation of his self-revelation and which in his wisdom he has determined to be the Word of God to mankind.

> If God speaks to man, he really speaks the language of this concrete human word of man. That is the right and necessary truth in the concept of verbal inspiration. If the word is not to be separated from the matter, if there is no such thing as verbal inspiredness, nevertheless the matter is not to be separated from the Word, and there is real inspiration: hearing of the Word of God, only in the form of verbal inspiration, hearing of the Word of God only in the concrete form of the biblical word.[14]

Hence Barth acknowledged that in the Bible we have to do with inspired, objective, reliable witness to God in which by the power of his own Spirit and Word God bears witness to himself in human words and statements.[15]

When *The Epistle to the Romans* appeared Barth was charged with putting forward 'a modern form of the dogma of inspiration', which he readily accepted. Thus in his preface to the third edition of his Commentary, Barth wrote: 'From the preface to the first edition onwards, I have never attempted to conceal the fact that my manner of interpretation has certain affinities with the old doctrine of verbal inspiration.'[16] This does not mean that Barth posited a direct identity between the words of Holy Scripture and the revealed Word of God, resting in the essence of either the human word or the divine Word. Nor did he hold that the revelation of God can be read directly off its pages, even though Holy Scripture cannot be separated from that revelation, for by its transcendent nature divine revelation is not restricted to or exhausted by the medium it freely brings into existence, but is the ever-new presence and speaking of the living God himself who is identical only with himself. In Holy Scripture, therefore, we have to do with *the majestic Word of the Lord God which he has stooped to speak in the frail human words of the Holy Scriptures* thereby constituting them through his grace as the unique authoritative written Word of God to mankind.

---

14 *CD*, I.2, 532.

15 Cf. *CD*, III.1, 200ff.

16 *The Epistle to the Romans*, tran. E. C. Hoskyns (London, 1933), 18.

It follows that our knowledge of the Bible as the Word of God is itself a divinely grounded event within the two-way relation God sets up between himself and us, an ever-new breaking through of divine revelation to faith and obedience.

Hence, it must be pointed out that while Barth thought of the Word of God in the strict sense as God himself, he also thought of it as the creative act of God, for God's act is itself speech and God's speech is itself act, as is evident both in the creation of all things in the beginning by his Word, and in the incarnation of his Word in space and time in Jesus Christ. God the Word is *God in action*. God speaking in Person and God acting in Person are one and the same. It is because the Word of God is creative act of God that it sets up an elliptical movement between God's self-revealing and our knowing of him, in which his Word breaks into the movement of our human thought and fills it with the content of his self-revelation. It is because the Word of God is creative act of God that it is recognised and heard by us through a corresponding effect generated in us by that act. This means that it is only through God that we can know God, and only through revelation that we can apprehend revelation. It is through its unique relation to this speaking and acting God as the sovereign Lord of all that is, that the Bible is and becomes and is recognised to be what it *is* as 'the Word of God'. That is why the Bible is the Word of God before we know it to be so, and why the Word of God is true before we know it to be so, for its truth as God's Word is not lodged in the Bible itself but in God from whom it comes and to whom it directs us.[17] There are several features in this coordination (as I have called it) between the Word and act of God and the Bible to which we must give fuller attention, for it was in discerning and working out their evangelical implications that Karl Barth became the great biblical theologian of our age.

The Concrete Character of Revelation

Revelation involves a real relation between God and man, the foundation of which is laid in God from whom it derives its force and permanence, but one that reaches across the infinite difference between God and man and penetrates into the actualities of his existence in the world. It is because revelation is God's own act done in his Word and in his Spirit that the Bible is so full of history, for God has not kept himself detached from the world

---

17 Refer to *Witness to the Word*, Barth's Commentary on John 1, lectures of 1925 and 1933, translated by Geoffrey Bromiley in 1986.

but has revealed himself to mankind within concrete situations of space and time. Indeed the only God we know, and the only God there actually is, is God clothed with his revelation who ceaselessly interacts with the world. The Bible is not to be regarded, then, as a history of developing religious ideas about God, or as an account of how we may find him or put ourselves into a right relation with him. It is the history of God's revealing and saving acts worked out through the specific space-time track of the covenanted relation he elected to establish with the people of Israel in the midst of world history, in order to mould it as the chosen instrument or servant of his revelation designed for all mankind, and thus in the fullness of time to bring that revelation to its fruition once for all in Jesus Christ. The Holy Scriptures came into being within that covenanted relation and partake of it both in its Old Testament prophetic form and in its New Testament apostolic form.

Because Barth thought of the revelation that came to the prophets and apostles in this way as nothing less than God himself, and because he thought of God's language as God's act, he used to describe the relation between the Word of God and the Bible in terms of 'contingent contemporaneity'.[18] By that he wished to keep in mind the fact that the bond between the Word of God and the Bible is not a static or necessary one but a dynamic one, freely established by God which he is pleased unceasingly to affirm and maintain through the real presence and activity of his Word. The mighty living Word of God is not encapsulated in the written words of the Bible, far less is that Word personally incarnated in the Bible as it is in the Lord Jesus Christ, for there is no hypostatic union between the Word of God and the word of man in the Bible. Nevertheless God has graciously accommodated his revealed Word to the written Word of the Bible, and has thereby adapted its written form to his self-revelation in a profoundly covenanted and sacramental manner such that we may hear the still small Voice of God himself speaking to us in the Bible in the form of human words and statements.

This calls for a dynamic, not a static, concept of verbal inspiration. All Scripture given by divine inspiration is and becomes what it really is through the presence and advocacy of the Holy Spirit. The Spirit of God is God in his freedom to be present to what he has brought into being through his Word and to realise its true end in himself through a relation of himself to himself.[19] While that applies in one way to the relation of all

---

18 CD, I.1, 145ff.
19 CD, I.1, 450f, 472.

creatures to the Creator, it applies in a peculiar way to God's relation with man, especially in revelation, when through his Spirit God makes himself present to man and thereby acts from within him to make him subjectively open and ready and capable for God, and thus to realise his revelation in him. It is in just that kind of way that we may regard the covenanted and sacramental relation of Holy Scripture to God in his revelation, for God freely and purposely makes himself present in the Scripture which he has brought into being through the activity of his Word, and thereby sustains it from within and from below through a relation of himself to himself, and thus is pleased to realise his revelation to us in and through it. This transcendent freedom of God in his Spirit to be present to us is what Barth (as we have already noted) speaks of as the 'contingent contemporaneity' of the Word and act of God.[20] It is that kind of divine creative and sustaining Presence which makes the Bible what it is and what it ever becomes as the written Word of God. While God himself infinitely transcends all the creaturely forms of our thought and speech, nevertheless he has freely and graciously bound his written Word to himself in such a way that we are bound to it as the direct canonical instrument of his divine truth and authority. To help us understand this further we may recall Barth's account of the relation between creation and covenant.[21]

By his Word God has freely brought the creation into being out of nothing, giving it a distinctive orderly reality of its own, utterly different from but contingent or dependent on God's own reality. The creation does not have any self-subsistence or ultimate stability of its own, but God continues freely and unceasingly to maintain it in orderly being and lawful structure through correlation with his Word, yet while God remains transcendently free over the universe, the universe itself is bound to the rational order and natural law imposed upon it by the eternal Word of God and as such depends on and reflects that Word. Barth thought of this covenanted correspondence between the creation and the Creator as operating in such a way that while the creation may be regarded as the external basis of the covenant, the covenant may be regarded as the internal basis of the creation. When we remember that for Barth the covenant freely and unilaterally established by God with the people of Israel was a specific redemptive form of that all-embracing universal covenant of grace operating in creation, we may understand why he regarded the covenanted

20 E.g., *CD*, I.1, 145.
21 *CD*, III.1, 95–329.

correspondence between the Word of God and the Bible as not altogether unlike that between the created order and the creative Word. While God has freely brought the sacred relation between his revelation of himself and the Scriptures of the Old and New Testaments into being and remains transcendent over them as the active subject of revelation and Lord of the Scriptures, he has nevertheless constituted the Bible as the external basis for our hearing and understanding of his Word, while it is his Word that constitutes the internal basis of the biblical revelation. Apart from that internal basis the Bible is nothing more than the word of man, but apart from the external basis which it has assumed in the Bible the Word of God does not reach us in a communicable and understandable form. Hence it may be said that the Bible is what it is as the written Word of God precisely through the divinely ordained bond between its creaturely form and God's self revelation.

The Exclusive Character of Revelation

If the Bible is what it is because of an inner divinely ordained bond between it and God, the Bible is thereby locked into the unique and exclusive character of God's self-revelation. Because God is One, his revelation is characterised by singularity.

> As a man can have only one father; as he is able to look at one time with his eyes into the eyes of one other man; as he can hear with his two ears the word of only one man at one and the same time; as he has been born once and dies but once—so he can believe and know only one revelation. It is quite possible to place alongside, each other, and compare a multiplicity of religions, but not a multiplicity of revelations. Whoever says revelation says one single revelation which has happened once and for all, irrevocably and unrepeatedly.[22]

Just as when we adopt one way of looking at things we set aside at the same time some alternative way of seeing them, so in our commitment to the exclusive claims of God's revelation in the Bible we find ourselves compelled to reject any alternative way of knowing him. Such is the inner logic of divine revelation that Barth discerned in the Old and the New Testaments alike. 'I am the Lord your God, you shall have no other gods

---

22 *God in Action*, 9.

before me.' 'I am the way, the truth and the life, no one comes to the Father but by me.'

> We must hold by the fact that the Word which calls us, the Word which forms the content of Scripture, is itself and as such in every respect the perfect and unsurpassable Word of God, the Word which exhausts and reveals our whole knowledge of God, and from which we must not turn aside one step, because in itself it is the fullness of all the information that we either need or desire concerning God and man, and the relationship between them, and the ordering of that relationship. At no point, then, and on no pretext, can we afford either to dispense with, or be turned aside from, the knowledge of Jesus Christ.[23]

This necessary exclusiveness of divine revelation is the ground for Karl Barth's consistent rejection of natural theology as some possible alternative way to knowledge of God, and that is the reason why he has been the most consistently committed biblical theologian of our day. There is no way of going behind revelation to know God, any more than we can know God behind his back, for there is no other God but he who comes to us clothed with his revelation to mankind. Thus the singular bond that obtains between the Bible and divine revelation means that there is a two-way relation between knowledge of God and knowledge of the Bible—there is no authentic knowledge of God except on the ground of the biblical revelation, for there is no God except this God who has once and for all revealed himself through his covenanted relation with Israel and through his sealing of that covenant in Jesus Christ his incarnate Word. That is why the volumes of Karl Barth's *Church Dogmatics* are replete with exegetico-theological examination of biblical data over every question, for it is only through his arduous wrestling with the Holy Scriptures that Barth has been able to gain his great insights into divine truth and make his unrivalled contribution to Christian theology.[24]

The Dynamic Character of Revelation

If the Word of God is itself the Act of God then in its divinely effected bond to the Word of God the Bible must share the dynamic character of God's

---

23 *CD*, II.2, 152f.

24 See the volume edited by John McTavish and Harold Wells, *Karl Barth. Preaching through the Christian Year: A Selection of Exegetical Passages from the Church Dogmatics* (Edinburgh, 1978 and 1985).

self-revealing through his Word and Spirit. If God's speech is God's act then the written form of God's speech in the Holy Scripture cannot be what it is inspired by the Holy Spirit to be, if its continuing link with God acting and speaking in Person is broken or disregarded. Even in its written form the Word of God in the Bible precisely as Word of God is and remains the free pure Act of God unqualified by anything outside of it. The Holy Bible is the Word of God as God himself utters it and thereby acts upon us, and remains the Word and act of God as God continues to utter it and act upon us. That is to say, even in its form as the written Word of God the Bible is and continues to be the Word of God communicated to us in virtue of the fact that God continuously coordinates it with the active presence of his Word and Spirit and thereby affirms, activates and substantiates it as his Word. Even in its written form generated by divine revelation in the Bible the Word of God encounters us and impinges upon us from beyond from moment to moment as what Barth calls *Ereignis* or *Event*. It was on that ground that Barth readily spoke of 'the identification between revelation and the Bible'. 'It takes place as an event when and where the biblical word becomes God's Word. . . . Thus in the event of God's Word, revelation and the Bible are indeed one, and literally so.'[25] How could the Bible be the Word of God otherwise, if the Word of God really is God in his act of self-revelation?[26]

The real clue in our understanding of the Word of God in its written, as in its revealed, form is the supreme event of the incarnation when the Creator Word of God, through whom all things were made, personally irrupted into our human and worldly existence in space and time by becoming man in Jesus Christ, although without ceasing to be the eternal Word of God. While that event took place once and for all, it does not cease to be event for, as the Word of God become man, it is and remains God in the act of his self-revelation. The singular nature of this event in the fullness of time is not easy to put into words, but in order to convey something of the unique dynamic character of the incarnation Barth uses the device of speaking of it both as '*completed* event' and as 'completed *event*'.[27] It is not a repeatable event, but is a continuing event which impinges upon us here and now throughout all history. 'The Word became flesh and dwelt

---

25 *CD*, I.1, 113.
26 Consult *CD*, I.1, the section on 'The Speech of God as the Act of God', 143–62.
27 *CD*, I.1, 165ff.

among us, full of grace and truth.'[28] How is that 'becoming' of the Word to be understood? Barth points out that God the Word remains throughout the inextinguishable *subject* of what happened. Thus the Word's becoming flesh is to be regarded as a sovereign divine act which does not come to a halt in its movement or pass over into some kind of static necessity. On the contrary, the Incarnation took place in the divine freedom of the Word, such that even in the state of becoming and having become flesh, the Word does not cease to be free and sovereign but remains the free sovereign active Word of God. He continues to be the subject and Lord of his becoming, so that the becoming cannot be thought of as passing over from being becoming into being something else: it remains the *living movement* of the Word become flesh—and must be apprehended as such.

Kierkegaard had already raised the question of the elusive nature of the notion of 'becoming' and of the difficulty we have in thinking and expressing it without transposing it into something altogether different through static concepts and terms.[29] By 'becoming', he pointed out, we are not here using the word to denote something on the way toward being or perfection, a 'becoming' which is eventually swallowed up in being like the possible which reveals itself as nothing the moment it becomes actual. 'Becoming' refers rather to the other side of being, to that which flows from being, to being in action in time as it continuously becomes what it really is. Just as in his becoming man God does not cease to be God, so the incarnate becoming takes place without any surrender of the being of the Word.[30] That is why in Barth's illuminating discussion of the reality of revelation and of the knowability of God his thought does not move from 'possibility' to 'reality', but from 'reality' to 'possibility',[31] and why in his doctrine of God he speaks of God's Being in his Act and his Act in his Being.[32]

It is in entire consistency with this understanding of the nature of the living God as revealed in the Incarnation, and of the Word of God as God in the act of his self-revelation, that Barth speaks of the Bible as ever 'becoming' the Word of God in coordination with the 'becoming' flesh of

---

28 John 1:14. See especially the discussion of this verse by Barth in *CD*, I.2, 132ff; and *Die christliche Dogmatik*, 182ff, 215ff.

29 S. Kierkegaard, *Philosophical Fragments*, tran. David H. Swenson (Princeton, 1936), 60ff.

30 Cf. *CD*, I.2, 159ff.

31 *CD*, II.1, 187ff; I.2, 1ff; II.1, 63ff—cf. my discussion in *Theological Science* (Oxford, 1969), 25ff.

32 *CD*, II.1, 257ff.

the Word of God in Jesus Christ. As any disjunction between God and his self-revelation through Christ and in the Spirit would empty the Gospel of any divine reality or validity, so any disjunction between the singular becoming man in the Lord Jesus Christ the incarnate Word of God and the ever new becoming of the Bible as the written Word of God, would empty the latter of its divine content and validity.

> The Bible, then, becomes God's Word in this event, and in the statement that the Bible is God's Word the little word "is" refers to its being in this becoming. It does not become God's Word because we accord it faith, but in the fact that it becomes revelation to us. But the fact that it becomes God's revelation to us beyond all our faith, that it is God's Word even in spite of our lack of faith, is something we can accept and confess as true to us and for us only in faith, in faith as opposed to unbelief, in the faith in which we look away from our faith and unbelief to the act of God, but in faith and not in unbelief, and therefore precisely not in abstraction from the act of God in virtue of which the Bible must become again and again his Word to us.[33]

That is to say, we must think of the nature and reality of the biblical content of revelation as deriving from and as ever grounded in the continuous self-revealing and self-giving of God through the Son and in the Spirit, for what God reveals of himself and his actual self-revealing are one and the same. It is ultimately the supreme truth of the oneness between God and the content of his saving revelation that is at stake here: what God is in his relations with us in space and time, he is eternally in himself and what he is eternally in himself he is in his relations with us in space and time.

Expressed otherwise, there is an unbroken consubstantial relation between the free continuous act of God's self-communication and the living content of what he communicates by divine revelation to us in and through the Holy Scriptures,. It is indeed only through their grounding in that relation that the Holy Scriptures are what they ever are and are what they ever will be. This is why the divine revelation in the written form of the Word of God must be continually given and be continually received in a living relation with God, as he addresses us and speaks to us in Person through the Bible. The Bible really is and becomes the written Word of God that it has been inspired by the Holy Spirit to be as through the same Holy Spirit it is ever newly made open to, and substantiated from, the objective

---

33 CD, I.1, 110.

pole of its witness in the transcendent reality of God who is who he is in the act of his self-revelation. That is the ground upon which Karl Barth took his stand in all biblical interpretation, and sought in every endeavour to speak of God as faithfully as possible under the compelling claims of the Word that God is. Because the Bible is uniquely coordinated with the self-revelation of God the Father through Jesus Christ his incarnate Son and in the Holy Spirit, Barth was convinced that our human apprehension of God clothed with the revelation mediated to us through the human words of the Bible is by the grace of God a real apprehension of him grounded in the depths of his triune being who nevertheless infinitely transcends all that we can think and say of him. God the revealer, God revealing himself and God revealed are one and the same in being and agency.[34]

2. The Mystery and Miracle of Revelation

What Karl Barth calls 'the mystery of revelation' has to do with the fact that while revelation is nothing less than God himself, it nevertheless concerns itself with man and involves a real relation between God and man effected by the grace of God within the concrete situations of space and time where man is found in this world. Since divine revelation is grounded in itself, God clothed with his revelation always retains his own transcendence, freedom and objectivity even when he communicates himself to us and gives himself to us as the object of our knowing. Hence authentic knowledge of God on our part mediated through his revelation carries with it an acknowledgment of the miracle by reason of which our meeting with the Lord God takes place and our knowledge of him is actualised. Because revelation is finally nothing less than God himself,

> It is *mystery*, i.e. a reality the possibility of which resides absolutely within itself; and therefore, also, we shall never, no, not in all eternity, be able to understand, derive, and substantiate it except out of itself. God is of and through himself. We correspondingly are able to meditate on revelation only if our thinking begins with revelation when it has spoken for itself. And, therefore, it is authority, i.e., truth which cannot be measured by the rule of any other truth beside it, however profound and valid that truth may appear to be. Rather it is truth which decides, and continues to decide what may be true. It is truth, then, with whose acknowledgment every truth must make its beginning;

---

34 Refer to *Die christliche Dogmatik*, 126ff; and *CD*, I.1, 295ff.

and without its acknowledgment even the profoundest truth is a deception and a lie.[35]

This mystery of revelation as identical with the Word of God, and yet as an irruption of that Word into our human existence effecting real meeting between God and man and man and God, has taken concrete, indeed corporeal, form in Jesus Christ the incarnate Son of God who was born of the Virgin Mary and rose again in body from the dead.

> The mystery of the revelation of God in Jesus Christ consists in the fact that the eternal Word of God chose, sanctified and assumed human nature and existence into oneness with himself, in order thus, as very God and very man, to become the Word of reconciliation spoken by God to man. The sign of this mystery revealed in the resurrection of Jesus Christ is the miracle of his birth, that he was conceived by the Holy Ghost, born of the Virgin Mary.[36]

Because the mystery of divine revelation has taken that singular, decisive form in the life and activity of Jesus Christ the Word become flesh, it is always in the last analysis by reference to the absolute miracle of God in Jesus Christ that Barth seeks to elucidate the mystery of revelation and of our knowledge of it. 'The singularity of the event of revelation conditions the singularity of the knowledge which it awakens and underlies.'[37]

On the one hand, revelation is the gracious condescension of God to enter into our human existence through the assumption of our human nature, manifest in the birth of Jesus; but on the other hand, it is also the triumphant raising up of our human nature from its alienation, corruption and darkness into union with the divine life, manifest in the resurrection of Jesus. The whole life and existence of Jesus on earth bracketed between his birth and his resurrection is the embodied actuality of God's revelation in which God has given himself to man and reconciled man to himself, thus creating for man, as Barth expresses it, 'the objective possibility' of revelation which is complemented by 'the subjective possibility' of revelation through the outpouring of the Holy Spirit.[38] It is thus that the reality of divine revelation has broken into our world of space and time

---

35 *God in Action*, 12f. Consult also *CD*, I.1, 162ff.
36 *CD*, I.2, 122.
37 *CD*, IV.2, 149.
38 *CD*, I.2, 25ff and 242ff.

in the Incarnation and continues through the Holy Spirit miraculously to actualise itself in our human understanding—after the manner in which the Lord Jesus was conceived by the Holy Spirit and born of the Virgin Mary, and after the manner in which he rose victorious over death emptying the tomb of Joseph of Arimathea and entered through closed doors to reveal himself to his disciples in the upper room.

The Inspiration of the Bible

If the supreme mystery of revelation has been embodied in Jesus Christ in that wondrous way, it must be in accordance with that very mystery and in union with it that the inspiration of Holy Scripture is to be understood. As Barth expresses it, 'the eventuation of the presence of the Word of God in the human word of the prophets and apostles, can only be regarded as a repetition, a secondary prolongation and continuation of the once-for-all and primary eventuation of revelation itself'.[39] By its very nature, then, Holy Scripture functions as a unique witness to divine revelation in its primary eventuation and as such ever points beyond itself to the transcendent Word that God himself is, and precisely in that service to the Word it is and ever becomes the divinely inspired eventuation of the presence of the Word in the human word of the biblical witness. This is not to say that the Word of God is tied to the Bible, but it is to say that the Bible is tied to the Word of God, and is thereby assumed under the power and disposal of the Word of God in such a way as to be constituted the Word of God to us. This is the miraculous thing about the Bible: that by the grace of God it can be and is made to be and is therefore believed to be 'the Word of God'.

Thus, to cite Barth again: 'Scripture is recognised as the Word of God by the fact that it is the Word of God. This is what we are told by the doctrine of the witness of the Holy Spirit.'[40] The miracle of divine revelation is not only that it crosses the infinite distance between the Creator and the creature, eternity and time, God and man, in order to effect a real relation between them, but that it breaks through the barrier of sin and guilt, alienation and darkness, which separates man from God, in order to effect actual reconciliation and communion between them. Divine revelation as the drawing near of God to man requires and calls forth a corresponding movement in which man draws near God. That is to say, divine revelation

---

39   CD, I.2, 534.
40   CD, I.2, 537.

completes its movement through the establishing of a two-way relation in communion between God and man and man and God in which God's self-revealing to man is faithfully actualised in a *vis-a-vis* within the mind and understanding of man. That is what has taken place in the Incarnation, through the hypostatic union of God and man in the one Person of the Lord Jesus Christ, and through the atonement, in the mediation between God and man accomplished in the reconciling life and activity of Jesus Christ from his birth to his death and resurrection. It is in the light of this revealing and reconciling activity of God brought to its fulfilment in Christ Jesus, the one Mediator between God and man, that we are surely to understand the miracle of the Holy Scriptures generated by the creative and reconciling Word of God out of frail, fallible human thought and speech.

Two interlocking aspects of this biblical miracle call for particular attention.

The Unassumed is the Unhealed

In the first place, if it is indeed a miracle that the Bible is the Word of God, then we must be careful not to play down in our understanding of it either the humanity of its form or the offence which can be taken at it—otherwise we would not be taking seriously its relation to the controlling actualisation of revelation and reconciliation in Jesus Christ. In that Jesus Christ is Word God become flesh, what is of decisive importance for God's self-revelation through him is the complete union of God and man in him, the completeness of both the Deity and the humanity of Christ. If he were not completely God he would not be identical with God's revelation; if he were not completely man he would not be to us the actuality of God's revelation.[41] That is why the early Church took exception to both ebionite and docetic approaches to Jesus Christ—rejecting alike a Christology 'from below' and 'from above' for a completely unitary approach to Christ as at once very God and very man. They quickly realised that a deficient view of his Deity or of his humanity would bring into question the very substance of the Gospel as God's revealing and reconciling gift of himself to man. Hence they insisted that in the Incarnation it was the *whole man*, in the unimpaired nature and integrity of his body, soul and mind, who was taken into union with the Person of the Son of God. While there would have been no Jesus had not the Son of God freely become man—the Incarnation

---

41 *CD*, I.2, 132ff. For Barth's early teaching about this, see *Die christliche Dogmatik*, 272ff.

was a pure act of Divine grace—nevertheless within that act of grace the man Jesus possessed full personal reality as true man in the one indivisible Person of the incarnate Son of God.

On the other hand, the ancient Fathers of the Church also insisted that in becoming man, and in making himself one with us, the Son of God assumed not some neutral human nature, but our actual fallen Adamic nature, and thereby made our sin and misery, our death and fate his own. He really became one with us as we actually are in our flesh of sin and alienation in mind. Otherwise our actual human nature, physical and mental, would not have been brought within the sanctifying and renewing activity of the Saviour. Thus they refused to separate incarnation from atonement, or the union of divine and human natures in Christ from his healing and reconciling work. In accordance with the New Testament they taught that Christ was absolutely sinless, but held that in the very act of taking our fallen Adamic humanity upon himself, the Son of God condemned sin in the flesh by his perfect holiness, and redeemed, renewed and sanctified that humanity at the same time. It was thus a primary doctrine of the early Church that 'the unassumed is the unhealed', or 'what Christ has not taken up has not been saved', which applies above all to the mind of fallen man, for it is in the dark depths of the mind that our sin, original and actual, has its root.

It is one of the most significant contributions of Karl Barth that he reintroduced this great evangelical principle back into dogmatic theology,[42] and thereby deepened our understanding of the interrelation not only between incarnation and atonement, but between revelation, reconciliation and redemption. Our concern at the moment is with his perception that this principle applies also to our understanding of Holy Scripture. The miracle that the Bible is the Word of God has to do with the fact that in generating it the Word of God has taken our fallen thought and speech upon himself in order to judge, heal, and sanctify it as the vehicle of his revealing communication to human beings. The miracle is that in the Bible the Word of God comes to us through the word of sinful, erring people to whom God has spoken and who bear witness to his speaking in frail, fallible, inadequate forms of thought and speech, which imperfect though they may be are nevertheless assumed and adapted by the holy Word of God to be the human medium by which God continues to communicate his self-revelation to mankind. Far from being contaminated by the transience,

---

42 CD, I.2, 151ff; also *Die christliche Dogmatik*, 265ff.

imperfection or inadequacy of the human medium, however, the Word of God is redemptively present in the biblical word in such a sanctifying, miraculous way that it achieves its end as the spoken and revealed Word of God in spite of what may be offensive. This implies a dynamic rather than a static notion of Biblical inerrancy. 'Verbal inspiration', Barth declares, 'does not mean the infallibility of the biblical word in its linguistic, historical and theological character as human word. It means that the fallible and faulty human word is as such used by God and has to be received and heard in spite of its human fallibility.'[43] The real offence of the Bible, then, is that as in the cross of Christ God makes such miraculous use of what he has assumed.

> This offence is therefore grounded, like the overcoming of it, in the mercy of God. For that reason every time we turn the Word of God into an infallible biblical word of man or the biblical word of man into an infallible Word of God we resist that which we ought never to resist, i.e. the truth of the miracle that here fallible men speak the Word of God in fallible human words, and we therefore resist the sovereignty of the grace in which God himself became man in Christ to glorify himself in his humanity.[44]

That is to say, what is finally at stake in a doctrine of the static concept of verbal inerrancy or infallibility of the Bible, is offence at the cross of Christ. Is this the reason why traditional doctrines of the inspiration of the Holy Scripture are strangely not brought into conjunction with the doctrine of atoning redemption?

Resurrection is Revelation

In the second place, if it is indeed a miracle that the Bible is the Word of God we must beware of playing down the corporeality of divine revelation or of detaching the Word of God from the earthen vessel in which it is mediated to us. The crucial issues here have to do with the corporeality of the resurrection and the redemption of the body. The fact that the Word of God has once for all become flesh in Jesus Christ establishes quite finally that God has not held himself aloof from our creaturely and historical existence, but wills to reveal himself to us within the subject-object and subject-subject structures and relations of our physical and personal being

---

43 *CD*, I.2, 533.
44 *CD*, I.2, 529.

in the world of space and time. The fact that in Jesus Christ God has not just come into man but has really become man and meets us and speaks to us *as man* (without of course ceasing to be God) means that God has veiled his revelation in creaturely flesh; but the fact that in Jesus Christ God meets and speaks to us at the same time *as God*, means that revelation takes place through an unveiling of what has been veiled.

It is the mystery and the miracle of divine revelation that God reveals himself as God in terms of what is not God, namely man, and that revelation is given to us only in terms of what it is not, in the actual humanity of those to whom it is given. Thus as in the incarnation of the Word of God divine revelation involves entry into our worldliness (*Welthaftigkeit* is Barth's term) or secularity. If God did not speak to us in worldly or secular form, he would not speak to us at all. Hence to evade the worldliness of his Word is to evade Jesus Christ. However, if God's revelation were not to shine through the very worldliness into which it has entered and with which it has clothed itself, it would remain veiled or hidden from us and thus fail to achieve its end as revelation. In the words of the Fourth Gospel, 'The light shines in the darkness, and the darkness has not overcome it'.[45]

It was, then, an essential element in Barth's doctrine of the Word of God that by its very nature and in virtue of its essential act, divine revelation involves both veiling and unveiling in which each serves the fulfilment of the other.[46] But it was also an essential element in his teaching that our understanding of divine revelation should begin with the resurrection of Jesus Christ from the dead, for it is from that revealing centre that the whole evangelical account of Jesus Christ is to be understood. This is made very clear by Barth in his commentary on St Paul's statement at the beginning of the Epistle to the Romans: 'concerning his Son Jesus Christ our Lord, who was born of the seed of David according to the flesh; and declared to be the Son of God with power, according to the Holy Spirit, through his resurrection from the dead.' The resurrection was both the establishing or declaration of the divine Sonship of Christ from above, and the corresponding discernment of it from below. It was certainly an occurrence within history, but it was also the point within history where it was intersected vertically from above, where the new world of the Spirit touched the old world of the flesh. 'The Resurrection is the revelation: the

---

45 John 1:5.

46 *CD*, I.1, 169f, 174ff; for further references see the entry under 'Revelation' in the *Index Volume* of the *Church Dogmatics*, 253.

disclosing of Jesus as the Christ, the appearing of God, and the apprehending of God in Jesus Christ.'[47]

The truth that Barth was so concerned to stress here is this: it was in the resurrection of Jesus from the dead that divine revelation in Jesus Christ became recognised by the disciples as identical with God himself. That is what actually governed the composition of the Gospels, for the understanding of Jesus Christ by the Evangelists, including their identification of him as the Son of God, flows directly from the resurrection. In fact it was in the light of the startling unveiling in and through the resurrection of who Jesus Christ really was that they finally presented all their reporting of Jesus. Thus they allowed the majestic *I am* of the risen Lord, regnant and triumphant over all the forces of darkness, to provide revealing enlightenment and objective depth to their report of the words and deeds of Jesus in such a way that their account of his life and mission provided the Gospels with a unifying intra-structure deriving from the witness of the disciples, and forced upon them by the intrinsic nature of the Son of Man himself.[48] The particular aspect of Barth's teaching to which I wish to refer now was his immense emphasis upon the *corporeal nature* of both the Incarnation and the Resurrection, and thus upon the realism of divine revelation to mankind in space and time. The issue at stake had been highlighted by the attack of Neo-Protestant liberalism upon the 'materialism' of early Christian theology which it sought to replace by a 'spiritualistic moralism'. This was very evident in criticism of the concept of two 'natures' in Christ. This modern Christology, Barth pointed out,

> has a horror of *physis*, of externality, of corporeality; it cannot take breath save in the thin air of moral judgment and of the soul's capacity for experience. It does not know what to make of what the New Testament calls *soma, sari, thanatos, zoe, anastasis* and the like. Biblical miracles are painful to it, apart from anything else, because every one of them is extremely 'natural'. What has it to say to Jesus' bodily resurrection, or to *natus ex virgine*? Horror of this means a strange impoverishment, but that is not of decisive importance here. What is important is that in all this there lurks a horror of the being of God in his revelation. . . . In refusing to acknowledge a 'natural' element in revelation, it refused to

---

47 *The Epistle to the Romans*, 30.

48 Cf. here my account of this in *Space, Time and Resurrection* (Edinburgh, 1976), 159ff; and refer to the section on 'The Royal Man' in *CD*, IV.2, 154–264.

acknowledge an ontological element. It was opposed to the realism of the biblical message of revelation.[49]

Modern liberal Christology stands for the transmutation of revelation into the subjectivities of religious consciousness and Christian experience. In sharp contrast to it Barth's insistence on the corporeality of the resurrection has the effect of confirming the corporeality, and thus the ontological realism, of the Word made flesh and so of the whole self-revelation of God in Jesus Christ from his birth to his death and resurrection. The virgin birth of Jesus and his resurrection from the dead constitute together the mystery and the miracle of divine revelation in its veiling and its unveiling. While the birth of the Son of God into the human race meant the veiling of revelation, the resurrection of Jesus meant the unveiling or revealing of his divine-human reality as the Son of God. Thus far from cutting our understanding of Jesus off from his concrete historical and earthly existence before the cross, the resurrection has the effect of gathering it all up and confirming its concrete factuality by allowing the historical Jesus to come to his own within the dimension of the risen Jesus, and the risen Jesus is discerned to have no other fabric than that in the life and mission of the historical Jesus. That is why Barth insists that 'the resurrection is revelation',[50] for it is the resurrection that really unveils and gives access to the historical Jesus, without in any way detracting from his physical and historical actuality, thereby enabling us to understand him in terms of his own intrinsic nature and truth as the Word made flesh, the Son of God become man. If we were to abstract from the Gospels the dimension of the resurrection, the actual picture of the historical Jesus they present would fragment, for the Gospels would then be considered apart from the unveiling or revealing activity of the risen Lord and so apart from the enlightenment that gives them their internal coherence. As it was through the same power of the risen Jesus that the eyes of the disciples were opened to understand the Scriptures, so it is with us.

It cannot be stressed too much that it is within the dynamic and objective frame of revelation reaching from the birth to the resurrection of Christ that the veiling and unveiling of revelation in the Bible must be understood. We have already seen that in accordance with the pattern established in Jesus' birth of the Virgin Mary the Word of God is

49 CD, I.2, 130.
50 *The Resurrection of the Dead*, tran. H. J. Stenning (London, 1933), Barth's exposition of 1 Corinthians 1:14, especially chapters II and III.

redemptively present in the assumption of human thought and speech as the creaturely medium of God's self-communication to mankind. It was thus in and through the sanctified assumption of our human language that the Bible came into being as the written form which the Word of God takes within our worldly conditions. Now we are to see that it is in and through the power and presence of the risen Jesus that the written form of the Word of God in the Bible becomes the vehicle of the living Voice of God as he speaks to us and reveals himself to us. As in the corporeal resurrection of Jesus Christ there was no abrogation of his human being and historical reality, but rather their confirmation and establishment, so here the risen Christ comes to us through the veiling of the Word in the Bible without in any way derogating or disparaging its human and historical reality, but on the contrary confirms and establishes it as the inspired objective reality of the Word of God in its historical and written form which we are bound to study with the utmost seriousness. The Holy Bible is thus to be cherished and interpreted with full theological realism as the Word of God. As the risen Lord came to his disciples in the upper room through closed doors, so by the power of his resurrection he continues to make himself present to us through the pages of the Bible, unveiling to us what has been veiled, and opening our eyes to understand the Scriptures. Resurrection is revelation, and revelation is resurrection. From this perspective it becomes clear why it is the ordained function of Holy Scripture to point away from itself to Christ and thereby to be the appointed place where he gives us access to his presence from within our worldly conditions. This is why Karl Barth used to speak of the bodily resurrection of Jesus as the starting and controlling point of all his biblical and theological thought. It is for this reason also that he welcomed and appropriated the hermeneutical principle of the Nicene Fathers and the Reformers, that while divine revelation is mediated to us exclusively through the Bible, the realities to which biblical statements refer are not to be interpreted in the light of those biblical statements, but biblical statements are to be interpreted in the light of the realities to which they refer.

3. Exegetico-theological Interpretation

Let us return to Barth's pivotal point that revelation means the incarnation of the Word, but the incarnation means entry into our worldliness. This worldliness is not something accidental to revelation but belongs to its essential movement, for by its very nature revelation is mediated to us in terms of what it is not, namely, the humanity and worldliness of those to whom it is given. This implies that from first to last all our understanding of revelation and all our interpretation of the Bible have to reckon with an inner dialectic or bi-polarity. We cannot penetrate behind the worldliness of revelation to its inner substance, any more than we can get behind the back of Jesus to the eternal Son of God. Nor can we divide between the form and content of revelation, between the human word of revelation and revelation itself, any more than we can divide between the human and divine natures in the one Person of Christ.[51] As in our understanding of Christ Jesus, the divine form and human form of revelation must neither be confounded nor separated, but must be apprehended in the integrity and mystery of their union. And as in our understanding of the historical Jesus Christ we look to the risen Lord himself to enlighten and give meaning to the whole of his earthly life and activity, so in our interpretation of the presentation of Christ in the biblical witness we seek to let the living Word of the risen Lord be heard and known in and through the human words of the Holy Scriptures and inform them with divine content.

As we have already noted it was Barth's arduous struggle to let the Word be heard in the words of the Bible that dominated his life and work as a pastor summoned to preach the Word of God to his congregation Sunday by Sunday. And it was in essentially the same dialectical struggle in which he engaged as a biblical and theological teacher in the University, to expose the Word in the words. There was no evading of the linguistic and historico-critical examination of the biblical text,[52] but all his concentrated exegesis pressed behind the many questions that arose to the one cardinal question as to the Word in the words by which they were all embraced. That is to say, after all the sweat and groans which serious exegesis involved, everything in the biblical texts had to be interpreted finally and primarily in the light of what they were speaking about.[53]

Objective Reference of Biblical Statements

Barth's wrestling with the Holy Scriptures gave rise to what he called dialectical theology, that is, one in which he sought to do justice to both

---

51 See *CD*, I.2, 492ff.

52 *The Epistle to the Romans*, Preface to the First Edition, 1. Cf. also *CD*, I.2, 466ff, 492ff, 722ff.

53 Consult again the Prefaces to *The Epistle to the Romans*.

ends of the bi-polar relation between the human and the divine, the words and the Word, the worldly form of revelation and its divine content. Faithful exegesis of the biblical text forced him to take seriously its basic semantic function as *witness* in which it points away from itself to the self-witness and self-revelation of God.[54] As is well known Barth made much of Grünewald's impressive painting of John the Baptist with his hand and index finger outstretched toward the crucified Christ. 'He must increase, but I must decrease', John cried.[55] That is precisely how biblical statements are to be regarded, as statements that refer away from themselves to divine objective realities. Biblical statements are true not because they capture the truth in themselves but because they refer to truth independent of themselves. A distinction is thus to be recognised between true statements and the truth of statements. Hence Barth took pains to reject any nominalistic identification of biblical statements with the truth, and pursued throughout a realist understanding of biblical statements as ontologically grounded in the truth and controlled by it. Biblical statements are true in respect of the fidelity of their objective reference to the truth—that is why they are to be understood and interpreted in accordance with the realities to which they refer, and not vice versa. This understanding of the nature and function of biblical statements Barth seems to have learned first from John Calvin,[56] and then from St Anselm.[57]

This attempt to interpret the Scriptures by following through the line of their witness and letting his mind come under the compelling claims of the objective reality to which they refer had the effect of throwing Barth into turmoil before the strange new world within the Bible that opened up before him. That is reflected very clearly in his astonishing handling of St Paul's Epistle to the Romans in which, as we have already noted, he was particularly concerned to clarify his own mind. He found himself increasingly under question before God as his own questions were turned back upon himself. It became clear that his questions about God were not

---

54 Cf. especially *CD*, I.2, 10ff, 223ff, 457–72.

55 John 3:30.

56 I recall Barth's account of Calvin's concept of the objective reference of biblical statements in a seminar in which we discussed the Address to Francis I of France, with which Calvin prefaced the *Institute*. See also Barth's preface to the third edition of *The Epistle to the Romans*, in which he praises 'the critical freedom of exegesis' used by Calvin.

57 See Barth's masterly handling of Anselm's thought in *Anselm: Fides Quaerens Intellectum*, tran. Iain Robertson (Richmond, VA, 1958).

really in earnest, for they were being asked only in order to escape hearing an answer that he could not understand or did not want to understand. The Bible on the other hand brings an answer and seeks the question corresponding to it. Thus under the impact of the dynamic objective reality of the risen Christ to which the biblical witness directed him, Barth's questions were themselves continuously questioned, critically questioned and turned inside out in such a way that the presuppositions behind his questions became more and more exposed.[58] Expressed theologically, Barth found that to be put in the right with God through justification by grace alone, meant that he himself with all his own ideas and presuppositions was put in the wrong—that was the cutting edge and devastating effect of St Paul's teaching: 'Let God be true and every man a liar'. Let God be true and Karl Barth a liar! Let God be true and Barth's Commentary on St Paul's Epistle a liar, and not least his dialectical method! True and faithful exposition of the Bible is that which refers away from itself to the one Word and Truth of the living God, before which all human witness is relativised.

That is to say, rigorous exegetico-theological activity has to reckon with a deep-seated conflict between the determining structure of our own conceptions and presuppositions and the coherent structure of the incarnate self-revelation of God in Jesus Christ, so that repentant rethinking has to take place at a very deep level.[59] That is why all Karl Barth's writing and the *Church Dogmatics* above all are full of questions, questions to which he gave expression under the questioning of the Word of God in order to let the living Truth of God disclose itself to him unhindered as far as possible by himself. It is particularly at this point that the strictly scientific procedure of Barth's exegetico-theological inquiry is so apparent. As in all precise science his questions are endlessly recast in the light of what becomes disclosed of the reality being investigated so that the conceptions on which the questions are based are progressively revised and adapted to the nature of the object.[60] No theologian in the whole history of the Church has submitted himself to such relentless questioning before the Word of God, and no works of Christian theology are so replete with such searching questions following exponentially on one another page after page in the *Church Dogmatics*.

---

58 Refer to chapters 3, 4 and 6 of *The Word of God and the Word of Man*.
59 See *CD*, I.2, the section 'Freedom under the Word', 695–740.
60 See our Editors' Preface to the English translation of *CD*, I.2, viif.

Reconciling Revelation

At the same time all this is found to take place within the circle of Karl Barth's understanding of the profound mutual interpenetration of divine revelation and reconciliation. Revelation does not achieve its end as revelation apart from reconciliation, for only through reconciliation can revelation complete its own movement within the human mind, evoking from it a corresponding movement of recognition and obedient reception whereby it becomes actualised. It is of course the Incarnation that shows us that divine revelation is given not apart from reconciliation but is mediated to mankind within the atoning life and death of Christ. In him we learn that revelation means the entry of the mind of God into our human darkness and alienation in order to redeem our understanding and to effect the reconciliation of our human mind with the mind of God. That is to say, the objective interpenetration of revelation and reconciliation in the Incarnation needs to be subjectively realised in our relations with God in and through Christ in such a way that there takes place a reconciling of the will and mind of man with the will and mind of God. But that is precisely what happens in faithful exegetico-theological activity in the progressive resolution of the conflict with the alien forms of thought which we bring to the understanding of the Word of God, in the course of which our understanding instead of being conformed to this world is transformed through the renewing of our mind under the power and redeeming presence of the crucified and risen Jesus Christ. Christ is risen! He cleaves his way through all our mental obstructions, entering through the locked doors of our minds to make himself present to us, until like St Thomas we put our fingers in his wounds and cry out 'My Lord and my God'.[61] Exegetico-theological activity of this kind, which is a painful wrestling with the Holy Scriptures, becomes a profoundly devotional movement of thought, in fact a form of what St Paul called 'rational worship'.[62] That is precisely the kind of movement in theological understanding which, as I have personally found, runs throughout the volumes of Karl Barth's *Church Dogmatics*, for again and again, as in my study of them I have shared the movement of his thought, I have been brought trembling to my knees in thanksgiving, prayer and adoration.

---

61 John 20:28.
62 Romans 12:1f.

Barth's Biblicism

We must now consider Barth's understanding of the relation between biblicist and theological thinking. He was not averse to being called a 'biblicist' because of his determination to be faithful to the Bible as the inspired Word of God, but, as we have seen, he did not believe that divine revelation could be read straight off the pages of the Bible for that implied a direct and static identity between the word of man and the Word of God in the Bible. While Barth was clearly committed to an objective concept of the divine inspiration of the Holy Scripture, his understanding of its verbal and propositional character was governed, not by rationalist or nominalist epistemological preconceptions, but by what the Bible says about itself as *witness* to divine revelation, which made him realise that biblical statements necessarily point away from themselves to God. They refer to the Truth of God independent of themselves, and so allow the Truth, as Calvin used to say, to retain its own Majesty over against them.[63] As such biblical statements fall short of the Truth to which they direct us, so that considered in themselves they have a measure of inadequacy which belongs to their nature as witness. Biblical statements would not fulfil their divinely appointed function if they claimed to contain the Truth within themselves or identified themselves with the Truth, or put themselves on the same level as the Truth. They are rightly to be interpreted, therefore, under the compelling authority of God's self-witness and self-grounded truth, and under the direction of his Word which it is their function to serve and not to usurp. Their function is not symbolic or conventional but signitive or semantic, one which they fulfil in objective or ontological reference to the Truth of God beyond themselves, from which they derive and upon which they are grounded. They are true statements in being truly related to the absolute truth which God is and by which they are relativised.

This biblical understanding of biblical statements and of how they are to be theologically interpreted was greatly reinforced by Barth's study of St Anselm.[64] Because of their objective reference biblical statements cannot be treated like fixed premises from which theological truths may be deduced, but as statements signifying the 'solid truth' of God upon which they are

---

63 John Calvin, *Institute*, Prefatory address to the King of France.

64 This arose out of a seminar on Anselm's *Cur Deus homo* held in Bonn during the summer of 1930 and published in 1931 as *Anselm: Fides Quaerens Intellectum*. The English edition appeared in 1960. See also my discussion in *Karl Barth: An Introduction to his Early Theology*, 182–93.

grounded. By their very nature, therefore, biblical statements have to be interpreted theologically in the light of the objective realities to which they refer. It is the business of the theologian to reflect upon what has been signified in the biblical text, and then to follow the signifying operation back to the reality signified, in order to let his understanding fall under the authority of its truth and take shape under the compulsion of its intrinsic intelligibility. Thus the quest for theological understanding begins strictly where biblical citations end, that is, at the relation between biblical thought and speech and their source in the truth and being of God.[65]

This does not mean that once we are in touch with the truth and being of God the biblical word may be left behind, far less kicked away, for we are quite unable to know God except on the basis of the biblical revelation. It is our specific task as theologians, at that point between the biblical citations and the realities they signify, to inquire into what we ourselves have to think and say on the basis and under the direction of the biblical revelation. Although, as Barth pointed out, this may require theologians to pass beyond the explicit statements of Holy Scripture and formulate propositions independently of their actual wording, as happened at the Council of Nicaea over the relation between the incarnate Son and God the Father,[66] nevertheless they must constantly be tested by critical reference back to the biblical witness. Because true theological concepts and statements refer to what is greater than we can ever conceive or express, they are essentially open-structured statements, always revisable under the continuing impact of divine revelation. In this event it belongs to the precision of theological statements that they fall short of the majesty and glory of God, for they are truly related to him only as they point beyond themselves in such a way as to behave as human statements in the service of the Word and Truth of God. After all, the Bible itself will pass away with this world, but the Word of God to which it refers and which it is inspired to communicate endures forever.

It should now be clear that Karl Barth's biblicism was of a rather deeper kind than is normally to be found. He did not build up his account of Christian doctrine by organising together biblical quotations and working out their conceptual content into some kind of systematic order. He certainly engaged in strenuous exegetico-theological interpretation of the biblical text ranging over the full extent of Holy Scripture in an unparalleled way, as

---

65 Anselm: *Fides Quaerens Intellectum*, 31ff, 40ff, etc.
66 Cf. Hilary, *De Trinitate*, II.2–5; Calvin, *Institute*, I.13.3–5.

we noted earlier. But for Barth true biblicism meant accustoming himself to breathe the air of divine revelation, and learning to think instinctively and speak naturally within it. Hence he was concerned above all to steep himself in the biblical witness, and to indwell its message in such a way that the truth of divine revelation became built into the very walls of his mind, and gave inner form to all his dogmatic conceptions and formulations of its material content. Unless theological insight and formation of this kind are already present, if only in incipient form, in his exegetical study of the Scriptures, the biblical theologian has not been engaging in genuine exegesis, for he has not been concerned to understand the Scriptures in terms of their all-important objective reference to the Word and Truth that God himself is. The decisive point in interpretation is not reached until there is inquiry into the reality signified. True interpretation takes place, therefore, where perception of the meaning of the biblical text and understanding of the reality it indicates are one.

Trinitarian Revelation

For Barth the paradigmatic instance of this kind of exegetico-theological inquiry is to be found in the disclosure of the trinitarian ground of our actual knowledge of God mediated through Holy Scripture, for there discernment of the objective meaning of the biblical revelation and understanding of God's self-revelation as Father, Son and Holy Spirit coincide. The all-important factor in this inquiry is the supreme truth that God is himself the content of his revelation: he reveals himself through himself and is himself what he reveals. Since revelation is God revealing himself we are concerned immediately in revelation with God the revealer, God who is the content of his revelation, and God in the act of his self-revelation, a fact which coincides with the content of the biblical witness to God as Father, Son and Holy Spirit. Barth discerned the biblical root of the doctrine of the Trinity in the condensed statement that *God reveals himself as the Lord.*[67] To express it otherwise, as Barth does, the one divine act of revelation is internally threefold: God is himself at once the Subject, Object and Predicate of revelation.[68]

There is no need for us here to discuss Barth's doctrine of the Trinity further—what concerns us now is that he did not build the doctrine through

67 *CD*, I.1, 306, 314,

68 This approach to the doctrine of the Trinity is evident already in *Die christliche Dogmatik*, 126ff.

adducing explicit biblical statements, so much as through an analysis of the basic structure of divine revelation in coordination with the reflection in the biblical witness to revelation. Exegetico-theological interpretation carried Barth into the heart of the elliptical movement set up between God's self-revealing and human knowing of him embodied in the Holy Scriptures, within which his own mind obediently took shape. While God may be known by us only through the Scriptures, the Scriptures themselves are to be understood only in terms of the revealing activity of God which gave rise to them. In his analysis of that elliptical movement Barth laid bare an illuminating correspondence between the trinitarian form of divine revelation and the trinitarian form of the biblical witness, within which he found the root of the doctrine of the Trinity.[69]

Quite clearly Barth's doctrine of the Trinity is grounded not simply on the text of Holy Scripture but in an in-depth examination of the inherent structure of biblical revelation imposed upon it through the three-fold act of God's self-revelation as Father, Son and Holy Spirit. Barth's theological inquiry always begins with careful attention to the biblical witness and takes the form of a movement of thought from below upward toward the objective ground of revelation, but it also takes the form of a movement of thought from above downward, from the constitutive revelation of God to the biblical witness, in course of which the understanding of the biblical witness is raised to a higher level. Thus there takes place a profound epistemological inversion in the human act of knowing under the control of God's self-revelation, in which a trinitarian structure becomes built into the foundation of exegetico-theological interpretation of the Bible and into the foundation of all Christian doctrine. Hence for Barth the formulation of the doctrine of the Holy Trinity takes place when under the actual impact of the Word of God the exegesis of biblical statements becomes matched to the divine reality to which they refer.

It was a primary principle of Barth's biblicism that no Christian doctrine can be properly grounded or rightly expounded except on the basis of the self-revelation of God attested in Holy Scripture. But it was also his masterful conviction that far from being one doctrine among others the doctrine of the Holy Trinity occupies a central authoritative place in the foundation of all true knowledge of God, and therefore must be allowed to exercise a controlling role in all theological explanation and dogmatic

---

69 Cf. *Die christliche Dogmatik*, 150: '*die ratio der Triniät ist die ratio der Offenbarung ... die ratio der Trinität wird erkannt in der ratio der Offenbarung*'. And see *CD*, I.1, 307ff.

formulation. That is the way in which he set out to write his great *Church Dogmatics*, as a theologian of the Word.

GENERAL INDEX

A

Alexander of Hales 64
allegory 26–30, 129–30
Ambrose 154
Anselm 69–96, 156, 219–20
Aquinas, Thomas 64, 97–31
Aristotle 25–26, 65, 98–131, 189
Athanasius 6–7, 44–45
atonement 15, 58–59, 62–63, 208–9
 limited 64–65
Augustine 1, 51–53, 73, 105, 109–13, 154

B

Barr, James 97
Barth, Karl 6, 18, 44–67, 191–223
Basilides 31, 33, 37
Bible. *See* Holy Scriptures (and Scripture Index)
Boethius 3, 97
Bultmann, Rudolf 1

C

Calvin, John 1, 8, 18, 194, 216
Cassian, John 3
Christ
 divinity of 62, 116
 humanity of 5, 13, 56, 62, 116
Chrysostom, John 1
Clement of Alexandria 34
Colet, John 151
communication 11, 18–19, 181–82
creation 42
Cyril of Alexandria 59

D

dogmatics 50–51, 192–223
dualism 5–6, 31–36, 46, 54, 63
Duns Scotus 4

E

Erasmus 150, 151–79
ethics 26
evil 42

F

faith 12, 34–35, 42, 61, 70–71, 128–29, 135

G

Gnosticism 30–37
grace 13, 45–46, 61, 65, 217
Grünewald, Matthias 216

H

Haggadah 20–21
Halakah 21
Hellenism 22–31, 180–81
hermeneutics
 biblical and general 11–19
 history of 1–9
 Jewish 20–21, 24–25, 27–30
Hesiod 25
Hippolytus 33
Hodge, Charles 54
Holy Spirit 11, 33, 44–46, 103, 203, 206–7
 sin against 65
Homer 25, 160
Hugh of St. Victor 3
Hume, David 8

I

idealism 186–88
Irenaeus 36–37, 45

J

Jerome 156, 162
John of Damascus 114
judgment 15

K

Kant, Emmanuel 8–9
Kierkegaard, Søren 203

L

law and gospel 43
Leo the Great 60
liberalism 55–56, 213
logic 26
Lombard, Peter 3
Luther, Martin 1, 60, 147, 178, 194

M

Mackintosh, H. R. 60, 191
Major, John 4
Marcion 38, 41–43
Mary, Virgin 60
Melanchthon 147
More, Thomas 154

N

Nestorianism 143
nominalism 97, 152, 177, 219

O

Origen 131, 154

P

Pelagianism 179
Philo 28–31
Plato 22–24, 75, 154–55
Plutarch 28

prayer 71, 219
Pseudo Dionysius 3

R

rationalism 55, 219
realism 5–7, 72–75, 158, 187
reconciliation 15, 56, 62–63, 218
redemption 35, 42
resurrection 206–14
Reuchlin, John 132–50
revelation 11–12, 13, 18, 48–51, 197–203, 210–11

S

Schleiermacher, Friedrich 8, 19, 54, 180–90
Scriptures, Holy 11–19, 71, 99–104, 115–31, 139–40, 146–50, 153, 176–79, 191–223
   inspiration of 15–16, 55–56, 198–200, 207–8
semantics 27, 73, 140, 216, 219–20
sin 59–60, 178
Stoicism 26–27

T

Tertullian 37–38, 51
Trinity 44–48, 66–67, 195, 221–23
truth 49–51, 78–91, 130, 178

U

universalism 64–66

V

Valentinus 31–33, 37, 40
Valla, Lorenzo 151
Vincent of Lerins 3
Virgin Birth 206–7, 212

W

William of Ockham 4

SCRIPTURE INDEX

Psalm 74:11 141
Psalm 107:20 157

Proverbs 12:18 157

Isaiah 9:6 141

John 1:1ff 141–42
John 1:5 211
John 1:14 202
John 14:6 11, 135, 142
John 14:9 141

Romans 1:4 211
Romans 1:5 12
Romans 3:4 217
Romans 8:3 14

Romans 16:26 12

1 Corinthians 1:28 141
1 Corinthians 13:12 14

Ephesians 2:12–22 15
Ephesians 2:18 67
Ephesians 4:21 12

Colossians 1:15ff 65

Hebrews 9:19f. 15
Hebrews 11:3 141

Jude 19 35

Revelation 19:16 141

www.ingramcontent.com/pod-product-compliance
Lightning Source LLC
Chambersburg PA
CBHW051641230426
43669CB00013B/2388